100 CLASSIC HIKES
UTAH

100 CLASSIC HIKES

UTAH

JULIE K. TREVELYAN

National Parks and Monuments | National Wilderness
and Recreation Areas | State Parks | Uintas | Wasatch

MOUNTAINEERS
BOOKS

MOUNTAINEERS BOOKS

Mountaineers Books is the publishing division of The Mountaineers, an organization founded in 1906 and dedicated to the exploration, preservation, and enjoyment of outdoor and wilderness areas.

1001 SW Klickitat Way, Suite 201, Seattle, WA 98134
800.553.4453, www.mountaineersbooks.org

Printed in China
Distributed in the United Kingdom by Cordee, www.cordee.co.uk
First edition, 2016

Copy Editor: Christy Karras
Series design: Kate Basart
Layout: Peggy Egerdahl
Cartographer: Pease Press
Cover photograph: *Double Arch, Arches National Park, Utah* © www.35mmNegative.com, Getty Images
Frontispiece: *Fisher Towers Trail*
The background maps for this book were produced using the online map viewer CalTopo.
For more information, visit caltopo.com.

Library of Congress Cataloging-in-Publication Data
Names: Trevelyan, Julie K.
Title: 100 classic hikes Utah : National Parks and Monuments/National Wilderness and Recreation Areas/State Parks/Uintas/Wasatch/Julie K. Trevelyan.
Other titles: One hundred classic hikes Utah
Description: First edition. | Seattle, WA : Mountaineers Books, [2016] | Includes index.
Identifiers: LCCN 2015037092| ISBN 9781594859243 (paperback) | ISBN 9781594859250 (ebook)
Subjects: LCSH: Hiking—Utah—Guidebooks. | Parks—Utah—Guidebooks. | Utah—Guidebooks.
Classification: LCC GV199.42.U8 T74 2016 | DDC 796.5109792—dc23
LC record available at http://lccn.loc.gov/2015037092

Mountaineers Books titles may be purchased for corporate, educational, or other promotional sales, and our authors are available for a wide range of events. For information on special discounts or booking an author, contact our customer service at 800-553-4453 or mbooks@mountaineersbooks.org.

Contents

South Central

Southeast

Hikes at a Glance

NO.	NAME	DIFFICULTY	SEASON	HIGHLIGHTS
HALF-DAY HIKES				
4	Wall Lake	Easy	Summer–Fall	Mountain lakes, views
6	Bald Mountain	Moderate	Summer–Fall	Spectacular views, wildlife
7	Lofty Lake Loop	Moderate	Summer–Fall	Mountain lakes, views
16	Mount Aire	Moderate	All year	Alpine scenery, pine forest, views
19	Mount Raymond	Hard	Spring–Fall	Expansive views, wildflowers
25	Cecret Lake	Easy	Summer–Fall	Stunning mountain scenery, wildflowers, lake
28	Stewart Falls	Easy	Spring–Fall	Waterfall, alpine views, wildflowers
34	Delano Peak	Easy/Moderate	All year	Mountain scenery, viewpoint, solitude
40	Emerald Pools	Easy/Moderate	Spring–Fall	Water pools, canyon views, long drop-offs
43	Canyon Overlook	Easy/Moderate	All year	Spectacular viewpoint, canyon scenery, sandstone formations
45	Spectra Point/Ramparts Overlook	Moderate	Summer–Fall	Viewpoint, limestone amphitheater, wildflowers, pine forest
48	Queens Garden	Easy/Moderate	All year	Hoodoos, canyon views, sandstone formations
49	Navajo Loop	Easy/Moderate	All year	Hoodoos, canyon views, sandstone formations
55	Lower Hackberry Canyon	Easy	Spring, Fall	Canyon vistas, creek, sandstone formations
62	Escalante Natural Bridge	Easy	Spring–Fall	Beautiful river canyon, natural bridge, river walking
65	Devils Garden (Escalante)	Easy	All year	Colorful, photogenic sandstone formations, natural arches
67	Spooky Gulch and Peek-a-Boo Gulch	Moderate	All year	Slot canyons, desert scenery
73	Hickman Bridge	Easy	All year	Natural bridge, wildflowers
75	Golden Throne	Moderate	All year	Canyon scenery, sandstone formations, great views
92	Mesa Arch	Easy	All year	Canyon views, expansive vistas, extremely photogenic
95	Windows Loop and Double Arch	Moderate	All year	Stunning views, natural arches
97	Delicate Arch	Easy/Moderate	Spring, Fall	Spectacular vistas, iconic natural arch, petroglyphs
98	Corona Arch	Easy	All year	Spectacular natural arch, canyon views

NO.	NAME	DIFFICULTY	SEASON	HIGHLIGHTS
SHORT DAY HIKES				
1	Naomi Peak	Moderate	Summer–Fall	Views, wildflowers
2	White Pine Lake (Logan Canyon)	Moderate	Spring–Fall	Mountain lake, meadows
3	Clyde Lake Loop	Easy/Moderate	Summer–Fall	Mountain lakes, views, meadows
9	Grandaddy Lake	Moderate	Summer–Fall	Mountain lake, great views, wildflowers, fall foliage
14	Frary Peak	Moderate	All year	Great views, Great Salt Lake scenery, wildlife
17	Gobblers Knob	Moderate/Hard	Summer–Fall	Pine forest, wildflowers, viewpoint
18	Lake Blanche	Moderate/Hard	All year	Gorgeous mountain lake, glacial cirque, views
26	Brighton Lakes	Moderate	Spring–Fall	Great mountain lakes, scenery
30	Silver Lake (American Fork Canyon)	Moderate	Spring–Fall	Mountain lake, views, waterfalls
31	Fifth Water Hot Springs/ Diamond Fork Canyon	Easy	Spring–Fall	Hot springs, waterfalls
35	Kanarra Creek Trail	Easy/Moderate	Spring–Fall	Gorgeous slot canyon, waterfalls
37	Snow Canyon	Easy/Moderate	Fall–Spring	Unique geology, colorful sandstone formations, desert wildflowers
46	Golden Wall–Castle Bridge Loop	Moderate	Spring–Fall	Unique geology, hoodoos, canyon views
50	Peek-a-Boo Loop	Moderate	All year	Hoodoos, canyon views, sandstone formations
52	Panorama Trail	Easy	Spring, Fall	Unique geology, sandstone formations
53	Willis Creek Narrows	Easy	Spring–Fall	Slot canyon, wildflowers
56	Wire Pass Trail/Buckskin Gulch	Moderate	Spring, Fall	Spectacular slot canyon, sandstone formations
61	Lower Calf Creek Falls	Easy	All year	Lovely waterfall, canyon vistas, lush plants, petroglyphs
64	Phipps Arch	Moderate	All year	Intriguing natural arch, canyon views, sandstone formations
66	Zebra Slot and Tunnel Slot	Easy/Moderate	All year	Slot canyons, extremely photogenic
69	Willow Gulch–Broken Bow Arch	Easy	All year	Gorgeous canyon scenery, spectacular natural arch
79	Crack Canyon	Easy/Moderate	All year	Great desert canyon, scenery
81	Ding and Dang Canyons	Moderate	All year	Slot canyons, canyon scenery
82	Goblin Valley	Easy	All year	Unique geology, hoodoos, desert views

NO.	NAME	DIFFICULTY	SEASON	HIGHLIGHTS
99	Negro Bill Canyon/ Morning Glory Natural Bridge	Moderate	All year	Gorgeous canyon, creek, lush plant life
100	Fisher Towers	Moderate	All year	Intriguing sandstone formations, desert canyon scenery, viewpoints

LONG DAY HIKES

NO.	NAME	DIFFICULTY	SEASON	HIGHLIGHTS
5	Notch Mountain Trail	Moderate	Summer–Fall	Mountain lakes and views, meadows
10	Amethyst Lake	Moderate/Hard	Summer–Fall	Mountain lake and views, wildflowers, fall foliage
12	Little Hole National Recreation Trail	Easy/Moderate	All year	River canyon scenery, whitewater views
13	Jones Hole Creek	Moderate	All year	Canyon views, falls, petroglyphs
15	Deseret Peak	Hard	All year	Viewpoint, surprising lushness, solitude
20	Desolation Lake	Moderate	Spring–Fall	Lovely mountain lake, fall foliage
21	Bells Canyon	Strenuous	Spring–Fall	Waterfalls, canyon views, solitude
22	White Pine Lake (Wasatch)	Moderate	Spring–Fall	Gorgeous mountain lake, pine forest, meadows
23	Red Pine Lake	Moderate	Spring–Fall	Mountain lake, wildflowers, pine forest, fall foliage
24	The Pfeifferhorn	Hard/Strenuous	Spring–Fall	Viewpoint, mountain scenery
27	Big Springs Hollow– Cascade Saddle	Hard	All year	Viewpoint, mountain views, meadows
29	Mount Timpanogos	Strenuous	Late spring–Fall	Viewpoint, alpine scenery, lake
32	Mount Nebo	Strenuous	Spring–Fall	Spectacular views, meadows, scenery
33	Notch Peak	Moderate	All year	Viewpoint, Great Basin vistas
38	Virgin River Narrows	Moderate/Hard	All year	Stunning canyon narrows, river walking
39	Observation Point	Hard	All year	Viewpoint, canyon scenery, sandstone formations
41	Angels Landing	Hard	All year	Stunning viewpoint, canyon views, long drop-offs
44	Rattlesnake Creek/ Ashdown Gorge	Moderate	Summer–Fall	Canyon scenery, waterfalls, natural bridge
47	Fairyland Loop	Moderate	All year	Hoodoos, canyon views, solitude
54	Lick Wash	Easy/Moderate	Spring–Fall	Canyon views, solitude

NO.	NAME	DIFFICULTY	SEASON	HIGHLIGHTS
LONG DAY HIKES (CONT.)				
57	Pine Creek Box	Moderate	Spring–Fall	River canyon views, sandstone formations, pine forest, solitude
59	Wolverine Canyon	Moderate	Spring, Fall	Petrified wood, canyon views, solitude
60	Little Death Hollow	Moderate	Spring, Fall	Slot canyon, sandstone formations
63	Escalante River	Moderate	Spring–Fall	Beautiful river canyon, lush plants
70	Pelican Canyon–Fishlake Hightop	Moderate	Spring–Fall	Mountain and lake views, solitude
71	Spring Canyon	Moderate	All year	Great canyon views, wildflowers, solitude
72	Cohab Canyon–Frying Pan–Cassidy Arch	Moderate	Spring–Fall	Natural arch, expansive canyon scenery, vistas
74	Navajo Knobs	Hard	All year	Viewpoint, canyon scenery, wide vistas
76	Upper Muley Twist Canyon/Strike Valley Overlook	Hard	Spring, Fall	Stunning desert views, unique geology, natural arches, wildflowers
77	Horseshoe Canyon	Easy	All year	Gorgeous canyon views, significant petroglyph panels
78	The Chute of Muddy Creek	Hard	All year	Canyon views, river walking
80	Little Wild Horse and Bell Canyons	Easy/Moderate	All year	Slot canyons, canyon scenery
83	Natural Bridges Loop	Easy/Moderate	All year	Gorgeous canyon scenery, natural bridges, ancient ruins, solitude
84	Collins Canyon	Moderate	All year	Canyon scenery, views, ancient ruins, petroglyphs
85	Kane Gulch	Moderate	All year	Canyon scenery, views, ancient ruins, petroglyphs
86	Bullet Canyon	Moderate	All year	Canyon scenery, views, ancient kiva, petroglyphs
88	Government Trail	Moderate	All year	Canyon scenery, views, pictographs
89	Mule Canyon	Easy	All year	Canyon scenery, ancient ruins
90	Dead Horse Point Rim Trail	Moderate	All year	Spectacular views, river canyon scenery, mountain views
91	Syncline Loop	Moderate	All year	Unique geology, expansive views, drop-offs
93	Chesler Park	Moderate	All year	Spectacular colorful sandstone formations, solitude
94	Big Spring Canyon–Squaw Canyon Loop	Moderate	All year	Canyon scenery, views, sandstone formations
96	Devils Garden Primitive Loop	Moderate	Spring–Fall	Spectacular canyon vistas, sandstone formations, natural arches

NO.	NAME	DIFFICULTY	SEASON	HIGHLIGHTS
SHORT BACKPACKS				
8	Naturalist Basin	Moderate/Hard	Summer–Fall	Abundant mountain lakes, views, wildflowers
36	Whipple Trail–Summit Trail Loop	Hard/Strenuous	Fall–Spring	Mountain meadows, lush plant life, interesting geology
42	West Rim Trail	Hard	Spring–Fall	Spectacular views, canyon vistas, sandstone formations
56	Wire Pass Trail/Buckskin Gulch	Moderate	Spring, Fall	Spectacular slot canyon, sandstone formations
87	Fish Creek Canyon and Owl Creek Canyon	Moderate	All year	Canyon scenery, ancient ruins, petroglyphs, natural arch
LONG BACKPACKS				
11	Kings Peak	Strenuous	Summer–Fall	Great mountain scenery, high mountain lakes, highest peak in state
51	Under-the-Rim Trail	Moderate/Hard	Spring–Fall	Solitude, hoodoos, canyon views
58	Death Hollow	Hard	Spring, Fall	Stunning river canyon scenery, high cliff walls, historic trail
68	Coyote Gulch	Moderate	All year	Spectacular canyon views, natural arch, lush plants

Legend

------ Featured trail	🔵 Trailhead	**8** Hike number
------ Optional trail or route	Ⓣ Alternate trailhead	‿ River or creek
········ Cross-country route	Ⓟ Separate parking	‿ǁ‿ Falls
------- Other trail	■ Point of Interest	⬭ Water
·—·—·— Horse-only trail	▲ Peak	⸢⸣ Park or forest boundary
—— Highway	⅄ Campground or campsite	⸢⸣ Wilderness boundary
—— Paved road	⬩ Park office or ranger station	⸢⸣ State or county boundary
===== Dirt road	⊼ Picnic area	⸢⸣ National boundary
⑮ ㉑⑮ Interstate highway	)(Pass	
⑥ ⑧⑨ ⑲① US highway	↔ Gate	Ⓝ⬆ True north (magnetic north varies)
⑨ ㉔ ⑫⑧ State route	)[Bridge	
㉔ ⑳⓪ Forest route	⸮ Spring	
㉔ County road		

Hikers along the trail through the gorgeous canyon to Lower Calf Creek Falls

Acknowledgments

Utah is hands down my favorite place in the world for outdoor exploration, and I am so very grateful I moved to the gorgeous middle of nowhere in 1999, thus allowing me to discover the truly stunning natural beauties of this state. Many friends hiked with me, gave me suggestions of new trails to explore, let me crash at their place while I traveled around the state hiking trails, pet-sat my mini farm for me while I was gone, were my contact person when I was hiking alone so someone would know where I was, were cheerleaders for me during the writing process, and offered their support and encouragement in countless ways. During this project in particular, many thanks to Robin Brodsky, Jennifer Howe, Karen Johnson, Kay Luther and Matt Ingoldsby (and Indi!), Amber Margolis, Melody Perdikis, Sasha Sadiq, Sallie Dean Shatz, Ellen Shinkle, Gretchen and Eric Suchman, Carrie and Aaron Torrey, and Melanie Webb. Hopefully I haven't forgotten anyone; if I have, my deep apologies and know that I really do thank you as well! My best hiking buddy, Pippin the wonder dog, accompanied me on as many trails as he was allowed, adding a great deal of fun and companionship along the way.

Prickly pear blossom

The entire team at Mountaineers Books has been communicative, friendly, and very accommodating to my pleas for more time. To all the employees of public land management agencies out there, I have deep gratitude for your time and energy in keeping both wild places and sometimes wild people protected from one another while you simply do your jobs. Also many thanks to the thousands of clients, students, and campers I have guided outdoors throughout the years; all of you taught me something and often made me laugh while I was privileged enough to explore beautiful wilderness areas with you.

My wonderful grandparents nurtured a deep love of the outdoors in me, taking me on extensive trips to the San Gabriel Mountains and to Yosemite National Park for nearly all the summers of my childhood, for which I am eternally grateful. Mostly, I owe a huge acknowledgment to my amazing mom, Halina J. Trevelyan, for taking me to my first national park when I was five, on my first overnight backpacking trip when I was nine, and overall instilling in me an abiding appreciation, respect, and love for the wild places in this world. Love you, Mom.

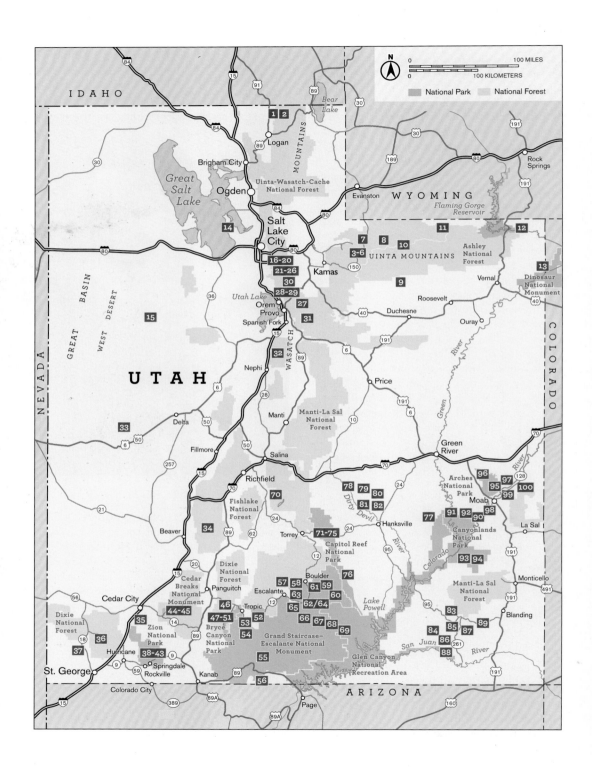

Introduction

Utah inspires the hiker's imagination and desire to explore like few other states due to its wildly diverse and gorgeous scenery. From its wildflower-dotted high alpine flanks to deep red canyon twists and turns, from sparkling mountain lakes tucked beneath the aerie folds of ancient volcanic basins to geologically wondrous sandstone carvings and monoliths that seem to defy gravity, Utah's hiking trails beckon to people of all ages, abilities, and nationalities. Within the state's more than 70 percent public lands lie some of the most breathtaking trails to grace the planet. These hikes range from nearly flat strolls of a mere half hour to heart-pounding multiday routes that include steep vertical ascents.

Following the criteria of "classic"—including best, most challenging, most popular, most scenic, and most representative of the state's natural beauty—hikes were selected to offer a range of difficulty, geography, topography, and interest to a variety of hikers. These 100 hikes allow visitors to the state to experience the breadth as well as depth of Utah's scenic trails. If you are a resident, the hikes are quintessential Utah and therefore belong on your must-do list.

Some hikes will appeal to casual hikers with limited ability and/or time, including those with young children or those whose physical makeup requires easy walks. Most of the trails will call to those desiring a longer excursion that serves up spectacular views or natural wonders without demanding more than a day's time. Some will spur the multiday adventurer to strap on a backpack and sleep out under the stars.

With literally thousands of trails to consider, final hike choice was necessarily subjective. Many people familiar with Utah hikes will, I'm sure, argue for their own favorite classics. While I agree that many other hikes are spectacular, quite frankly, choices had to be made. As for some cherished lesser-known hikes, although it is frustrating to discover what seem to be hordes of people at what were once little-known trailheads, I side with Edward Abbey: "The idea of wilderness needs no defense. It only needs defenders." If people have experienced firsthand the beautiful hiking trails in threatened wilderness areas, and if they both know how to travel those trails lightly and understand that places must remain as uncultivated as possible by heavy-handed human "conquering" of the land itself, they are far more likely to become vocal defenders of these amazing landscapes.

Overall, this selection of 100 routes represents a sampling of Utah's most classic hikes. Guided by that frame of "classic," the hikes chosen showcase outstanding scenery, the fascinating geologic features specific to Utah, and/or definitive adventures that are part and parcel of the state's natural legacy. The hikes were chosen primarily for their natural features rather than cultural or historical significance, but as Utah contains an exceptional amount of awe-inspiring evidence of ancient human inhabitation, several of the trails do focus on ancient rock art or ruins as well as beautiful natural scenery.

Although Utah is famous for its canyoneering hikes, no technical hikes (those that absolutely require the use of ropes, cams, harnesses, or similar equipment) are included in this book. Slot canyon hikes do make an appearance, but only if the entire length can be hiked on foot, although some hand-and-foot scrambling, small drops, potential wading, or possibly even swimming through water-filled potholes may

View from Amethyst Lake Trail

be necessary. A few hikes suggest using a rope or chain as a handhold for additional safety, but they are not considered technical in the usual sense of the word. All hikes that may require agile scrambling or the use of a handhold are clearly identified.

Other considerations were routefinding and trail access. The vast majority of trails included here do not demand any intensive routefinding other than bringing a good map and being cognizant of usual trail markers such as cairns; those that do require some cross-country travel or routefinding and thus demand very strong navigational skills are specifically labeled. Knowing how to read and use a topographical map is strongly recommended. Relying solely on a GPS unit has gotten more than one hiker hopelessly lost or even in trouble. In the wilderness, good old-fashioned map and compass skills generally are a reliable bet.

Because some of the state's most fascinating hikes are in its many remote sections, plenty of its trails are accessible only via travel on daunting dirt roads. Many of the dirt roads included here are drivable with two-wheel-drive passenger cars, weather and road conditions permitting. Hikes that may demand more rugged vehicles (high clearance and/or four-wheel drive) are clearly labeled in the hike notes. In general, most hikes are accessible by passenger vehicles under good conditions (please note that the definition of "good" conditions may vary wildly at different times of the year, as well as for different types of drivers!).

A striking variety of terrain graces Utah. In the north are many trails heading into the high country of the Uinta Mountains and the Wasatch Range. Some of the Intermountain West's largest alpine expanses, the mountains here are a hiker's dream of forestland, mountaintop views, and wildlife. High elevations, crystal-clear lakes, the scent of pines, the sight of colorful wildflowers, and breathtaking classic alpine scenery tend to be the main draws. The Uintas boast more than 450,000 acres of stunning wild lands. The Wasatch Front rears up behind the largest urban center in the state, from Salt Lake City and its environs all the way south past Provo. Quick access to hiking trails and the ability to rapidly ditch crowds by heading just a little farther into the backcountry make the trails here inviting to casual visitors as well as residents. Families can find hikes that will work for even their youngest members, while those looking for more adventure can find nearby trails to challenge them.

The famous red-rock canyons, bizarre hoodoos, huge sandstone monoliths carved into wild shapes by impressive millennial forces of nature, and overall stunning unique geography of southern Utah has long captured the imagination of people worldwide. The high mesas and deserts of the grand Colorado Plateau have created an elaborate wilderness experience for generations of hikers, perhaps most notably in the very southern portion of the state. The Colorado Plateau actually extends as far north as Dinosaur National Monument in Vernal, although most people do not realize that.

Utah's five national parks—Arches, Bryce Canyon, Canyonlands, Capitol Reef, and Zion—are all on the Colorado Plateau. They attract most of southern Utah's visitors, although an increasing number are discovering the spectacular hiking trails of lesser known but just as beautiful Cedar Breaks National Monument, Grand Staircase–Escalante National Monument, and the San Rafael Swell. Elemental forces at work over time, mostly volcanic and seismic, have created a playground of sandstone buttes, windswept mesas, deep red canyons that can surprise with ribbons of greenery running through the wetter ones, and sweeping vistas that astound not only for their scattered jumble of variegated shapes and colors but the sheer immensity of blissfully untamed nature to admire and explore.

Contact information for each hike's land management agency is included at the end of this book, and these agencies are your best source of information on current road conditions, weather, blockages, or any other up-to-date information about a particular trail. While all the information here is as recent as possible, by their nature, trails can change over time, as can the driving routes leading to them, so make sure you are aware of any such differences before you attempt any hike.

GETTING STARTED

If you are a novice hiker, numerous resources will help you get started. Many websites and blogs focus on hiking, often with excellent tips for those new to it. Local gear outfitting stores may offer classes or even guided trips. Local hiking clubs can also be a good way to dip your toes into the hiking world, with the benefit of more experienced hikers who can share tips and techniques. Start with easier trails to work up your stamina and fitness, which will only increase

An example of Utah's unique geology

your enjoyment as you slowly tackle longer and harder hikes.

WHAT TO TAKE

Having certain essentials along on a hike can make the trip more fun, not to mention be extremely valuable should the situation turn challenging or even dangerous. The Ten Essentials are highly recommended for every hiking trip, no matter how short. Originally created in the 1930s by The Mountaineers, the updated version is as follows:

1. Navigation: Nothing beats solid map and compass skills. While a GPS (global positioning system) is fun to have and can be quite useful, it won't always be completely reliable because technology can fail, especially in remote, rugged backcountry areas of Utah. Carry the appropriate map for your chosen hiking area and know how to use it, or make sure someone with you does.

2. Sun protection: Sunscreen, lip balm with SPF, sunglasses, a hat that covers the face and neck, a loose-fitting long-sleeved shirt, and long pants all go a long way toward protecting your body's biggest organ—your skin—from the potentially damaging and even life-threatening effects of sun exposure.

3. Insulation: Bring extra clothing layers to keep you dry and warm. These can be lightweight but still afford valuable additional protection if needed.

4. Illumination: A hands-free headlamp is your best option, along with extra batteries. A flashlight also works.

5. First-aid supplies: Small first-aid kits for hikers are easy to buy complete or assemble on your own. Make sure you are familiar with everything in yours and how to use each item. Restock it regularly.

6. Fire: A small lighter is very easy to carry and is perhaps one of the simplest, quickest ways to make fire and warmth if necessary. Other firestarters include waterproof matches, candles, canned heat, and many similar devices.

7. Repair kit and tools: A good knife is still a hiking essential due to the variety of needs it can address. For overnight trips, small repair kits for shoes, tents, and clothing are also easy to buy and carry.

8. Nutrition: Extra ready-to-eat food should always have a place in your pack. Energy bars, a bag of nuts, and dried fruit are all good choices.

9. Hydration: Water is your friend. Bring more than you think you will need (one general rule: at least a gallon per person per day, particularly in desert areas), and consider also having a way to purify water, as most backcountry sources are not safe to drink otherwise. Check with land managers before you go to find out about the availability of water on longer routes.

10. Emergency shelter: Carry a tent or bivy sack for overnight trips. On a day trip, emergency shelter can be as simple as a small reflective emergency blanket or a large trash bag—or several.

PERMITS AND FEES

Land management agencies often require use fees in order to help maintain the incredible natural areas they manage. Contact information for each hike is included, and it's highly recommended you check in first with said agency to discover what, if any, fees are necessary. In some areas, a use permit is required to be displayed on your vehicle's dash or even carried with you. Make sure you understand and have abided by all permit and fee requirements of a specific area before setting out on the trail.

TRAIL ETIQUETTE

For both personal enjoyment and preservation of the land, follow some general guidelines of trail use. People hike for different reasons, but probably the most common one is to experience an immersion in nature, no matter for how long or how far away. It's all too easy to disrupt someone else's enjoyment of solitude and beauty, but listed below are easy things to remember that can make everyone's experience much more pleasant.

Red Pine Lake Trail

Leave No Trace

With parts of wild Utah being almost literally "loved to death," treading very lightly on the land is essential to ensure its preservation for future generations, not to mention anyone who comes down the trail immediately after you do. Much of Utah's arid desert landscape is extremely fragile and can retain the sign of careless human incursion for decades afterward. The basic premise of Leave No Trace, which is actually a national organization, is essentially to leave the wilderness in at least the same condition, if not better than, you found it. Picking up trash—even the tiniest pieces, whether or not you were the one who dropped them—is a prime example of the Leave No Trace principles. Altogether, the principles are simple and easy to follow:

Plan Ahead and Prepare

Know your route, your season, and the abilities of every member of your hiking party. Have a clear understanding of the hiking area's regulations, including the number of hikers and any especially protected sites. Understand what sort of weather you might encounter that time of year and choose your gear accordingly while also being prepared for anything. Check on road and trail conditions before your trip to help ensure a smooth, fun excursion.

Travel and Camp on Durable Surfaces

Use established trails and campsites. In some areas you will see a crisscrossing network of trails that might be confusing; these so-called social trails are made by people who decide a certain route is the way to go without either realizing or caring where the actual trail lies. Don't add to the madness. Walk single file on trails and be sure to avoid trampling fragile vegetation. Stay at least 200 feet away from lakes and streams when camping, and contain your campsite to the minimum space necessary. In the backcountry, if there are no popular, established campsites, choose the least impacted and least fragile area to set up your camp.

Dispose of Waste Properly

The standard mantra is pack it in, pack it out. Don't leave your trash behind, and don't assume that if it's food you can toss it into the woods or canyons and it will biodegrade naturally. An apple core doesn't belong on a remote desert mesa top, nor do orange peels belong in the untouched meadow that was your lunch site. Pack out all food pieces and trash you either create or find. Toilet paper and any hygiene products should be packed out; carry self-sealing plastic bags for this purpose as well as paper bags if you prefer to not have a visual. Solid human waste needs to be left buried beneath dirt in a "cathole" that is six to eight inches deep and at least 200 feet from any water source. There is perhaps nothing more disgusting than seeing soiled toilet paper or human waste lying on top of the ground or poorly "hidden" just beneath a rock in the backcountry.

Leave What You Find

Utah is well known for its amazing proliferation of ancient cultural artifacts, such as arrowheads and rock structure ruins, and even more ancient natural artifacts, such as dinosaur bones and tracks. Stumbling across such finds as these while on a hike can make the overall experience that much more fascinating and memorable. Being able to see the actual fingerprints of people dead for centuries pressed into the mud that adheres to wood or rock parts of ancient dwellings can be an extraordinary moment as you recognize a human connection with those who lived here long ago. Seeing rock art, gazing at a huge dinosaur track left in stone, or coming across a potsherd (broken clay pottery piece) provides distinct evidence of, and sometimes an awe-inspiring sense of kinship with, people and creatures who passed here hundreds, thousands, or millions of years ago.

However, remember that such artifacts are not only rare and precious, they are also heavily protected by both state and federal laws. Many of the larger land management agencies now use hidden cameras at some sites because, unfortunately, some people believe these artifacts are for their personal enjoyment or even profit. Native American artifacts in particular have seen horrific looting for more than a century now for the express purpose of individual gain, and this is tragic on levels ranging from personal to national. Increased federal and state crackdowns on such illegal looting and trafficking have gotten the point across to some, but others may simply find work-arounds for their own selfish, very thoughtless, and very temporary gain. If you see any suspicious activity, report it immediately.

Although it may be tempting to touch or paper-trace rock art, pocket that perfect little arrowhead, or make a cast impression of a dinosaur track, please don't. Touching rock art can help destroy it over time, as the oils in our hands can alter the surface's natural composition through staining and darkening, not to mention erosion, as well as interfere with dating methods used to determine how old such art might be. In addition, contemporary graffiti left on or near ancient ruins or rock art does nothing to enhance

Brighton Lakes Trail

a site but rather makes it far less striking and historically educational—and is, of course, also illegal. Instead, take pictures and make memories, then leave everything in its original place for others to see and enjoy in the future.

Minimize Campfire Impacts

Before building any fire, be certain to check on any current fire restrictions or permanent bans. Open flames are not allowed in many backcountry areas of Utah, and all five national parks ban fires outside of some designated campgrounds. Rather than building an unsightly old-school campfire ring encircled by large rocks (which you may find at established sites; if so, go ahead and use it), if you need to cook food or absolutely require the warmth of a fire (only, of course, in an area that allows open fires), use a camping or backpacking stove, a fire pan, or a mound fire. Use only dead and downed wood from outside the camp area. Keep the fire small and make sure everything burns. Completely douse the fire with water when done, and scatter the ashes. Nothing you scatter should be larger than a pencil eraser.

Respect Wildlife

Wild creatures and their habitats are more vulnerable than people may think. Observing them from a distance allows them to keep as much of their natural routine as possible while enabling you to see wild creatures in their natural home. Keep your food to yourself and your pets on a leash when required.

Be Considerate of Other Visitors

Little can mar the bliss of hiking in the outdoors more than insensitive, excessively loud, discourteous, or even dangerous other people. Please do not succumb to the urge to talk on your cell phone if you have a signal. Yield the trail to those who have the right-of-way, such as pack or riding stock, and realize not everyone on a trail will be in the same shape or have the same outdoor background. If the trail is precarious in sections and large numbers of people are on it, step aside for those less skilled or more fearful to let them pass in safety.

San Rafael Swell wild horse

SAFETY

Any hike can be dangerous, depending on the weather, physical factors, and your level of preparation. Generally speaking, the less managed an area is (national forests, Bureau of Land Management), the more rugged the terrain. In Utah, however, extremes of landscape and weather mean that even within highly managed national parks, some trails can still potentially be quite hazardous. Utah's weather often dictates the safety parameters of hiking. From flash floods to lightning strikes to extreme heat to snowstorms, the weather here should be regarded with the deepest respect. Check the local weather forecast for your hiking area and make sure you can still reach the trailhead in your vehicle that day. In some areas at certain times of the year, heavy rains can make dirt roads impassable and even dangerous to drive. This is an important consideration not only heading out to the trail but for your planned return; be aware that midafternoon summertime thunderstorms in mountain and desert canyon areas can wipe out your road.

As the second most arid state in the nation, Utah demands that you keep yourself well hydrated while hiking. Always carry more water than you think you will need. Your pack will only get lighter as you drink it, after all. Those from even mildly wetter climates (that is, almost every other state and many other countries) tend to sharply feel the aridity of the air, which can dramatically affect their physical ability to hike. Southern Utah summer temperatures can soar, making midday or even midmorning treks an exercise in misery or worse if you are hiking in a lower-elevation or desert environment. Dramatic summer storms and lightning can spring up during high-altitude hikes in any part of the state; make sure you do not head above tree line if a storm seems even remotely nearby. In general, simply be very aware of the time of year and the forecast, and plan your gear and your trip accordingly.

In the southern Utah canyons, mid- to late summer monsoons often help create fascinating yet potentially deadly flash floods. The ground saturates very quickly and can only hold so much water at a time, so the significant amount of precipitation that collects from these storms cannot just dissipate into the earth; it needs to flow somewhere. Following the path of least resistance as well as the force of gravity means storm water plunges into the canyons, filling them very quickly. August tends to be the wettest month, but heavy rain and flash floods can occur regularly from July through September, and even during other months.

The rule of thumb while hiking in southern Utah, particularly during summer monsoon season, is to avoid any drainage (canyon) if a storm threatens, either overhead or even miles away. Obviously the narrowest of slot canyons are to be avoided, but even larger canyons can become raging torrents. Flash floods have occurred as much as several hours later and as far as 100 miles from the storm epicenter, a phenomenon that can happen when various drainages pour into one another for miles upon miles. If you even slightly question the possibility of rainfall, leave the canyons and head for higher ground. If you are camping, never camp in a dry wash or streambed.

Basic survival skills, wilderness smarts, the ability to rescue yourself, and simple common sense are all highly recommended tools in your hiking arsenal. As documented accidents have proved over the years, the Utah wilderness can be greatly enjoyed but should never be underestimated. If in doubt about the abilities of any member in your hiking party, it might be best to turn back or maybe not even head out that particular day at all. Use all the resources at your disposal, both in this book and from the varying land management agencies, to make sure you stay safe, have a great time out on the trail, and return home with wonderful memories.

Prickly pear cactus in Snow Canyon State Park

Devils Garden Primitive Loop Trail

HOW TO USE THIS BOOK

The hikes are divided into geographical sections. Each trail includes information on distance, approximate time to complete the hike, elevation gain, level of difficulty, season, US Geological Survey (USGS) topographical map, and land management agency contact information.

The round-trip distance given is for the entirety of the hike. Any hikes that are one-way or loop hikes are so indicated. If a vehicle shuttle is recommended, that is noted.

The amount of time needed to finish any given hike will, of course, vary greatly with each individual hiking party, depending on a variety of factors including weather, physical fitness, stops along the trail, the length of stops, and the weight of a pack. The time given for each hike is meant to be a general guideline only. Remember, the more difficult the hike in terms of elevation gain or terrain, the longer you should expect to be on the trail and the more time you should allow to complete it.

The elevation gain includes the total amount of elevation gained on a trail, regardless of how often you descend before ascending again or how much you descend before climbing.

Difficulty is subjective, as people often have different ideas of what is easy and what is hard. In this book, it is based on trail length, elevation gain, level of wilderness immersion (backcountry as opposed to front country), and any particulars that might make a certain trail tougher to navigate, such as any cross-country travel or very steep or rocky sections that demand careful foot placement. In Utah, many trails have significant elevation gain or start out at high elevation; these factors play into the ratings, meaning that even a short hike that begins at 9000 feet may be marked as moderate rather than easy. The ratings used are as follows:

Easy. Mostly flat, short (4 miles or less), or both. Some shorter hikes that have significant elevation gain may be marked as easy/moderate.

Moderate. Longer, with some inclines or slight elevation gain. May include uneven terrain or sections that require closer attention to navigate.

Hard. Steeper elevation gain, longer. Some obstacles such as stream crossings or rock scrambling. May require routefinding.

Strenuous. Very steep and/or quite long, somewhat technical sections or sharp drop-offs. Requires a good level of fitness and agility.

Anyone who is new to hiking or not physically ready to hit the trail may quickly realize a trail labeled "moderate" is actually more difficult than expected, so assess the fitness and skill level of everyone in your hiking group before attempting any trail.

The best seasons for hiking are generally noted; criteria for best season include weather, the possibility of enjoying seasonal particulars such as wildflowers or fall foliage, heat or cold, and accessibility if the trailhead is reached via a dirt road. Many hikes are accessible year-round, but that doesn't necessarily mean they are most enjoyable at any old time of year. Many trails are technically considered closed during winter months when snow levels might hamper access, but hiking, snowshoeing, or even cross-country skiing might be just as fun during the colder months. Utah's southern and lower-elevation areas are also notable for their high temperatures and the possibility of monsoon storms during the summertime. Many people can only visit during the summer, so caution is a good thing to have when contemplating tackling a trail beneath the hot summer sun.

The name of the appropriate USGS 7.5-minute topographical, or contour, map(s) that covers the particular hiking trail is included. It's generally advisable that you carry and know how to read such maps. Some trails are very straightforward and don't necessarily require a map to navigate, but many of the longer or more backcountry trails demand using and interpreting the correct topographical map. As a rule, it's always a good idea to carry a detailed map whether or not you know the trail, just to be on the safe side.

Each trail falls under the jurisdiction of a land management agency, sometimes more than one, depending on the trail length or route followed. Contact them to find out about any recent developments that may alter any given hike.

A Note about Safety: Safety is an important concern in all outdoor activities. No guidebook can alert you to every hazard or anticipate the limitations of every reader. Therefore, the descriptions of roads, trails, routes, and natural features in this book are not representations that a particular place or excursion will be safe for your party. When you follow any of the routes described in this book, you assume responsibility for your own safety. Under normal conditions, such excursions require the usual attention to traffic, road and trail conditions, weather, terrain, the capabilities of your party, and other factors. Keeping informed on current conditions and exercising common sense are the keys to a safe, enjoyable outing.

—*Mountaineers Books*

Opposite, top: Snow can come early to the High Uintas, as seen along the trail to Amethyst Lake in October.

Opposite, bottom: Wildflowers along the trail to Naomi Peak

Northeast

The northeastern part of Utah can be hard to define because what would be the state's northeastern corner is neatly sliced out. For this book, the northeast includes the Bear River Range, the Uinta Mountains, Flaming Gorge National Recreation Area, and Dinosaur National Monument, all of which are quite different from one another. The Bear River Range and the Uintas are classic alpine mountain regions. Flaming Gorge and Dinosaur claim more desert environs, although both of those areas are typified by the same major river, the Green River, running through them.

Actually considered the far northern part of the sprawling Wasatch Range, the Bear River Range runs from Idaho into Utah and is a beautiful area with stunning mountain peaks, lakes, and trails. Tremendous exploration can be had along its crystalline streams and pine-dotted mountainsides, with a generous helping of solitude thrown in. The Uinta range is unusual in that, unlike most other North American ranges, it runs east-west. Covering about 150 miles in length, the Uintas contain the highest peaks in the state and vast tracts of wilderness that can allow you to hike for days without running into roads or, often, other people. Well over a thousand lakes—some estimates put the number closer to two thousand—dot this area, with a multitude of trails connecting and interconnecting them.

Flaming Gorge includes land and water in Wyoming and Utah and attracts large numbers of visitors who want to hike, fish, boat, and generally recreate in its 207,000 acres. Ancient history still shows up in the form of petroglyphs and pictographs left behind by the Fremont Indians. The area got its name when famed explorer John Wesley Powell and his crew witnessed sunlight hitting its red rocks during their 1869 expedition down the Green River. Miles downstream, Dinosaur National Monument is a trove of fossils that wow the public. Hiking, camping, and river rafting are also significant draws in this sunbaked landscape.

1 *Naomi Peak*

Roundtrip: 6.6 miles
Hiking time: 3–4 hours
Elevation gain: 1950 feet
Difficulty: moderate

Season: summer–fall
Map: USGS Naomi Peak
Contact: Uinta-Wasatch-Cache National Forest, Logan Ranger District

Getting there: From Logan, drive northeast for 22 miles on US Highway 89 to the Tony Grove turnoff. Turn left (north) here and drive 6 miles to trailhead parking. **Notes:** Fee required. Vault toilets at parking area.

The highest peak in Cache County, 9980-foot Naomi Peak commands lovely views but isn't quite as demanding as hikes to many other Utah peaks. Located just inside the boundary of the Mount Naomi Wilderness area's 44,523 acres, Naomi is also the highest peak in this federally designated roadless area. That means this is a gorgeous playground of relatively untouched wild landscapes that can be enjoyed without some of the more unsightly marks left on less protected places. From the top you can survey vast tracts of land: deep canyons to the west,

Along the Naomi Peak Trail

Idaho's mountains to the north, and Wyoming to the east. Summer wildflowers sprinkle across the landscape, while the temperature can vary by as much as twenty degrees from trailhead to summit on a windy day. Mostly, though, stellar alpine views are the lure for this accessible high peak. Even the start of the trail is pretty; it originates from scenic Tony Grove, an outdoor playground for the elite social class during the late nineteenth century.

From the Tony Grove trailhead, head north through a little meadow toward the trees. Barely 0.25 mile in, you come to the junction with the White Pine Lake trail; bear left for Naomi Peak. Just under 1 mile in, the trail curves more west. Soon you begin to pass through several small, grassy open areas lightly tossed with boulders. A large bowl opens up in another 0.1 mile, around which the trail circles before reaching a rocky section. Here, the trail ascends via switchbacks. At 1.25 miles reach a rock band that stretches out above the subalpine basin below. Once you top out over a ridge, the trail drops 150 feet into another meadow basin, leading you across it and toward the next cliff band to ascend via more switchbacks.

As you reach the summit ridge, you'll see the boundary sign, 3.2 miles in, informing you that the Mount Naomi Wilderness extends to the west. You'll also be able to see the deep ravines of steep mountains and the start of views that reach out to the horizon. From here it is only 0.2 mile to the peak itself and only a gradual incline the remainder of the way to the top. Although here

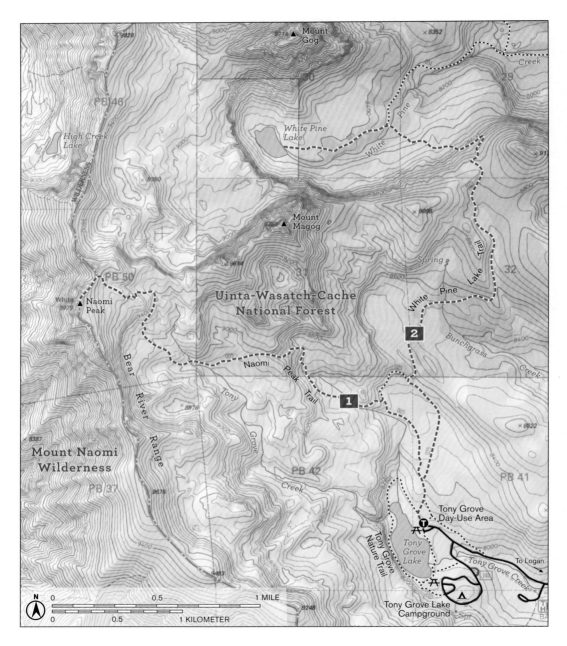

the trail fractures into multiple little paths beating their way up to the top, it is a simple matter to pick your way up the final, slightly rocky ascent to stand at the highest point in the Bear River Range. The views from Naomi Peak are utterly stunning in every direction, giving a clear sense of the amount of rugged wilderness all around. Scan the surroundings for elk, deer, and moose. Once you are ready to leave, just retrace your steps back down the mountain.

2 *White Pine Lake (Logan Canyon)*

Roundtrip: 7.6 miles
Hiking time: 3–4 hours
Elevation gain: 1200 feet
Difficulty: moderate

Season: spring–fall
Map: USGS Naomi Peak
Contact: Uinta-Wasatch-Cache National Forest, Logan Ranger District

Getting there: From Logan, drive north for 22 miles on US Highway 89 to the Tony Grove turnoff. Turn left (north) here and drive 6 miles to trailhead parking. **Notes:** Fee required. Vault toilets at parking area.

Probably the most popular lake hike in the Bear River Range, this incredibly scenic trail delivers outstanding alpine meadows, summer-time wildflower displays, tall stands of white fir and Engelmann spruce, rugged mountain peaks grazing the skyline, and a classic alpine lake nestled into a glacier-carved limestone basin. While the lake itself isn't as grand as others in the state or even the immediate area (Tony Grove Lake, by the trailhead, is significantly larger), its setting makes it spectacular. Cirque lakes are usually quite beautiful, with the contrast of waters nestled beneath the rugged cliffs roughly sculpted into submission by ancient, slow-moving ice sheets. A great day hike, this can also be a pleasant backpack for families or those who simply wish to linger in the backcountry a little longer.

From the Tony Grove trailhead, head north through the small meadow. During the high summer season, this initial section may be carpeted in wildflowers, while fall will see the colors beginning to explode on deciduous trees. Just a quarter mile along, the trail forks; take the right

White Pine Lake and Naomi Peak share a trailhead.

Hikers on the trail to White Pine Lake

turn to White Pine Lake. From here continue for 2 miles, gaining elevation with every step. You are climbing the ridge that separates Tony Grove Lake from White Pine Lake, which means you also start to gain in views as you ascend.

Through this section, the trail bisects meadows ringed by tall trees. Limber pines are found in this area; sometimes confused with bristlecone pines due to a slight similarity in appearance, limber pines are so named because their branches are pliable. The open meadows allow for generous views, primarily of the biblically named Mount Magog, which towers 1375 feet above White Pine Lake.

Enter a rustling aspen grove 1.7 miles along the trail. The trail opens up again after a short ways, soon leading into a gully slicing across the earth. Follow this glacial arroyo as the path goes through it, then takes you up its side to the ridge above the White Pine Basin, 2.4 miles in. From here you will drop 400 feet fairly quickly, traveling down switchbacks to reach the basin floor. Heading almost due west, the trail shoots you along another 1.2 miles, leveling out before it crosses a creek. The lake is set into a small meadow, with excellent campsite spots along its eastern end. Tall fir and spruce trees dominate some sections, and the high limestone cliff band rears up behind. When you are ready to head back, remember that you face a 400-foot climb back out to the ridge before the trail drops you back down to the trailhead parking area.

3 Clyde Lake Loop

Loop: 5.2 miles
Hiking time: 3–4 hours
Elevation gain: 600 feet
Difficulty: easy/moderate

Season: summer–fall
Map: USGS Mirror Lake
Contact: Uinta-Wasatch-Cache National Forest, Heber-Kamas Ranger District

Getting there: From Kamas, drive east on Mirror Lake Scenic Byway, State Route 150, for 27 miles. The signed turnoff for the Crystal Lake area will be on your left. Turn left (west) and drive 0.8 mile to a fork; turn right (north) and drive another 0.9 mile to Crystal Lake trailhead parking. **Notes:** Fee required; pay at self-service kiosks along highway or at ranger stations. Vault toilets, overnight camping, large parking lot. Mild routefinding may be required. Insect repellent handy in summer.

Appropriate for those wanting a leisurely exploration, Clyde Lake is another stunner of a hike that demonstrates the alpine beauty of the Uintas while introducing you to but some of its thousands of lakes. Clyde Lake is only one of the lakes on this loop, which will take you past no less than sixteen of them, more if you opt for side trips. Mountaintops, green meadows, majestic pine trees, and summer wildflowers or fall colors all add to the beauty of this trail. If you keep a sharp eye out, you might spot squirrels, chipmunks, and even the bright white mountain goats that enjoy hanging out on the high rocky slopes above the loop. Those seeking an immersive experience can camp overnight by one of the lakes and even cast a line, or you can simply enjoy this as a day hike that yields tremendous views for not much effort.

From the parking lot, find the trailhead marked with the small wooden sign for Notch Mountain Trail, which leads due north. Follow this 1 mile to Wall Lake, almost immediately passing Lily Lakes and catching glimpses of Bald Mountain and Reids Peak rising skyward to your right (east) through openings in the trees along the way. The trail skirts the eastern side of lovely Wall Lake. Entering the trees, the trail now winds briefly east, then back northward, though more sweeping views are somewhat obscured here by the ample pines. Pass small but pretty Hope Lake 2 miles in, then reach a rocky quartzite ledge section through which the trail switchbacks and takes you upward. This is the most strenuous section of trail yet, but the views when you reach the top are well worth the relatively short climb. At the top, a little meadow opens up. If you momentarily leave the trail and walk southwest on top of the quartzite shelf, the views to the east and south are very satisfying.

The trail becomes a long, narrow wooden boardwalk over a marshy section, which may or may not actually be wet all the way. Wind again through trees until you come upon a cairned trail fork at 2.5 miles. To your right, a trail heads north toward Notch Mountain. Directly before you, the trail continues west. Keep going west. You'll almost immediately see the lower of the Twin Lakes on your left; soon the upper and

The uppermost of the Twin Lakes along the Clyde Lake Loop

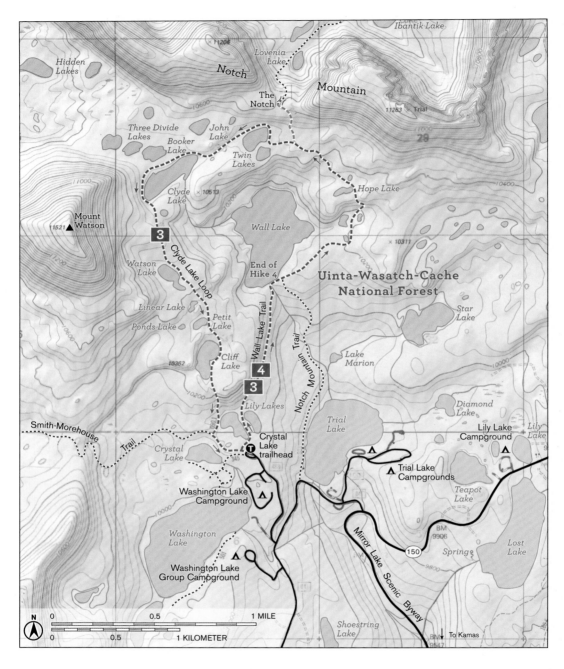

larger Twin Lake will come into view above it. Here you will start to come across a bewildering multitude of hiker paths, most of them leading to campsites or simply trodden by the confused. Keep circling around the Twin Lakes' north sides, then head generally southwest. The imposing Mount Watson to the west is a good landmark to keep in your sights if you temporarily lose the trail here and there. In 0.2 mile you will reach Clyde Lake.

The trail follows the western shoreline of this lake, gently curving you almost due south once you reach the lake's far end. Hike along beneath the imposing bulk of Mount Watson, rising to your right (west), for 0.4 mile to Watson Lake. You'll pass a succession of small lakes as you wind your way back to the trailhead: tiny Linear Lake, then Petit Lake, then the larger Cliff Lake. Pass through a wooded section and drop down 250 feet in elevation to reach the western Lily Lake. Here you reach another trail junction, with the Smith-Morehouse Trail heading off to your right (west). Stay on the trail going more left (east) to reach the parking area, 2 miles after Clyde Lake.

Extending your hike: At the cairned spur trail leading north to The Notch, head uphill for 0.3 mile. Somewhat tougher than any other part of the described loop due to the 120-foot elevation gain in this brief section, the side jaunt is well worth it to reach the top and be able to take in spectacular views to the south as well as over The Notch to the north. Looking down over the northern vistas reveals many other lakes and mountains to explore, including Lovenia Lake almost directly below. Return south back down this spur trail to rejoin the Clyde Lake Loop, adding a total of 0.6 mile to this hike.

4 *Wall Lake*

Roundtrip: 2 miles
Hiking time: 1–2 hours
Elevation gain: 300 feet
Difficulty: easy

Season: summer–fall
Map: USGS Mirror Lake
Contact: Uinta-Wasatch-Cache National Forest, Heber-Kamas Ranger District

Getting there: From Kamas, drive east on Mirror Lake Scenic Byway, State Route 150, for 27 miles. The signed turnoff for the Crystal Lake area will be on your left. Turn left (west) and drive 0.8 mile to a road fork; turn right (north) and drive another 0.9 mile to the Crystal Lake trailhead parking. **Notes:** Fee required; pay at self-service kiosks along highway or at ranger stations. Vault toilets, overnight camping, large parking lot. Insect repellent handy in summer.

Displaying the significant beauty of the lake-strewn Uintas, the Wall Lake Trail is a delightful blend of alpine lake, pine-tree pathways, and scenic mountain views, all of which make this a truly classic hike.

Wall Lake is a beautiful lake nestled into a stunning setting that can be reached with minimal effort, making it an ideal hike to showcase the area for the very young, the less fit or agile, or those with less time. It can be tacked onto a longer hike or a backpacking trip, or done in addition to a separate hike in the same day, giving more ambitious hikers even more bang for their buck. The trailhead is in an area with a plethora of other lakes, trailheads, and camping facilities ranging from tent sites to RV parking. Holidays and weekends can be fairly crowded at this popular and easy-to-reach area, so a midweek trip may allow for more solitude if that's what you prefer.

From the parking lot, find the trailhead marked with the small wooden sign for Notch Mountain Trail, which leads due north. The wide, rock-lined path ambles through towering pines, quickly skirting by the edges of small, grassy meadows and passing through two scattered bodies of water known as Lily Lakes. The trees provide shade, and the view at every turn, from the simplest to the most grand, is photogenic. As you walk under a canopy of spruce and firs, you will catch occasional views of Bald Mountain and Reids Peak to your right, with a few spots on the trail allowing for nearly

Wall Lake on a serene summer day

unobstructed views. Summertime can see colorful wildflowers liberally dotting the meadows, and fall hikes show off reds, oranges, and golds on the trees and lower-lying shrubs. There are some small rises along this section of trail, but for the most part it is an easy stroll in the woods on a well-defined path.

As you approach Wall Lake 1 mile in, you'll see a small stream rumbling down a rocky course from beneath a constructed bridge. From here, the trail winds up the hillside to the left of the stream. A small rise in the trail comes just before you reach the lake, and the walk up lets you have a splendid first view of the lake spread out in the basin, tucked up beneath the rock "wall" on its west side. Directly to your north rises Notch Mountain, its appearance immediately making clear the reason behind its name. There are numerous spots around the lake at which to sit, play, eat lunch, camp, or fish if desired. The entire shoreline is rocky, but some sandy "beaches" smooth it out. When you're ready to leave, simply retrace your steps on the trail back to the parking area.

5 *Notch Mountain Trail*

One-way: 9.7 miles	*Season:* summer–fall
Hiking time: 7–9 hours	*Map:* USGS Mirror Lake
Elevation gain: 930 feet	*Contact:* Uinta-Wasatch-Cache National
Difficulty: moderate	Forest, Heber-Kamas Ranger District

Getting there: From Kamas, drive east on Mirror Lake Scenic Byway, State Route 150, for 29 miles. The well-signed dirt parking area for Bald Mountain will be on your left (north) side. *Shuttle vehicle parking:* From Kamas, drive east on Mirror Lake Scenic Byway for 27 miles. The signed turnoff for the Crystal Lake area will be on your left. Turn left (west) and drive 0.8 mile to a fork; turn right (north) and drive another 0.9 mile to the Crystal Lake trailhead parking. **Notes:** Fee required; pay at self-service kiosks along highway or at ranger stations. Vault toilets at trailhead. Insect repellent handy in summer. Shuttle vehicle required.

A long and rewarding hike, the Notch Mountain Trail whisks you by gorgeous alpine lakes, reveals miles upon miles of mountains within the sprawling Uinta-Wasatch-Cache National Forest, and offers a true sense of the area's grandeur without requiring an overly lengthy or rutted dirt-road drive. If you are camping in the area, this trail is but one of many you can explore. The Notch Mountain Trail, however, showcases some of the best views around, which makes it an ideal candidate for sharing some of northern Utah's most classic scenery. While you will gain elevation, you

Typically enticing Uintas scenery on the Notch Mountain Trail

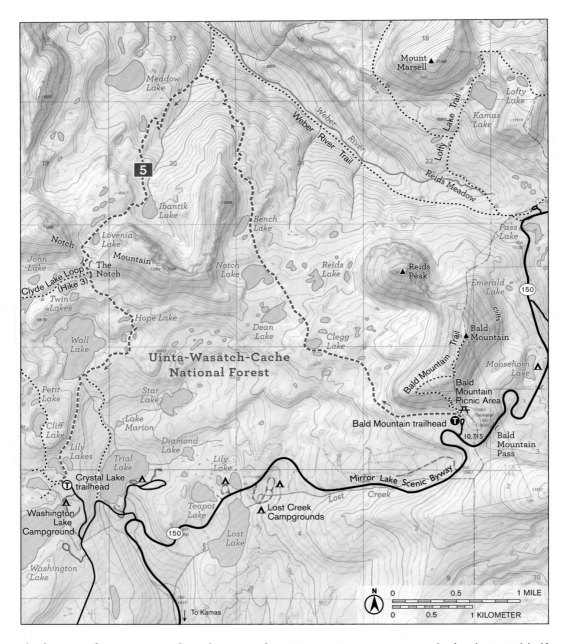

also lose significant amounts along the way, making this trail unusual in the otherwise upwardly mobile hikes of the Uintas.

From the Bald Mountain trailhead, go first north and then almost immediately west (left) on the signed Notch Mountain Trail path. Bald Mountain rises to your right for the initial half mile as you slowly descend toward the first lake of interest on the way, Clegg Lake at 1.7 miles in. Small compared to other lakes on this trail, Clegg is mighty in its refined beauty. After the trail curves around the southern end of the lake, it heads in a more northwesterly direction. The next mile features three more lakes the trail directly passes: Dean, Notch, and Bench. Sometimes popular with people who enjoy casting a line or wanting to pitch a tent for the night, these glacial lakes are all beauties. Past Bench Lake you continue dropping in elevation for the next 1.5 miles. About 4.5 miles in, turn left (south) at a junction with the Weber River Trail to remain on the Notch Mountain Trail.

As you meander along, passing tall, elegant spruce trees and small meadows, you have a mile and a half before you reach what many hikers consider one of the most, if not the single most, beautiful lakes in the entire region: Ibantik Lake. Rippling teal-colored waters against a backdrop of severe mountain ridges make this a classic alpine scene and lure many to spend the night alongside its shores. This is also where you are likely to begin encountering more people, as many hike north to this lake from the terminus point of your route. Continue south along the trail, passing Lovenia Lake to the east as you approach the climb up the trail's eponymous

notch. When you reach the top of the notch in Notch Mountain, about 1.3 miles past Ibantik Lake, you are at the height of the trail's elevation gain and standing at 10,655 feet.

The views from here are tremendous—both to the north behind you and to the south before you—and you deserve a well-earned rest stop to enjoy and take photos. From here, drop 0.3 mile down the switchbacks to a flatter portion. Cairns usually mark the trail; turn left (east) for the shorter distance to the parking area. (Turning west will take you only a slight bit longer; see the Clyde Lake Loop trail, Hike 3, for more information on this section.) Hope Lake spreads out to your right as you pass through a marshy meadow to drop down quartzite switchbacks. Pass Wall Lake, a large reservoir popular with the fishing crowd, on the right. From here only 1 mile remains to the terminus trailhead where your shuttle vehicle awaits, and it is an easy, scenic mile spent on a broad path winding through the tall trees and allowing occasional glimpses of Bald Mountain and Reids Peak to your left (east) along the way.

6 *Bald Mountain*

Roundtrip: 4 miles	**Season:** summer–fall
Hiking time: 3–4 hours	**Map:** USGS Mirror Lake
Elevation gain: 1160 feet	**Contact:** Uinta-Wasatch-Cache National
Difficulty: moderate	Forest, Heber-Kamas Ranger District

Getting there: From Kamas, drive east on Mirror Lake Scenic Byway, State Route 150, for 29 miles. The well-signed dirt parking area for Bald Mountain will be on your left (north) side. **Notes:** Fee required; pay at self-service kiosks along highway or at ranger stations. Vault toilets at trailhead. Lightning danger due to exposure.

Accessible directly from the Mirror Lake Scenic Byway, Bald Mountain is a marvelous lung-burner that affords those who reach its rocky top incomparable 360-degree views across a rolling landscape of mountains and lakes as far as the eye can see. Although short in length, this hike's elevation gain means you will be exercising those lungs on the way up. A trailhead point for a maze of hikes that lead deep

into the wilderness, Bald Mountain is also home to a herd of mountain goats the sharp-eyed can sometimes easily spot, due to their bright white coats, as they lounge or graze on the steep sides of the mountain. Some exposure may make a few hikers careful with their steps, and it also makes this hike too treacherous for small children.

From the parking area, walk toward the trailhead by the restrooms and trail kiosk. You are almost immediately presented with a trail fork: choose the one leading right (northeast). The trail leads directly toward Bald Mountain but switchbacks to the right as soon as you begin to ascend. Long, swooping switchbacks curl along the side of the mountain as you climb. The views the entire way are utterly open and arresting, although you will want to watch your steps rather than the scenery in some sections. Crumbled rock and shrubs make this seem like an almost desert-y hike, although you are smack in the Uintas and surrounded by mountains. Some of the many area lakes will become visible as you get higher. Pass dwarf conifers and other ambitious little pockets of hardy small vegetation as you climb the switchbacks for 0.6 mile before reaching a long, wide boulder field on an inclined plateau.

Here, the trail flattens out before swerving eastward and again generally uphill. Now you've reached the last gasp of plant life, which gives up

almost all semblance of holding on as the path strikes out through the boulders. This sort of exposure means excellent views but makes this a poor choice of trail on any day that threatens lightning. As you reach the eastern edge of the mountain again, almost directly above where your hike began far below, the trail will take you right to the edge. Views to the east are stunning, as is the drop-off on your right-hand side. The trail sharply angles back westward and tightly switchbacks again, passing beside large boulders and taking you ever uphill. One section requires a bit of a hop, skip, and a jump, with a yawning precipice dropping off to the east, but it is easily doable by those who are sure of their feet and not afraid of heights. At almost 2 miles in, you are very close to the summit when you reach the stone stairway that seems to lead right into the sky itself.

When you tumble onto the wide, rocky top of Bald Mountain, the views really open up in every

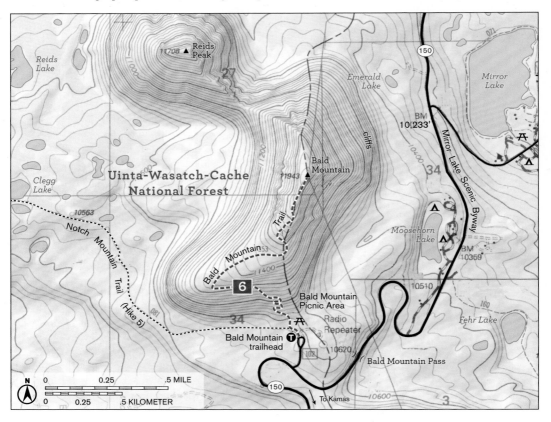

Majestic views from Bald Mountain

direction. Fancifully constructed rock cairns may decorate some of the rock ledges, and boulder seats are available for you to sit and take in the views, which are truly astounding as you survey the vast wilderness that seems to extend in every direction. Return via the same route.

7 Lofty Lake Loop

Loop: 4 miles
Hiking time: 3–4 hours
Elevation gain: 900 feet
Difficulty: moderate

Season: summer–fall
Map: USGS Mirror Lake
Contact: Uinta-Wasatch-Cache National Forest, Heber-Kamas Ranger District

Getting there: From Kamas, drive east on Mirror Lake Scenic Byway, State Route 150, for 32 miles. Turn left (north) into the Pass Lake parking area. **Notes:** Fee required; pay at self-service kiosks along highway or at ranger stations. Vault toilets at trailhead. Insect repellent handy in summer.

Lofty indeed, this loop hike takes you past lakes, over saddles, and to breathtaking views, and gives you a great introduction to the beauties of the High Uintas. With classic high alpine lakes cradled in rocky bowls or tucked beneath towering rock walls, tall green pine trees, large meadows filled with waving grass and sometimes deep rivulets of streams, and a trail that is moderate enough for many hikers yet pleasantly challenging for beginners, this hike

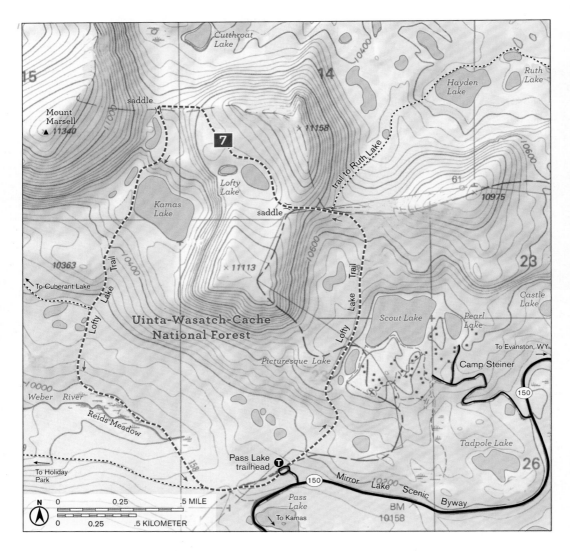

can make for a very beautiful day in the mountains. This popular trail might be a little crowded on weekends and holidays, but sometimes you will have it mostly to yourself. Spectacular views from the high points are an added bonus to this loop that passes by or allows you to view five lakes. The change in terrain from tree-ringed meadows to barren above-timberline spots also makes this a topographically diverse hike.

From the parking area, set out eastward on the signed Lofty Lake Loop trailhead in the middle of the lot. The route meanders eastward through spruce and fir, rising and falling as it goes. Several small log bridges straddle stream rivulets that run down over the path in places. Soon you pass small Picturesque Lake to your right (east), quickly followed by the far larger, beautiful Scout Lake at 0.5 mile. Naturally, Scout Lake is home to a scout camp, on the opposite shore, so be prepared for hordes of excited kids running around during the busy (but brief) summer season. Fall yields more tranquility.

After leaving Scout Lake, the trail continues northward and heads determinedly uphill. Slowly, the scenery opens up as you head above timberline. The trail winds ever upward through yellow and cream-colored boulders scattered across the landscape. Turning west, the trail dives right into a boulder field where it may be easy to temporarily lose the trail, although cairns usually mark it. Simply keep moving upward and it will soon be visible again. Hardy little bushes and shrubs grow from cracks in the rocks; by now the tall pines are below you. When you reach the saddle, you are at 10,900 feet, the highest point in this trail. From here you look down onto Lofty Lake to the north, with the trail easily visible skirting around it to the east.

Drop down and follow the trail north and then northwest past Lofty Lake, 1.5 miles into your hike. It leads to a spectacular overlook to the north from which you can see Cutthroat Lake and a seemingly endless expanse of adventuring opportunities. The trail now heads down and due west toward Mount Marsell before it curves south again. Pass through a flat meadow with an excellent view of Reids Peak directly before you, far in the distance. The trail drops down a rocky hill to Kamas Lake, 2 miles in. The rocky shores of the lake offer plentiful places to sit and relax or have lunch. Once it leaves the lake, the trail continues to descend, passing meadows on the way. Pass the trail fork toward Holiday Park and keep an eye out for signs to Pass Lake trailhead and State Route 150 to ensure you remain on the correct trail, which is still heading south before it curves eastward again to deposit you back at the parking area.

Looking northward from the overlook above Cutthroat Lake

8 *Naturalist Basin*

Roundtrip: 15.8 miles
Hiking time: 8 hours–2 days
Elevation gain: 1350 feet
Difficulty: moderate/hard

Season: summer–fall
Map: USGS Hayden Peak
Contact: Uinta-Wasatch-Cache National Forest, Heber-Kamas Ranger District

Getting there: From Kamas, drive east on Mirror Lake Scenic Byway, State Route 150, for 35 miles. Turn right (south) into the Highline Trail/Butterfly Lake parking area. **Notes:** Fee required; pay at self-service kiosks along highway or at ranger stations. Vault toilets at parking area. Insect repellent handy in summer.

With its veritable explosion of lakes, Naturalist Basin is a popular area with those who love the Uintas, yet it is far less frequented the farther along the trail you get and into Naturalist Basin itself. The choices of a multitude of beautiful lakes at which to relax, eat lunch, fish, explore, or camp along the way stop many people before they complete the entire loop. For those seeking more solitude, doing the whole loop can yield wilderness immersion with fewer people to encounter. Engelmann spruce, lodgepole and ponderosa pines, grassy meadows, and rocky ridgelines all make this a classic mountain hike. Those wanting to do this trip as an overnight should set up camp near the end of the lollipop loop that explores the basin's lakes so they can do the 4.5-mile loop as a day hike. Whether you opt to do this trail as a long day

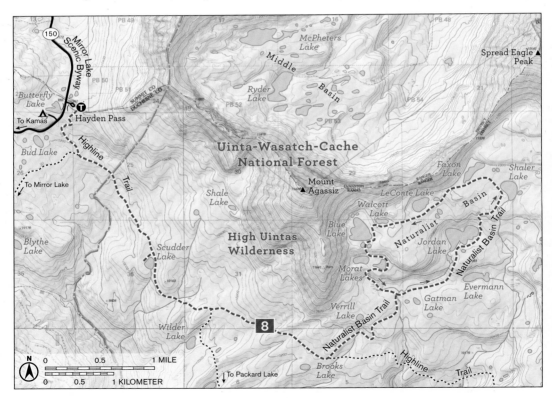

Lakes abound on the Naturalist Basin Trail.

hike or an overnight trip, Naturalist Basin is a rewarding example of some of the best scenery in the High Uintas.

The Highline Trail shoots off south from the parking area. Two miles down the trail a sign points you to Scudder Lake, up a short spur trail to your right; taking this spur to and from the lake will add 0.4 mile to the entire hike, but Scudder is a pretty place to visit. Gorgeous meadows that can be strewn with wildflowers in the summer make this section quite scenic, as do the views of Mount Agassiz and Hayden Peak, visible in the distance to the east.

At 3 miles from the trailhead, a signed junction indicates Packard Lake. Keep going east on the Highline Trail for another 1.2 miles, where the junction to Naturalist Basin Trail awaits. Veer left and walk northeast for 1 mile, traveling

somewhat uphill until the route finally opens up at a wide green meadow ringed behind with the gray laccolithic rise of the Uinta crest. From here you begin the basin loop. Somewhere in here, or at one of the closer lakes (the large, popular Jordan 1 mile northeast, or smaller Morat 1 mile northwest), is where you'll likely want to camp if this is an overnight trip.

Take the right fork and head east to reach Jordan Lake. The largest lake in the basin, Jordan is settled into an alpine visual delight, edged by tall pines and the high lift of the mountains. The trail contours around the east side of the lake, turning more northward at the top. Shortly thereafter you reach Shaler Lake, where the trail bends to the northwest as it beelines for Faxon Lake, 0.3 mile away. Keep heading southwest toward small LeConte Lake, passing on its eastern side and continuing toward puddle-like Walcott Lake and then larger Blue Lake. Head south and a little east again to skirt the Morat Lakes, where the trail passes by the east edge of the eastern lake. If you get a little turned around, there is a trail, traversing directly between the lakes, that will take you straight back to the main trail. From here you have half a mile to reach the end of the Naturalist Basin loop, where you will find the remaining 1 mile of the Naturalist Basin Trail leading southwest back down to the Highline Trail. Retrace your footsteps back to the parking area.

9 *Grandaddy Lake*

Roundtrip: 6.4 miles
Hiking time: 4–5 hours
Elevation gain: 940 feet
Difficulty: moderate

Season: summer–fall
Map: USGS Grandaddy Lake
Contact: Ashley National Forest, Duchesne/Roosevelt Ranger District

Getting there: From Salt Lake City, take I-80 east 25 miles to US Highway 40 and drive 4 miles south to exit 4. Take State Route 248 11.8 miles east to Kamas. At the stoplight turn right onto Main Street/State Route 32. Drive south 2 miles to State Route 35/West Main Village Way (has stop sign) and turn left (east). Drive 37.5 miles to a well-marked road heading north along the North Fork of the Duchesne River; turn left here and pass a Forest Service sign for Stockmore Guard Station. Continue 11 miles to Hades Campground; about 4 miles in the road will become maintained gravel. Just past Defa's Dude Ranch on your left, look for a dirt road signed 315 heading off to the right (northeast). Follow this road 5.8 steep mountain miles to the Grandview trailhead parking.
Notes: The final 5 miles of steep, one-lane dirt road to the trailhead may be impassable by low-clearance or non-4WD vehicles, depending on weather and season. The road is not suitable for very large vehicles or for drivers unaccustomed to narrow roads with steep drop-offs. Can be very crowded on weekends and holidays. Insect repellent handy in summer.

As the largest natural lake in the Uinta range, Grandaddy Lake would already hold some renown. The dazzling setting, however, catapults it into serious popularity. It's simply gorgeous, and enough of a hike that the effort to reach the trailhead seems very worthwhile. On early summer trips you may spot blooming flowers: the delicate, well-named white globeflower; the very pretty pink spring beauty; and the graceful yellow glacier lily may peek up from the forested floor or be scattered through meadows. Although easily doable in one day, this hike is an excellent choice for an overnight trip so you can really enjoy the area. Plenty of campsites are scattered along the ragged shoreline of the 170-acre lake. The entire Grandaddy Basin actually holds a plethora of lakes from which you can string together a multinight backpacking extravaganza with virtually endless routes. But as the highlight of this area, Grandaddy Lake should be high on your list to visit.

From the trailhead, a rocky path leads you up, winding through the towering pine trees. After 2 miles of heading uphill, you reach the high point of this trail, Hades Pass at its lofty height of 10,640 feet. Walking just a little ways beyond the pass offers thoroughly breathtaking views into the seemingly unbroken passages of wild mountain country unfolding as far as the eye can see. Heart Lake and Grandaddy Lake present themselves to you far below, urging you along the next 1 mile down to reach a trail junction, as you drop 340 feet in the process. Going left at the trail divergence sends you to Betsy Lake; turn

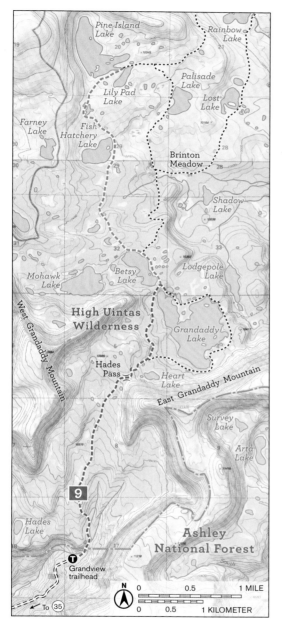

Fall color turning along the way to Grandaddy Lake

right and head 0.2 mile southeast to reach the northern end of huge, lovely Grandaddy Lake.

Ringed by a thick forest of pines, with some grassy meadow areas meeting the shore at points, this is truly a nature setting—especially when viewed from far above, where you get the sense of how much country lies beyond it. Although there may be a significant number of other people here, depending on what time of year and when in the week you do this hike, if you feel a need for solitude you can continue along the shoreline to find a quiet little nook from which to enjoy the blue-green waters. When you are done exploring and enjoying the lake, return to the parking area via the same trail.

Extending your hike: Endless options exist here to make this a longer day or an overnight trip. For just a little more, head north from the trail junction to reach Betsy Lake almost immediately. You can wander along the shoreline for up to 0.5 mile on the trail, then return the same way. This will add a total of about 1 mile to your hike.

For a longer (possibly overnight) excursion, continue north from Betsy Lake for 2.5 miles to Pine Island Lake, which is also large and extremely scenic. Return via the same route, adding a total of 5.6 miles to your hike.

10 *Amethyst Lake*

Roundtrip: 12.4 miles
Hiking time: 7 hours–2 days
Elevation gain: 1950 feet
Difficulty: moderate/hard
Season: summer–fall

Map: USGS Christmas Meadows, Hayden Peak
Contact: Uinta-Wasatch-Cache National Forest, Evanston–Mountain View Ranger District

Getting there: From Kamas, take State Route 150 (Mirror Lake Scenic Byway) east for 46.3 miles to Christmas Meadows Road, signed for Christmas Meadows Campground, and turn right (south). **Notes:** Fee required; pay at self-service kiosks along highway or at ranger stations. Vault toilets, campground, picnic tables, and fire rings at trailhead. Insect repellent handy in summer.

The fast and fit hiker can complete this beautiful, popular trail in one day, and many do just that. For full enjoyment and more solitude during the evening and early morning, however, a more leisurely overnight trip is suggested. For a more tranquil hike, try to come on a weekday or earlier or later in the season. Best hiked from mid-July through late September, this very popular

Amethyst Lake on a sunny day

area is often overrun with vehicles and people during the height of the summer season. But even with the crowds, this gorgeous hike is a gem to remember.

Beginning 200 yards past the Christmas Meadows Campground, the trail heads south, skirting the eastern side of the meadow basin for 2 miles. Stillwater Creek is a scenic accompaniment to your stroll through this section. Look for deer and moose grazing on the grasses, as well as the inevitable fellow hikers and horseback riders on the trail, as you pass through rustling aspen trees.

Watch for a wooden High Uintas Wilderness Area sign at 2.3 miles. Barely 200 yards later, you will come to a junction. Take a left turn at the sign for Amethyst Lake. From this point the trail climbs steadily up, which your lungs and legs will take note of as you gain 600 feet in 0.5 mile. Let the burble of Ostler Fork's cascading falls, which tumble down just beside the trail, make a pretty soundtrack to urge you uphill. As soon as the trail levels out again, pat yourself on the back—the steepest pitch is now done. You'll still be going uphill, but it's a much gentler incline from here.

Occasionally you can glimpse two peaks, Ostler and LaMotte, through breaks in the trees. Their very rugged stance gives you plenty of assurance that you are in the high country, as does the fact that they are generally still spotted with snow during the summer months. You'll know when you reach Amethyst Basin because it's the poster child for gorgeous mountain meadows, complete with a meandering creek, healthy-looking pine trees, a carpet of green grass, and the frame of Ostler Peak to the south. If you make this a two-day trip, the meadow is a good place to pitch your tent.

From the meadow, Amethyst Lake is a mere 0.8 mile farther. If you're there in abundant sunshine you will see the riveting blue from which the lake, cradled in its basin just below the talus slopes of Ostler Peak, gets its name. Return back to the parking area via the same trail.

Extending your hike: If you crave more solitude for overnight camping, head due west for less frequented Ostler Lake and set up camp there. There is no trail to Ostler Lake, but it is easy to find if you have a map and compass. You can visit Amethyst Lake in the morning before heading back down. Amethyst Lake does have campsites set back in the trees from the water. Lake BR-24 (which is so beautiful it really deserves a far better moniker) is between Ostler and Amethyst and also provides excellent campsites.

11 *Kings Peak*

Roundtrip: 29 miles
Hiking time: 2–4 days
Elevation gain: 4100 feet
Difficulty: strenuous
Season: summer–fall

Map: USGS Kings Peak, Gilbert Peak NE
Contact: Uinta-Wasatch-Cache National Forest, Evanston–Mountain View Ranger District

Getting there: From Evanston, Wyoming, drive 35 miles east on I-80. Take exit 39 south to State Route 414. Drive 6 miles and turn right (west) on State Route 410. At 6.8 miles down the road, SR 410 makes a sharp westward bend while a gravel road goes straight. Take the gravel road south for 12 miles to the fork. Take the left fork to Henrys Fork and drive 10.8 miles to the trailhead parking. Roads on the way in should be signed for Henrys Fork. **Notes:** Vault toilets at parking area. Snow usually bars access until midsummer. July and August are usually the best months, but beware of thunder and lightning storms. May be crowded over holiday weekends, especially initial portions of the trail. Insect repellent handy during summer.

As the highest peak in Utah at 13,528 feet, Kings Peak receives much attention. A long, hard hike demanding at least one night for most people, if not two nights, it rewards with backcountry beauty, lush alpine meadows, the graceful whisper of tall pines, and the feeling of being on top of the world—or at least the state. Although there are different routes to the top, this is the traditional, shortest trail followed by thousands of summit hopefuls every year.

The high backcountry of the Uintas beckons en route to Kings Peak.

(Thankfully, you are unlikely to encounter all of them on one trip.)

Extremely fit backpackers might make the top in two days, or even one; most people will enjoy a slower pace, taking three to four days. Remember that hiking above 10,000 feet is far more taxing than you'd think. It is not remotely suggested that you wear a full backpack to actually summit Kings Peak; most hikers simply day hike it with a small daypack, stashing their larger packs at a base camp. Alpine views, rugged peaks, abundant wildlife, and the chance to top out on Utah's highest point all make this hike a must-do for peak baggers. If you don't particularly want to bag a peak but simply enjoy mountain hiking, the views alone are well worth forays into the gorgeous basins here, especially throughout the Henrys Fork section.

From the Henrys Fork trailhead, follow the trail southwest as it roughly parallels the right (west) side of the Henrys Fork River. The views along this section are very pretty, and for the first 5.5 miles you only gain about 700 feet in elevation. Pass the spur trail to Alligator Lake in about 2.5 miles and continue on, unless you want to take the 0.8-mile trek to and from that lake. This can also be a decent campsite if you're making a longer multiday trek or don't start your hike until late in the day.

Cross a small bridge over the creek at 5.5 miles and keep going, now on the east side of the creek. This is also known as Elkhorn Crossing; the North Slope Trail crosses here and offers a somewhat longer alternate route (see Extending your hike). Stay on your southward-leading trail. Pass Dollar Lake on your left at 7.3 miles; this can make a good campsite for the night that allows the next day to be about summiting with only a daypack. Dollar Lake is picturesque, with lovely views of the mountains. The relative flatness of this first day's hike also means you can conserve most of your energy for the next day. Those who are uber-fit will, of course, press on past this lake.

Keep heading south on the trail to Gunsight Pass at 10.5 miles, about 1600 feet higher than the trailhead. At 11,888 feet, the views from this pass into Painter Basin are outstanding and

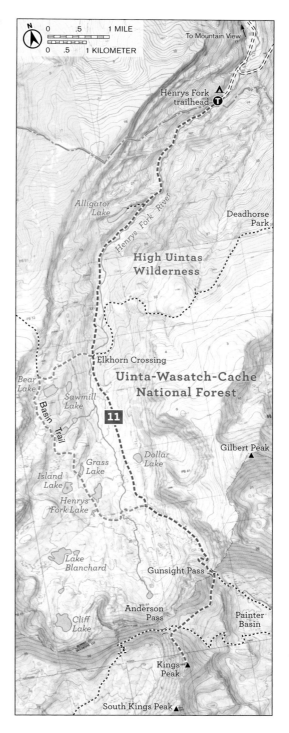

deserve some time to admire. From here, you roughly aim for Anderson Pass, 4.6 miles away. If you're comfortable with shortcuts and are an experienced hiker, you will likely see a more direct path, as there are some hiker-made trail marks. However, the shortcut is extremely steep and covered in loose boulder scree, so it is not recommended—frankly, you'll probably not save much time since you have to take so much additional care ascending this way. Also, Anderson Pass is 800 feet higher than Gunsight Pass, and at this point you're probably not interested in adding any more elevation than necessary to your hike. Remain on the correct trail described here, which takes you through Gunsight Pass.

Do not drop down into Painter Basin on the most traditional version of the trail, as you will lose 500 feet of elevation. A very prominent rock cairn at the height of the pass points you to the hiker-marked trail heading off to your right (south). Follow this until you reach a fairly steep ridge. After the breathless scramble up, views into the gorgeous Painter Basin should help assuage the burn in your lungs and legs. Contour around the ridge and head toward the flatter part approaching Anderson Pass toward Kings Peak. From here, the going can be slow as you pick your way through. Kings Peak is—as mountains of its stature tend to be—a treeless, rock-covered summit that can strike some as very unappealing during the final push.

Achieving the last 1500 feet of this slog (and several false summits along the way) is an effort. There is no easy way through the rock pile that basically makes up the final portion of trail, which is a loosely used term for this section. The ultimate beauty of the hike is in the view payoff at the top. The 360-degree views are astounding, although if a storm is approaching you'd best enjoy them very quickly before hustling back down so as not to become lightning bait. From here, follow your same route back down, retracing the trail back to your campsite or even directly to the trailhead, depending on your level of fitness and eagerness to finish this most epic of peak-bagging trails.

Extending your hike: If you'd like a little more leisure time, take this side route on your way to Kings Peak and enjoy a night by a passel of lakes. At the North Slope Trail junction, also known as Elkhorn Crossing, turn right to head west along the Basin Trail. Along the 5.6 miles of this trail diversion, pass by Bear Lake, Grass Lake, Island Lake, and Henrys Fork Lake. More dot the area, and campsites abound in this spectacularly pretty basin. It can be quite crowded in this area. The trail loops right back into the main trail, coming out past Dollar Lake.

1 2 *Little Hole National Recreation Trail*

One-way: 7.2 miles
Hiking time: 3–4 hours
Elevation loss: 230 feet
Difficulty: easy/moderate

Season: all year
Map: USGS Dutch John, Goslin Mountain
Contact: Ashley National Forest, Flaming Gorge/Vernal Ranger District

Getting there: From Vernal, drive north on US Highway 191 for 41 miles to Flaming Gorge Dam. Just past the dam, turn right on the road to the boat launch. Park here. To drop off the shuttle vehicle, drive an additional 2.4 miles north on US 191 to Little Hole Road/Forest Road 075 and turn right. Drive 6 miles to the parking area. Commercial shuttle services are locally available. **Notes:** Fee required. Shuttle vehicle required. Toilets at both trailheads.

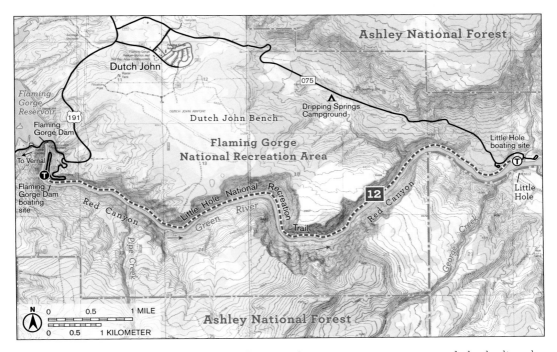

Skirting the north side of the Green River from Flaming Gorge Dam up to Little Hole, this incredibly scenic, mellow hike is an enjoyable ramble. Gently curving through Red Canyon, the river and trail genuinely deserve the National Recreation Trail label. In this west to east route, rolling hills crest down to the river, tumbled with dark boulders and dotted with rubber rabbitbrush and sage, along with pine trees in the deeper parts of the canyon, where the rim soars 1000 feet overhead. You may spot river otters at play in the water or sunning themselves on the rocks, or catch sight of the trout that lure many to bring their fishing rods on this hike. In the springtime, bald eagles may be watching the river to do a little fishing themselves.

The trail is immediately lovely; the waters and vegetation contrast nicely with the pale red color of the cliffs as you descend via switchbacks to the river. The trail hugs the cliff walls as it goes downward, with drop-offs that may give those truly nervous about heights some pause, although for the majority of hikers this is nothing of concern. Native grasses and shrubs line the trail as it nears the river, and large boulders extend into or thrust up from the water here and there the entire way.

In some brief sections the trail is a wooden boardwalk leading over tricky boulder sections or beneath cliffs where the water comes nearly to the cliff edges. In the placid sections, the river can be so clear as to be crystalline, allowing you to see every single thing in the water. The views seem to reflect the classic colors of the state's southern portions—green water and trees, red rocks, brilliant blue sky, depending on the weather—but they are also fairly common in this dry northeastern corner of Utah.

For the first few miles you will likely share the river with people fishing, but after that they tend to peter out until you reach the end of the trail. River runners sometimes float by. When you reach the rapids sections in the latter part of the hike, starting at about 3.5 miles in, watching a rafting party come down and negotiate these technical parts of the river can be fun.

The Little Hole National Recreation Trail meanders alongside the Green River. (Photo by Kay Luther)

Huge ponderosa pine trees show up on occasion, and keep an eye out for the flat, broad paddles of the prickly pear cactus. In the spring, the blooms can be enchanting, varying from yellow to pink and all shades in between. As you walk, now and then you will notice how the water does indeed appear to be very green, especially when vegetation lines the river bottom in calm sections, gently floating beneath the surface. While the history of how the Green River got its name is a little murky, it seems a safe bet that some early explorer such as John Wesley Powell noted the brilliance of the color. The beautiful, serene trail officially ends at the Little Hole take out, although you can actually keep hiking for some ways down the river.

13 Jones Hole Creek

Roundtrip: 7.9 miles
Hiking time: 5 hours
Elevation gain: 424 feet
Difficulty: moderate

Season: all year
Map: USGS Jones Hole
Contact: Dinosaur National Monument

Getting there: From US Highway 40 in Vernal, turn north on US Highway 191, go 5 blocks to 500 North and turn right (east). After 2 miles veer left (north) onto Diamond Mountain Road. Go 35 miles to the Jones Hole Fish Hatchery and park in the lot there. The trailhead is signed and easy to find from the parking area. **Notes:** Fee required. Roads may be impassable if wet.

Jones Hole is in Dinosaur National Monument, a fascinating place in itself. The Jones Hole Trail winds alongside Jones Hole Creek through a 2000-foot-deep river canyon, eventually depositing you at the confluence with the Green River. The creek originates from a limestone spring, its flowing waters etching the canyon with deep, curving strokes over millions of years and creating what is today a very nice hike. Although you won't see dinosaur bones, other delights beckon: intriguing ancient petroglyphs, a positively lush riparian scene in the midst of what is otherwise a sere landscape, and the fun of playing in a small waterfall in nearby Ely Creek on hot days. If it floats your boat, you also have the added bonus of casting a line into the well-stocked creek. Half shaded, half exposed, the trail can be super hot in the height of summer, so leave as early as you can and take more water than you think you'll need. Spring and fall hiking here is excellent.

From the parking area at the fish hatchery, set off downstream (south) through fragrant sagebrush and scrubby, resilient junipers and pinyons. For 4 leisurely miles, you are surrounded by box elder and cottonwood trees and greenery on the banks where they happily soak up the water. At 1.5 miles, a wooden bridge crosses the creek, taking you to its west side. A worn footpath leads to the Deluge Shelter pictographs, centuries-old Fremont Indian rock art, colored in deep brick and ocher tones, depicting animals and, perhaps, flights of ancient imagination.

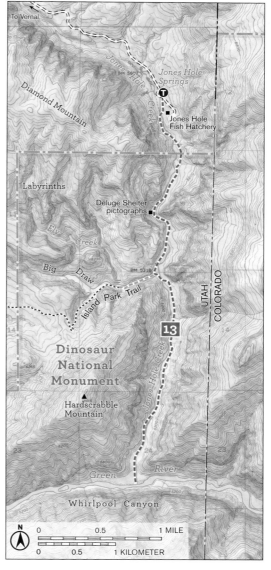

Ancient pictograph of a bighorn sheep near the Jones Hole Trail

Just over 2 miles from the trailhead, you reach the campsite area. From here, the trail continues another 1.8 miles down to the Green River, becoming progressively drier and hotter, although still lovely, as it approaches. At the river, the clear water and bank-carpeting green grasses invite relaxation and enjoyment of the scene. Keep your eyes peeled for wildlife, which come to the area for water. It's possible to spot deer, marmots, many bird species, and even bighorn sheep close to the river if you're lucky. You may also spot river rafters lazing down this section of the river or setting up at the river traveler-only (from mid-May through mid-September) campsites there. Hikers there off-season are allowed to camp at the river sites; check with the monument for the specific dates. Once you've taken everything in, return to the trailhead the same way.

Extending your hike: From the Deluge Shelter, it's an easy 0.3-mile walk to Island Park Trail. Then walk about 0.25 mile on Island Park Trail to Ely Creek, where a 12-foot waterfall spills over a terraced rock face and invites you to stand under it on the hottest days. Surrounding Douglas fir and silver-barked birch trees add shade and the natural wind chime sounds of rustling leaves on breezy days. Fun tip: if you're in a larger hiking party when it's later in the season and the waterfall is low, to experience the best deluge have several members seat themselves in the small pools immediately above the falls. Proper wedging of behinds will temporarily dam the water, allowing it to build up. Brave souls may then position themselves at the bottom of the falls, awaiting an extremely chilly drenching once those at the top all move at the same time.

Opposite, top: Moose graze in Albion Basin near the trail to Cecret Lake.

Opposite, bottom: Red Pine Lake as viewed from the trail to The Pfeifferhorn

North Central

The Wasatch Mountain Range sprawls from the Idaho border to nearly halfway through Utah, covering about 250 miles north to south. Tall peaks, beautiful rocky cirques with alpine lakes nestled into them, pine trees towering above trails, and wildlife ranging from bears to moose to chipmunks all make these mountains a nearby playground for hikers who choose to settle in or visit local areas. Mountain peaks topping 10,000 feet can be climbed after work because the trailheads—and short trails—are 20 minutes or less from Salt Lake City.

The Great Salt Lake is one of Utah's most striking features, and Antelope Island, resting in its waters, teems with wildlife and trails. This landlocked lake of salt water also explains why you will see seagulls flying around everywhere and perching on lampposts in grocery store parking lots. But the island is also home to bison, antelope, and an array of other wildlife unexpected so close to human civilization.

The Great Basin, which actually covers most of the western half of Utah, is a dry area characterized by vast distances, tenacious life, and the surprise of mountain peaks rising over 10,000 feet high. While hiking in this region is wildly less popular than in the Wasatch, the Great Basin still fascinates due to its differences, and it offers hiking trails that show off its unique qualities.

14 *Frary Peak*

Roundtrip: 6.8 miles
Hiking time: 3–4 hours
Elevation gain: 2100 feet
Difficulty: moderate

Season: all year
Map: USGS Antelope Island
Contact: Antelope Island State Park

Getting there: From Salt Lake City, take I-15 north to exit 332, Antelope Drive. Head west from the highway for 7 miles to the fee station on the causeway, then continue 6.9 miles to the island itself. Drive south for 0.6 mile to Antelope Island Road and turn left (east). Keep driving 5.2 miles to the Frary trailhead sign and turn right up the paved road for 0.5 mile to the dirt parking lot. The paved road is sometimes closed, which would add an additional 1 mile roundtrip to the hike. **Notes:** Fee required at pay station on causeway into the island. Trail closes and parking lot gates are locked at night. Trail may be closed for several weeks or more in the spring during bighorn sheep lambing season; call ahead to inquire.

Antelope Island lies in the Great Salt Lake, and you may find yourself thinking of oceans when you spy the plentiful seagulls that happily call the area home. At forty-two square miles, Antelope Island is the largest of the islands in this huge lake. Its size supports a significant number of species, including mule deer, bighorn sheep, bison, bobcats, coyotes, porcupines, badgers, and pronghorn antelope (of course). Up to six million birds visit annually, which makes this a birder's paradise. Several hikes are scattered across the island, but the ascent to Frary Peak will afford you the best views and the certainty that you earned them with its 2100-foot elevation gain. Named after island homesteader John Frary, who claimed the place as his own at the end of the nineteenth century, the peak offers a quintessentially Utah experience due to its location in the unique Great Salt Lake.

Gazing over the Great Salt Lake from the Frary Peak Trail

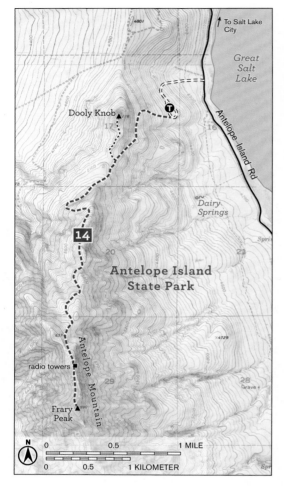

From the parking lot, head west and immediately uphill as the trail switchbacks its way over the first hills. Large, dark quartzite boulders tumble across the landscape that otherwise contains waving grasses and extensive views, even from the starting point, across the lake to the Wasatch Mountains in the east. As the well-beaten path winds around, over, up, and down the golden hills, it slowly draws you west. One mile in there is a spur trail heading north, which leads to Dooley Knob. Just 0.25 mile beyond the spur is a cluster of boulders in the northern morning shadow of the ridge you will quickly and sharply ascend. The mini boulder field is fun, as the trail passes directly between two

large boulders that make it almost cavelike for a few strides. As you once again trek uphill, the trail turns in a more southerly direction just as you ascend toward a ridgeline that is wide and relatively flat for a ways.

As the trail weaves mostly along the contour line leading to Frary Peak, you will understand why summer is not the best time of year for this hike, because there is no shade virtually the entire way. But a clear winter day or a springtime excursion up here reveals the stunning views as you continue climbing. Wooden markers efficiently note the mileage for you along the way, but despite the significant elevation gain, the combination of stellar views and generally gradual ascent make this hike robust but not extensively grueling.

At 2.4 miles you might think you're about to achieve victory, but you'll quickly realize you've reached a false summit. Still heading south and up from here, you'll spot radio towers on the ridge ahead and slightly east. The seemingly artistically posed limbs of dead trees here and there provide stark relief against the backdrop of the lake water and mountains to the east. Once you reach the radio tower at 2.9 miles, the trail leads off and down to the right (west) rather than across the ridgetop as might be expected. That route is blocked by deliberately placed branches, although people have clearly trodden a path in what seems to be the most direct route to the peak. Trust instead the path that seems to drop straight down the side of the mountain as you pick your way down with care. Wooden steps shoved into the dirt path with rebar appear now and again, giving some support on slightly sketchier portions of the trail.

After the drop, the trail scrambles directly up the hillside through scrubby juniper trees, waving grasses, and a profusion of jagged boulders that help create the peak itself. The last few hundred yards command the most rugged ascent of the entire hike and should not be attempted if conditions are icy or very wet, because a slip could result in a long fall. As soon as you reach the pinnacle of Frary Peak, the world opens up around you in a complete panorama spreading out in every direction. Return to the trailhead via the same route.

15 *Deseret Peak*

Loop: 8.1 miles
Hiking time: 4–6 hours
Elevation gain: 3613 feet
Difficulty: hard
Season: all year

Map: USGS Deseret Peak East, Deseret Peak West
Contact: Uinta-Wasatch-Cache National Forest, Salt Lake Ranger District

Getting there: From Salt Lake City, drive west on I-80 for 20 miles to State Route 36 (exit 99). Drive 3.8 miles to State Route 138 and turn right (southwest) there. Drive 10 miles to Grantsville and look for the brown Forest Service sign directing you to South Willow Canyon. Turn left and drive 5 miles to the South Willow Canyon sign. Turn right and drive 7.3 miles to the south end of the Loop Campground and park by the trailhead.
Notes: Vault toilets at parking area. Camping and picnic areas available, for a fee. Free parking for day hikes only. Can be very hot in summer.

Undervisited due to the far greater popularity of the Wasatch Range to the east, Deseret Peak is the highest summit in the Stansbury Mountains, a range in the mostly arid Great Basin of the state's western portion. Yet while the surrounding scenery appears to be barren and dry, the trail to the top is surprisingly lush, with stands of aspen trees, an abundance of meadows, burbling streams, and best of all, a pleasant lack of other people. The cramped Wasatch Front metro area tends to herd the majority of hikers to the trails near there, leaving this area blissfully empty of crowds. A green oasis in the vast beiges of the desert around it, Deseret Peak is a charming, beautiful hike, although its elevation gain is definitely demanding.

From the campground trailhead, follow the trail up South Willow Canyon, passing through aspen trees as you go. You'll ascend 500 feet the first 0.7 mile, at which point you cross a stream and come to a trail split. Take the left fork to Deseret Peak and trek through a densely wooded area filled with pine trees. Animals that live in the area include mule deer, elk, and squat little marmots. Depending on the season, you may stumble across orange-red Indian paintbrush or purple daisies. From here you head through the Mill Fork drainage, rising half a mile up switchbacks to a rocky ridge. From this point onward, the tree growth lessens as you ascend. Small meadows pop up along the way, along with rock fields that are evidence of

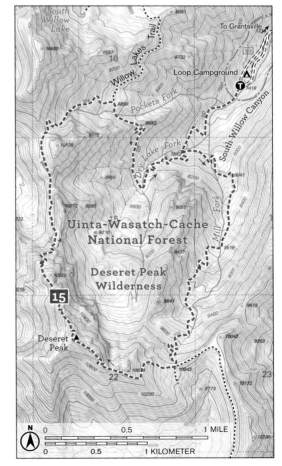

The Deseret Peak Trail is lusher than it first appears.

the occasional cold-season avalanche tumbling down the mountain. Here is where you will feel the burn for sure, as you climb over 2100 feet in 1.8 miles.

Another tree-filled saddle greets you, indicating the final rise is just ahead. The views from here are already tremendous. Prepare for the last, grueling 0.5 mile to the peak, during which you'll rise 1000 feet. At the top of Deseret Peak, the views just soar in every direction. You'll be able to see the Wasatch, out past the Great Salt Lake and its mudflats, and more mountains to the west in the Great Basin range. From here the loop trail continues northward, staying on the ridge for a short ways before dropping in elevation. While the route may be somewhat less visible in this section, you will reach Pockets Fork after 1.6 miles and a loss of 1200 feet. Here the trail veers right (east), meeting up with the Willow Lakes Trail in 0.7 mile. Turn right and continue another 1.5 miles back to Mill Fork. From here it is an easy final 0.7 mile to return to the trailhead.

16 *Mount Aire*

Roundtrip: 3.4 miles
Hiking time: 3–4 hours
Elevation gain: 2000 feet
Difficulty: moderate

Season: all year
Map: USGS Mount Aire
Contact: Uinta-Wasatch-Cache National Forest, Salt Lake Ranger District

Getting there: From Salt Lake City, take I-215 south to 3300 South/3900 South exit. Turn left onto Wasatch Boulevard, drive one block north, then turn right (east) on 3800 South. Drive 6 miles up Mill Creek Canyon to the Elbow Fork trailhead parking area on the east side of the road, just where the road smartly turns to the right. **Notes:** Fee required. Vault toilets at trailhead. Crowded on weekends. Snowshoes may be necessary in winter, when road is closed to vehicles at Maple Grove gate, requiring an additional 1.5 miles on foot to reach the trailhead.

keeps the vegetation through here well watered and lush and gives rise to the enormous trees that make for lovely shade in the summer. Look for maples, Douglas firs, and, of course, the white trunks and limbs of the aspen trees whose leaves pleasantly rustle with any whisper of a breeze. Flowers are abundant along this section in the warmer months, and you may catch sight of butterflies as well. The overall feel through here is green and vital. Cross wooden footbridges several times along the trail. If you really need a breather, small wooden benches also beckon you to take a load off for a minute or just sit and enjoy the area.

The steep Mount Aire Trail runs through a beautiful forest.

Short but steep, Mount Aire is a great leg-burner that rewards your effort with gorgeous forest trees and high alpine scenery. Although the summit is only 8820 feet, the commanding views are a very nice payoff for such a short trail. The lack of switchbacks until the very end makes this quite a demanding trail with its nearly unrelenting climb, which is why it's rated as more difficult than you would think for such a short distance. Shady in the summer, reasonably easy to snowshoe in the winter, filled with flowers in late spring and early summer, and dotted with fiery leaf color around late September through early October, the hike to Mount Aire can be the perfect way to work off excess energy after work or simply experience some classic Wasatch scenery if your time is otherwise constrained.

From the Elbow Fork trailhead, almost immediately come to a trail fork; take the left-hand one signed for Mount Aire. The presence of a little creek for the first 0.8 mile from the trailhead

In 1 mile you will find yourself cresting the saddle, where the vantages begin to stretch out as you now climb higher than the trees that mostly blocked the view until now. Although a welter of possible trail directions and lack of signage may confuse you, your destination is to your right, or north. You should see the mountain in front of you as soon as you turn in that direction. The trail to Mount Aire angles east toward the summit, which does have some switchbacks on the final approach. Don't get too excited by the thought of long, flat portions, though; these switchbacks head up the mountain and still require muscle effort to propel yourself up them. They are also more rock-strewn than the lower portion and have sharper drop-off edges, although not of the sort that have yawning chasms below.

When you reach the summit at 1.8 miles from the trailhead, a rocky cairn marks the actual high point. Although the far-off roar of traffic from I-80 well below in Parleys Canyon to the northeast may be a little jarring, the endless sea of mountain hills and peaks rolling off in all directions should help realign your sense of being in the wilderness. From here, retrace your steps down the trail back to the parking area.

17 Gobblers Knob

Roundtrip: 4.4 miles
Hiking time: 2–4 hours
Elevation gain: 3100 feet
Difficulty: moderate/hard

Season: summer–fall
Map: USGS Mount Aire
Contact: Uinta-Wasatch-Cache National Forest, Salt Lake Ranger District

Getting there: From Salt Lake City, take I-215 south to 3300 South/3900 South exit. Turn left onto Wasatch Boulevard, drive one block north, then turn right (east) on 3800 South. Drive 7.7 miles up Mill Creek Canyon to the Alexander Basin trailhead parking area on the south side of the road. **Notes:** Fee required. Crowded on weekends.

Wild geranium is common in the Wasatch.

You can access Gobblers Knob in a few different ways (see Hike 19 for an alternate route), but this is the most direct—and steepest—route to the popular peak. A sharp scramble up and long-ranging views make this otherwise relatively simple hike one to check off the list. For a real treat, do this hike in the summer, when wildflowers are blooming in astonishing numbers in the Alexander Basin. There is also a network of trails in the area that allow for connecting longer hikes or exploring different routes if you are so moved.

Ascend seemingly straight uphill for the initial 1 mile of trail. Many have dubbed this the steepest trail in the Wasatch Range, but switchbacks through here ease the burn of the ascent somewhat as you head up the trail, which is densely surrounded by fir trees. Meet the junction with Bowman Fork Trail, which zips off to your right (west) at 1.1 miles, but remain on your trail, going straight ahead. Don't be alarmed if you're huffing and puffing quite a bit. Covering over 1000 feet in elevation in about one mile of hiking tends to do that. A little farther on, you'll see the glaciated bowl of Alexander Basin opening up as you head toward it, reaching it in another 0.4 mile. Once in the basin, know that you've now covered 1640 feet. Only 0.7 mile remains, but spare some breath for the remaining 1500 feet of gain still to conquer.

If you've timed your hike for the spring flowers, riots of blues and pinks and purples and yellows will greet you in Alexander Basin, although they've probably already been nodding

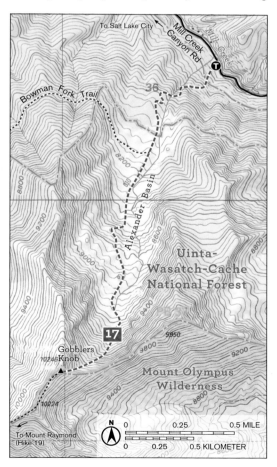

Heading toward Gobblers Knob on the Alexander Basin Trail

along your trail for a ways. Made up of several meadows, the section through the basin isn't quite as demanding, although you are still gaining elevation. As you face the looming rim above you, Gobblers Knob stands proudly to the right. Continue on, aiming toward the east end of the summit. Carefully climbing out of the basin and up the very steep pitches here lands you on a saddle from which you head west for another several hundred yards, still climbing some, to the top of the knob. Once you've achieved the summit at 10,242 feet, the views are outstanding. After you've recovered from the ascent, return to the parking area via the same trail.

18 *Lake Blanche*

Roundtrip: 5.8 miles
Hiking time: 3–4 hours
Elevation gain: 2600 feet
Difficulty: moderate/hard

Season: all year
Map: USGS Mount Aire, Dromedary Peak
Contact: Uinta-Wasatch-Cache National
Forest, Salt Lake Ranger District

Getting there: From Salt Lake City, take I-215 south to the 6200 South exit. Turn left and drive southeast for 1.7 miles on 6200 South, which becomes Wasatch Boulevard. Turn left at Fort Union Boulevard and drive up Big Cottonwood Canyon for 4.3 miles. At an S curve in the road, pull into the Mill B South parking area to your right and follow it 0.2 mile to the trailhead parking. **Notes:** Vault toilet at trailhead. Crowded on weekends. Watershed restrictions apply: no pets, no swimming. Winter access can make the route longer, and snowshoes may be needed.

Extremely popular and extremely scenic, Lake Blanche makes for a demanding hike to a gorgeous lake flanked by rugged high peaks, one of which in particular, 10,320-foot Sundial Peak, is fascinating for its truly distinctive shape. Situated in a glacial cirque, Lake Blanche has beauty in spades, and its trailhead is mere minutes from downtown Salt Lake City. For this reason it tends to be beloved by locals and can get quite crowded, but it is still well worth a visit. The elevation gain is fairly significant, but it isn't a march straight up the mountain, so most hikers in reasonable shape will not find it terribly demanding.

Lake Blanche nestled in its alpine cirque

From the trailhead at the eastern side of the parking lot, the trail follows Big Cottonwood Creek, bears right, crosses a bridge, then very quickly launches you uphill. Aspens and pines shade you through this section as the trail makes its way up the east side of the canyon. The steady ascent becomes more pronounced 2 miles in. Debris evidence from winter avalanches and rockslides piles up here and there. Seeing the remnants of trees mown down as if they were blades of grass provokes sober reflection on the powerful forces of nature that shape this landscape. The trail cuts directly over an old rockslide in the switchback section; look for brightly colored flagging tape that indicates you are indeed still on the correct trail.

Just under a mile more hiking takes you to quartzite slabs that still bear the striated marks of a glacier's action during the most recent ice age. Almost right afterward, you top a little rise and can see Lake Blanche spread out in the bowl, with the two-knobbed Sundial Peak stabbing the sky above it. The overall setting is very reminiscent of *The Sound of Music*; climb up the rock slabs immediately north of the lake to get the best views and photos. Return to the parking area via the same trail.

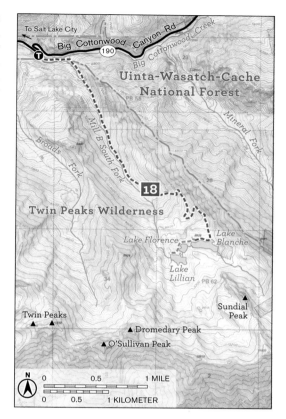

Extending your hike: Continue on the trail around the western side of the lake to drop into the little bowl below, where you will find the smaller but just as pretty Lake Florence and Lake Lillian; altogether, the lakes are referred to as the Three Sisters. This will add a total of 0.5 mile to your hike.

19 *Mount Raymond*

Roundtrip: 8 miles
Hiking time: 5–6 hours
Elevation gain: 3100 feet
Difficulty: hard

Season: spring–fall
Map: USGS Mount Aire
Contact: Uinta-Wasatch-Cache National Forest, Salt Lake Ranger District

Getting there: From Salt Lake City, take I-215 south to the 6200 South exit. Turn left and drive southeast for 1.7 miles on 6200 South, which becomes Wasatch Boulevard. Turn left at Fort Union Boulevard and drive up Big Cottonwood Canyon for 8 miles. Pull into the Butler Fork parking area on the left. **Notes:** Vault toilets across from trailhead. Crowded on weekends. Watershed restrictions apply: no pets, no swimming.

Usually, 10,000-plus-foot alpine peaks with excellent views from the top involve a fair amount of travel time to access—and that's just the driving part. One of the joys of living in or visiting Salt Lake City is that spectacular trails are close enough to make some fantastic hikes only half-day outings. Mount Raymond certainly qualifies as an alpine peak with its 10,214 feet of rise, and getting to the top takes you only 8 miles. Granted, there's over 3000 feet of elevation to surmount on the way, but this trail is so pretty and fun, and the outlook from the top is so far-reaching, that it easily makes the cut as a must-do local hike.

From the trailhead, hike alongside burbling little Butler Fork, gaining altitude and swiftly entering the Mount Olympus Wilderness. In the midsummer months, the nearby water makes this a colorful haven for wildflowers, which may be bursting out in glorious color if you hit the trail at the right time. In 0.5 mile the trail forks; take the left turn toward Mill A Basin and head into

a flurry of aspen trees. You'll shortly be greeted by a series of switchbacks to help you climb. You finally reach a ridge leading you north, about 1.6 miles into the hike. Head on until you see another trail sign about 0.4 mile along. To the right is the trail to Dog Lake, and to the left, Mill A Basin. Take the left fork and amble onward to cross the hillside of Mill A Basin. Your destination is clearly visible before you, barely 2 miles ahead.

Close to the top of Mill A Basin another trail bisects yours, running southwest off to your left. Your trail, however, continues on and upward. Reach Baker Pass in 0.2 mile and feel justified in stopping to catch your breath, as you have now ascended 2220 feet since the start of the trail. Here, you are at the equivalent of a freeway interchange, with four trails converging on this one spot. Turn sharply left to begin the final, 900-foot climb up to the top of Mount Raymond just 0.6 mile hence.

At first this section of trail along the ridgetop seems very straightforward, but the final 0.3 mile

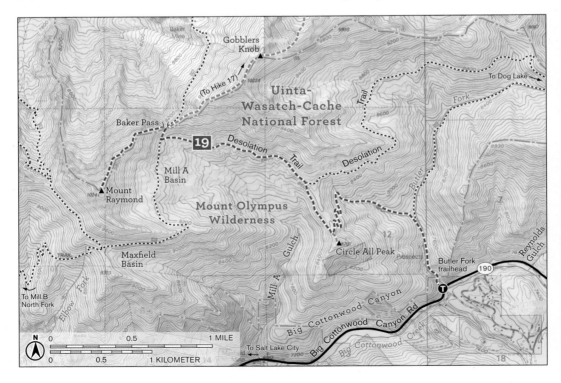

Heading to Mount Raymond

may give some hikers serious pause when they are presented with a thin slice of ridgeline that seems to be a Rubik's Cube of large quartzite and limestone blocks. Although unseasoned hikers or those with significant fear of heights might look at this part and firmly decide they've gone far enough, those who are more experienced or simply unafraid of what seems to be a treacherous portion of the trail should have little problem navigating—on all fours if necessary—this steeply inclined ridge.

At the top of Mount Raymond, the views are breathtaking and the panorama extends in every direction. Once you are done enjoying the sights from the top, return to the parking area the same way you came up.

Extending your hike: At the ridge just above the switchback section, a short spur trail heads off to the south (left as you head up the trail). This takes you only 0.2 mile and another 150 feet up to Circle All Peak, from which you can see Kessler Peak and the Broads Fork Twin Peaks Massif to the south. This worthy addition to your day will add a total of 0.4 mile to your hike.

Some people also like to nab two peaks in one day: Gobblers Knob (approachable in a very lovely different way in Hike 17) is but 0.8 mile and the same 900 feet of elevation gain from the four-way trail junction at Baker Pass. From that point, head northeast to Gobblers Knob, returning the same way. Tacking this on to your day will add a total of 1.6 miles to your hike.

20 *Desolation Lake*

Roundtrip: 7.4 miles
Hiking time: 5–6 hours
Elevation gain: 2500 feet
Difficulty: moderate

Season: spring–fall
Map: USGS Mount Aire
Contact: Uinta-Wasatch-Cache National Forest, Salt Lake Ranger District

Getting there: From Salt Lake City, take I-215 south to the 6200 South exit. Turn left and drive southeast for 1.7 miles on 6200 South, which becomes Wasatch Boulevard. Turn left at Fort Union Boulevard and drive up Big Cottonwood Canyon for 9.1 miles. Pull into the Mill D North Fork parking area on the left. **Notes:** Vault toilets across from trailhead. Crowded on weekends. Watershed restrictions apply: no pets, no swimming.

A picturesque mountain lake with rippling or smooth blue-green waters, tucked into a bowl surrounded by a blanket of pine trees, Desolation Lake (referred to as Lake Desolation on the USGS map but known locally as Desolation Lake) is a well-traveled hike in the Wasatch, despite the elevation gain. The trail is straightforward, there are only a few mighty uphill charges that must be fiercely tackled (or slowly plodded, depending on the desire of your legs and lungs), and the rewards are more than satisfying for such a short

drive from the city. Although this can be a popular route and thus is perhaps best avoided on summer weekends if you value privacy over scenery, don't let the presence of others keep you from experiencing this pretty trail and beautiful lake.

Hit the trail from the parking lot and right away start to gain elevation, a steady yet relatively mellow ascent in this section. Here the trail passes through aspen trees, their white trunks an eye-catching contrast to the other natural colors of their leaves, other plants and trees, and the

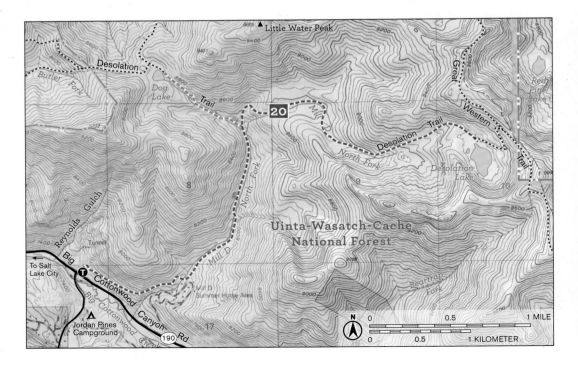

Desolation is a classic mountain lake beauty. (Photo by Sallie Shatz)

earth itself. Gorgeous in summer when the aspen leaves are green, this is even more striking when fall colors race through the groves and a plethora of deciduous trees, about to shed their leaves, herald the season with an explosion of golds and reds. In springtime, flowers dot the edges of the path. The trail gently rises as it heads east along the contour of the mountain fold for 0.8 mile, where it then meets up with Mill D North Fork and curves left to head north for another 1 mile. At this point you find a trail junction, with the pronounced left (west) turn taking you to Dog Lake and the right (east) turn bringing you onto the actual Desolation Trail. Take the right fork and continue.

After the junction the trail becomes remarkably steeper. The trail does level out in sections throughout the remainder of the hike, though. Passing through scattered meadows in the mostly forested walk, you sometimes will be able to glimpse nearby peaks rising high above the trees. This final 1.8 miles to the lake is quite scenic. Immediately before you reach the lake there is a last climb, and then you suddenly are there. Called Desolation due to the lack of trees around its immediate shoreline, the lake is down in a glacier-carved bowl about 550 feet deep. Campsites are available back in the trees for anyone wishing to spend the night. From the lake, return to your vehicle on the same trail.

Extending your hike: Add the short jaunt to Dog Lake on the way back as an added bonus. This is a pretty little lake, worth a visit if you have time and the inclination after your trip to Desolation Lake. At the signed trail junction, take the west turn and proceed 0.6 mile to Dog Lake. Return the same way, adding a total of 1.2 miles to the entire hike.

21 *Bells Canyon*

Roundtrip: 9.5 miles
Hiking time: 8 hours–2 days
Elevation gain: 4150 feet
Difficulty: strenuous

Season: spring–fall
Map: USGS Draper
Contact: Sandy City; Uinta-Wasatch-Cache National Forest, Salt Lake Ranger District

Getting there: From Salt Lake City, take I-15 south to the 9000 South exit. Turn left and drive east for 6 miles, during which the street name changes to 9400 South and then to East Little Cottonwood Road. Find the Granite trailhead parking at 3470 East Little Cottonwood Canyon Road. **Notes:** Restrooms at trailhead. Crowded on weekends and holidays. Watershed restrictions apply: no pets, no swimming. Routefinding may be required. Map reading skills useful. Very steep trail. Trekking poles may be useful. Massive water flow can affect trail conditions in springtime.

Steep mountainsides, cascading waterfalls, accessibility, and a choice of how far to hike—you can turn around at the first waterfall or march all the way to the upper reservoir—all serve to make Bells Canyon (rather confusingly also called Bell Canyon, but they are one and the same) a very popular hike. Yes, it starts in a residential neighborhood. But the swiftness with which you reach wilderness is impressive. Yes, it can be crowded on weekends, but most people stay within the lower reaches of the trail. If you are fit, surefooted, and have sturdy lungs, making it all the way will afford you not only beauty but a stronger sense of wilderness serenity as the crowds melt off with each intense step higher. Many choose to attempt the upper reservoir as an overnight trip, an option suitable only for strong hikers who can manage carrying a pack up the steep trail. (Camping somewhere near the second waterfall is a good bet; you can make it to the upper reservoir the next day while only carrying a light daypack.) The rewards, however, are solitude and beauty just a stone's throw from a metropolitan area.

From the Granite trailhead (another trailhead, Boulders, is in a nearby residential neighborhood), the trail immediately climbs up switchbacks.

Sagebrush, scrub oak, and little shade mark this portion of the trail. Arrive at the Lower Bells Canyon Reservoir in 0.75 mile. For those with small children or little inclination to continue, this might make the perfect short outing. Depending on the water level, this reservoir can be very pretty, complete with ducks and mountain views. Pressing onward, take the utility road as it heads to the left and around the reservoir. A sign points the way to Bells Canyon on your left. Woody, shaded, and pleasant through here, the trail also features some small meadows. Cross a little footbridge and head into the canyon. The stream keeps you company on your left (north) side as you hike. Granite rocks litter the trail and require a little negotiation here and there.

Look for a spur trail 1.7 miles along. Take this down to your left in order to get a remarkable view of the lower falls. The way down the hillside here is very steep, with loose rock and dirt making the footing very sketchy. Descend carefully, clinging to trees if necessary. The waterfall cascades 50 feet over rocks, presenting a sheet of slithering beauty that creates a cooling spray, especially early in the season when snowmelt adds to its grandeur. The rocks can be extremely

Bells Canyon curving back into the Wasatch

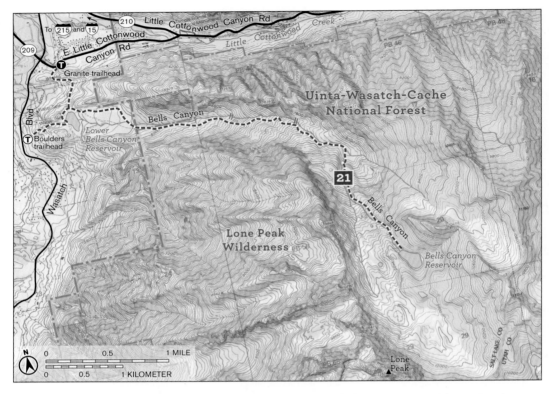

slippery here. Exercise caution and common sense. From here, climb back up the shale hillside to the trail and continue upward along it.

The trail here is pretty much vertical, so you really need to concentrate on it rather than any views. When you reach 2.6 miles you are in a clearing that opens up for some views down into the populated valley. An enormous boulder juts out of the earth here. Just past it find the usually cairned spur trail leading left to the second waterfall. Although smaller than the lower one, this falls is still quite striking as it sluices down the rock face. Many people call it a day here and return to the parking area. To reach the upper reservoir, however, continue on up. The trail from here is generally not as well marked, so the knowledgeable use of a topo map can be quite helpful.

Back on the main trail, the minus is how much more difficult the climb is about to get. The plus is how many fewer people you will now encounter, which is always better when also trying to safely navigate challenging terrain. The preponderance of granite rocks underfoot makes this portion of trail very tricky, since the rocks tend to shift, not to mention provide the natural version of a stair-climbing machine. A wet day or snow would make this part of the trail potentially very dangerous, and tackling it is not recommended in such weather. In dry weather, however, the utterly stunning views down the canyon as you continue to climb up through the forest are gorgeous.

Small clearings, as well as the side of the trail, can be filled with summertime flowers such as fireweed, Indian paintbrush, and monkeyflower. The occasional aspen tree and tons of ferns line the trail as you head up, up, up. Eventually, less tree and more rock occurs as you get closer to the cirque in which the upper reservoir lies. Once you reach Upper Bells Canyon Reservoir, 4.75 miles in, you're at 9388 feet, a height well earned on your arduous but beautiful hike. Descend back to the parking area the same way.

22 *White Pine Lake (Wasatch)*

Roundtrip: 9 miles
Hiking time: 5–7 hours
Elevation gain: 2500 feet
Difficulty: moderate

Season: spring–fall
Map: USGS Dromedary Peak
Contact: Uinta-Wasatch-Cache National
Forest, Salt Lake Ranger District

Getting there: From Salt Lake City, take I-215 south to the 6200 South exit. Turn left and drive southeast for 5.7 miles; the street name changes to Wasatch Boulevard. Turn left (east) at Little Cottonwood Canyon and drive 6 miles to the White Pine trailhead parking lot on your right. This is also the parking area for Red Pine Lake. **Notes:** Vault toilet at trailhead. Crowded on weekends. Watershed restrictions apply: no pets, no swimming.

Ambling along a wide track through a forest of pines and aspens and rising up high to an alpine cirque that holds a large, beautiful lake, this trail is lovely, and long enough to be challenging to some hikers but not overwhelmingly so. Located at 10,000 feet, the waters sometimes appear aquamarine in color when the light hits them just right. Actually a reservoir that holds the water corralled by a little dam, White Pine Lake is a simply breathtaking sight. This is also a relatively easy hike that contains no major obstacles on the way, except, of course, the elevation gain, which in a few spots is certainly noticeable. Complete with forest ambiance and natural growth, this is a good stroll to a beautiful spot.

The trail departs the parking area and heads south, sharing the first 0.8 mile with the Red Pine Lake Trail. This initial section is paved for a brief way, though that soon gives way to dirt. It dips down toward Little Cottonwood Creek, crosses a footbridge, then rises to stay on the eastern wall of the canyon in an easy ascent. You may notice the trail is fairly wide; this used to be a mining road, first constructed as part of a maze of roads used by miners with dreams of striking it big. Those dreams never materialized, and this road was closed to vehicles decades ago. The ensuing natural revegetation of the area has left it so that most hiking this trail will likely not even realize its original purpose was to allow wheels to turn over it.

When you reach the trail split, take the sharp left turn to remain on the White Pine Trail. From

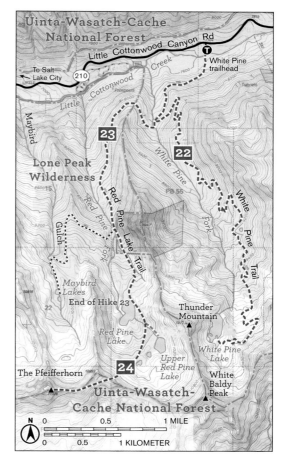

here you will start to feel the climb. The trail first heads northeast, but it soon returns to its southerly direction toward the lake. The forest

rises around you, and several small meadows also provide ample beauty. You can find abundant displays of spring wildflowers, particularly after wet winters. Little streams and springs make appearances as well, adding to the lushness of the region. These streams can sometimes require involved searching for good places to cross without getting your feet wet—or simply resigning yourself to just splashing through them.

When you finally reach the rim just above the lake, the scenery is utterly breathtaking, with the lake nestled into the bowl beneath the rock face of White Baldy Peak. Drop down 0.2 mile to reach the lake itself, which sports some campsites for those who wish to spend the night. Vegetation along the shores is sparse due to the elevation, although large pines ring it on the ridge side. Once done with your visit to the lake, return to the parking area on the same trail.

The bridge over Little Cottonwood Creek on the way to the Wasatch's White Pine Lake

23 Red Pine Lake

Roundtrip: 7 miles	**Season:** spring–fall
Hiking time: 4–5 hours	**Map:** USGS Dromedary Peak
Elevation gain: 1900 feet	**Contact:** Uinta-Wasatch-Cache National
Difficulty: moderate	Forest, Salt Lake Ranger District

Getting there: From Salt Lake City, take I-215 south to the 6200 South exit. Turn left and drive southeast for 5.7 miles; the street name changes to Wasatch Boulevard. Turn left (east) at Little Cottonwood Canyon and drive 6 miles to the White Pine trailhead parking lot on your right. This is also the parking area for White Pine Lake. **Notes:** Vault toilet at trailhead. Crowded on weekends. Watershed restrictions apply: no pets, no swimming.

The popularity of this hike is due to two things. One, it's close to a major metropolitan area. Two, it is a stunning example of classic alpine beauty, with rugged mountains, thick stands of aspen and pine trees, summer wildflowers, fall colors, flowing streams, and striking views down Little Cottonwood Canyon. Plenty of wildlife calls this area home, from chattering chipmunks to mighty moose. Not so long as to dissuade those unused to hiking or those simply pressed for time, the trail to Red Pine Lake is a gem among Wasatch mountain hikes.

Follow the initially paved trail south and down to Little Cottonwood Creek, and cross the water via a small wooden bridge. Now the trail begins to take you up the canyon on a wide, flat road that used to allow vehicles. Whispering aspen leaves surround the trail, as do the wide, spreading branches of spruce. Some views down canyon are very pretty before you wrap back around a bend in the mountain. Slightly less than one mile in, the trail to White Pine Lake departs off to your left (east). Head straight on the trail south to Red Pine Lake and cross another footbridge a short ways on. At this point you have risen almost 500 feet from the trailhead. In 0.5 mile you enter the Lone Peak Wilderness. Views from here to the north look far, far down into Little Cottonwood Canyon.

The hiking becomes significantly steeper 1.7 miles from the trailhead. Another trail splits off to your right at 2.5 miles, leading to Maybird Lakes; remain on your trail directly ahead, still heading south and upward. A coniferous forest and talus slope mark this section of trail. You'll know you're in the final pitch, about 0.5 mile from the lake, because the trail becomes practically sheer. After this steep push, however, the hike is suddenly gentler, allowing you to catch your breath for the last several minutes to the lake. After you've enjoyed your time beside the water, return by the same trail back to the parking area.

Extending your hike: Visit Upper Red Pine Lake with an additional 0.5 mile and another 400 elevation feet of effort. Walk around the east side of Red Pine Lake to find one of the trails that leads to the upper lake. While no trail here is officially maintained, the route is relatively obvious. Return the same way.

Red Pine Lake is just spectacular.

24 *The Pfeifferhorn*

Roundtrip: 10 miles
Hiking time: 7–9 hours
Elevation gain: 3600 feet
Difficulty: hard/strenuous

Season: spring–fall
Map: USGS Dromedary Peak
Contact: Uinta-Wasatch-Cache National Forest, Salt Lake Ranger District

Getting there: From Salt Lake City, take I-215 south to the 6200 South exit. Turn left and drive southeast for 5.7 miles; the street name changes to Wasatch Boulevard. Turn left (east) at Little Cottonwood Canyon and drive 6 miles to the White Pine trailhead parking lot on your right. This is also the parking area for Red Pine Lake. **Notes:** Vault toilet at trailhead. May require some routefinding. Exposure on the boulder scramble near the top.

Called Little Matterhorn Peak on the map, The Pfeifferhorn does somewhat resemble the famed peak in Switzerland. This Utah mountaintop is a rugged blast up—way, way, up—but the sublime subalpine scenery along the way and the magnificent views from the top make it is worth the lung and leg effort. There are several ways to access the summit, but the most common route is from Red Pine Lake. Although this hike is only 1.5 miles longer than the trail to Red Pine Lake, the elevation gain in that last push almost doubles what you climb to the lake. A long day hike for most, this also makes for a good overnight trip with a planned

It's hard to believe this alpine mountain overlooks a major metropolitan area.

camp at the lake. Either way, prepare for a solid hiking experience that will put you close to what feels like the roof of the world, or at least of these mountains.

Head south from the White Pine trailhead to cross Little Cottonwood Creek, then head into the canyon. The trail rises gently for the first mile, and it is wide, reflecting its past life as a road, although vegetation has reclaimed most of it. In just under a mile the trail forks, with the hard left turn going to White Pine Lake; keep walking due south toward Red Pine Lake. As the trail rises, you'll feel the elevation gain slowly but surely. Old avalanche routes disfigure the landscape somewhat at the 2-mile mark. The trail splits off again at 2.5 miles, with a right turn leading to Maybird Lakes. Continue south on the main trail.

When you reach the lower Red Pine Lake, circle around its east edge to continue up generally toward Upper Red Pine Lake, but find the more lightly traveled trail to The Pfeifferhorn veering off right before you reach the upper lake. As you head up this way, you will see the peaks ahead and to your right; the large one primarily in your field of vision is not the summit you are aiming for but rather a false summit you will eventually hike behind. As you ascend, keep an eye out for rock cairns, but if you don't see any, simply aim for the tree-covered hillside southwest of the upper lake. Go for the spur ridge about 0.25 mile above, then traverse it southwest toward the main ridge about another 0.25 mile away. The last push here is very steep and exposed. The saddle makes for excellent photos of the lakes below and allows you impressive views over the spectacular wild landscape.

Head west along the saddle toward The Pfeifferhorn. Pass beneath a lower peak to your right (north) before you reach the most exposed, vertiginous section of the trail: a 100-yard-long ridgeline that is often appropriately described as a knife edge. While those who are comfortable with heights and rock scrambling should have little issue with this part, for some it may be too much. After this section, only a 500-foot scramble up a chute to one side of the pyramid-shaped Pfeifferhorn awaits you. The scramble appears more intimidating than it is, particularly if you've already made it this far. The views from the very top are stunning, to say the least, stretching out in every possible direction and giving your eyes a feast to examine. Once you are ready to depart this sky-high perch, carefully descend and return to the trailhead the same way you came up.

25 *Cecret Lake*

Roundtrip: 1.5 miles	**Season:** summer–fall
Hiking time: 1–2 hours	**Map:** USGS Brighton
Elevation gain: 420 feet	**Contact:** Uinta-Wasatch-Cache National
Difficulty: easy	Forest, Salt Lake Ranger District

Getting there: From Salt Lake City, take I-215 south to the 6200 South exit. Turn left and drive southeast for 5.7 miles; the street name changes to Wasatch Boulevard. Turn left (east) at Little Cottonwood Canyon and drive 11.1 miles to the parking lot on the left (north) side of the road. **Notes:** Vault toilet at trailhead. Crowded on weekends.

Although the name implies the hidden quality of this trail, the secret is long out. Very popular due to its brevity and beauty, Cecret Lake (sometimes spelled Secret Lake, or even Seacret Lake due to a long history of spelling variations by different parties, beginning with the miners who originally named it) is an easy hike that is tailor-made for families, those less agile or swift

Cecret Lake, a little gem in Albion Basin

of foot, or anyone short on time but long on desire to experience some of the gorgeous backcountry of the Wasatch. Just above Albion Basin, Cecret Lake is another glacially created body of water that sparkles in the sunlight on clear days. Lush meadow sections can be dotted with color. The season to see this lake is short because of its nearly 10,000-foot altitude and the existence of nearby Alta ski area, so carve out time during the brief summer months to head up here.

From the trailhead, hike south. Cross the little stream and pass beneath one of the ski resort chairlifts within the first 0.1 mile. The trail briefly joins a dirt road here, then veers off to the right at a split 0.3 mile in. The path winds up the rock-covered slope in switchbacks before depositing you at the lovely lake. Midsummer hikes yield a cornucopia of wildflowers in rioting color, while early fall hikes see the mountains ablaze with the color of the changing leaves. Although the trail officially ends as soon as you reach the northeastern shore of the lake, you can explore all around it. While this is perhaps not precisely backcountry, since it is so easy to reach from the

city, the basin will certainly have you fooled when you take in its beautiful mountain setting. After enjoying the lake, return to the parking lot the same way you came in.

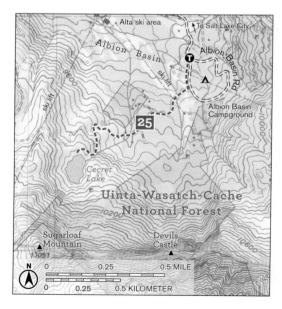

26 Brighton Lakes

Roundtrip: 4.5 miles
Hiking time: 2–3 hours
Elevation gain: 1200 feet
Difficulty: moderate

Season: spring–fall
Map: USGS Brighton
Contact: Uinta-Wasatch-Cache National
Forest, Salt Lake Ranger District

Getting there: From Salt Lake City, take I-215 south to the 6200 South exit. Turn left and drive southeast for 5.7 miles; the street name changes to Wasatch Boulevard. Turn left at Fort Union Boulevard and drive up Big Cottonwood Canyon for 15 miles to the Brighton ski resort. Pull into the large parking area by the Brighton Center lodge. The well-marked trailhead for Lake Mary/Catherine Pass is just south of the lodge. **Notes:** Restrooms at resort lodge by trailhead. Crowded on weekends. Watershed restrictions apply: no pets, no swimming.

Seeing three beautiful lakes in one easy fell swoop makes this trail very popular with families and day hikers. Mary, Martha, and Catherine are all different enough from one another to maintain interest, and, frankly, just a lovely example of a little string of lakes left in this area by ancient glacial action. An excellent introduction to mountain hiking for kids or newbies, this route has enough elevation gain to make such hikers feel victorious upon reaching the lakes, but the shortness of the trail prevents it from seeming too daunting. Although some may not feel as partial to this trail due to the potential hordes of people on it during summer and holiday weekends, for others it's very comforting to know there are plenty of other hikers present, particularly if they run across a moose. Consider yourself lucky if you do see one of these hulking yet oddly graceful forest denizens, and definitely keep your distance from their often quite unpredictable movements, which can involve running at speeds of up to 35 miles per hour.

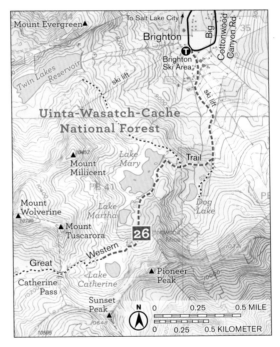

Head up the mountain as directed by the signs indicating the way to Lake Mary, the first body of water on the trail. In the summertime, you may see hordes of wildflowers as well as people. Indian paintbrush, lupines, striking columbines, and more can all grace the mountainsides by July. This first length of the trail is steep, but views help alleviate the workout. Leave the open hillsides behind as you dive into the woods at the half-mile mark. At 0.8 mile, a trail sign points you to the left for Dog Lake; continue ahead on your trail toward Lake Mary. You'll reach the northeast corner of the lake, which is actually a reservoir, in just another 0.2 mile, where it spreads out in its rocky little bowl. The largest lake on the hike, Mary is striking with the large granite boulders and slabs that trace its shoreline. Mount Millicent, Mount Wolverine, and Mount

The Brighton Lakes hike is stunning in summertime.

Tuscarora are ranged beyond the lake, all of which adds tremendous scenic charm to the area.

The trail follows along the eastern shoreline before leaving it to quickly reach Lake Martha. Barely higher in elevation than Mary, Lake Martha is much smaller but still very pretty, nestled as it is just below the looming crags of Mount Tuscarora, its shoreline dotted here and there with tall pines. From here, the trail goes on another 0.6 mile to a sharp double-back to the north before curving back south again. At a trail junction, go left to reach the shores of Lake Catherine in barely 0.1 mile. Somewhat larger than Martha, Lake Catherine is the highest lake on this trail, situated at 9940 feet. Although the trail continues on, for this hike, return to the trailhead from here via the same way you came in.

27 Big Springs Hollow–Cascade Saddle

Roundtrip: 11.5 miles
Hiking time: 6–9 hours
Elevation gain: 3770 feet
Difficulty: hard

Season: all year
Map: USGS Bridal Veil Falls
Contact: Uinta-Wasatch-Cache National Forest, Pleasant Grove Ranger District

Getting there: From Orem, drive 5.8 miles east up US Highway 189 (Provo Canyon) to Vivian Park. Turn right (south) onto South Fork Road and drive 3.3 miles to Big Springs Park. Turn right here and drive another 0.2 mile to the trailhead parking. **Notes:** Popular with mountain bikers. Trail can be snow-covered in winter; snowshoe or ski accessible.

Grassy green meadows, tall shading trees, magnificent views, and serious elevation gain—all hallmarks of most hikes in the Wasatch—are a beautiful part and parcel of this lovely trail nestled into the gorgeous Provo Canyon area. Easily reachable from the metropolitan hustle and bustle, this trail quickly propels you into the backcountry with a tinkling creek,

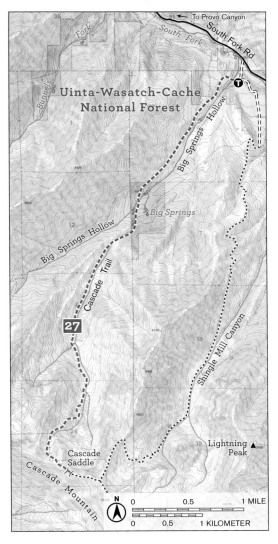

bit more solitude, hiking Big Springs Hollow to Cascade Saddle might be a good choice.

From the parking lot's west end, start out on the wide dirt path heading southwest and slightly uphill from just past the information kiosk. Low hills and scrub oak greet you first, though they soon give way to steeper inclines and taller aspens and maples. Autumn hikes can give you quite the color display from these trees, while the warmer months offer flowers and lovely green vegetation happily growing near the creek. Look for red penstemon and delicate purple clematis flowers in early summer. Because this is a multi-use trail, mountain bikers sometimes whiz along here, so beware their passing; horseback riding is also allowed on the trail here, so remember that hikers must always yield to horses.

The initial Big Springs Hollow Trail is shaded by aspens and pines.

chattering birdsong, a large number of colorful butterflies in warmer months, and far-ranging scenery to behold from the Cascade Saddle. The relatively easy first part of this hike, up to Big Springs, can make for a great family outing. The most strenuous elevation gain doesn't occur until you aim for the saddle itself. Although popular with locals, this trail doesn't see quite the huge influx of hikers that ultra-popular nearby Mount Timpanogos does, so if you're seeking a wee

View from Big Springs Hollow Trail

Reach a small meadow in 0.25 mile and continue with pretty views of Cascade Mountain drawing you on. In the first 1.8 miles, to the trail fork, the going is relatively easy and pleasant. Wooden bridges cross over the creek a few times through this section. At the trail junction, a left turn indicates Big Springs in 0.5 mile. Many people head there, then turn back once they reach Big Springs at 2.3 miles from the trailhead. Lush and well watered, the area around the springs is very pretty and can make for the perfect little hike.

Take the right at the trail junction for the Cascade Trail, which will lead you to the Cascade Saddle. As the trail gets closer to the saddle, the incline begins to markedly steepen. From the spring to the saddle you will gain 3100 feet, so if you start to huff and puff, you have good reason. At first the climb up from the spring isn't terribly taxing, but within half a mile you should start to really pay attention to it. The footing here starts to get rocky and loose underfoot; this is more noticeable and potentially treacherous on the descent. The trail also, however, takes you through more meadows now dominated by towering pines and sometimes decorated with mule deer and other high-mountain wildlife. The entire trail, actually, is good for spotting the wild denizens of the area, particularly if you have sharp eyes and hike without making too loud an announcement of your presence. If you're really lucky, you might even spy a moose foraging in the woods. Enjoy such an encounter, but be sure to give these large, unpredictable creatures a wide berth.

When you reach a rocky cirque you attain the steepest portion of the trail; luckily, it also means you are close to the saddle. When the trail finally tops out on the saddle 5.75 miles in, the wow factor comes into play as you take in the views. Sunlight sparkles off the water of Utah Lake to the west, and you really get a sense of the wild country surrounding you in the form of peaks and valleys. From here, other trails branch off; simply return to the parking area via the same trail you came up on, watching your footing on the steep, rocky path as you descend.

28 *Stewart Falls*

Roundtrip: 3.8 miles
Hiking time: 2–3 hours
Elevation gain: 650 feet
Difficulty: easy

Season: spring–fall
Map: USGS Aspen Grove
Contact: Uinta-Wasatch-Cache National
Forest, Pleasant Grove Ranger District

Getting there: From Orem, drive east up US Highway 189 (Provo Canyon) for 7 miles
to State Route 92, the first left after the tunnel. Drive north on SR 92 past Sundance
Mountain Resort. Trailhead parking is immediately after the Forest Service fee booth
on your left at 4.5 miles. **Notes:** Fee required. Maximum group size fifteen. Can be very
crowded on weekends and holidays. Restroom at parking area.

Tall and graceful as they tumble down the mountainside, tiered Stewart Falls is a beautiful example of an alpine waterfall in the Utah mountains. Very popular due to the ease of reaching this 200-foot-high falls, the Stewart Falls hike is an excellent choice for families or those with limited time. The moderately easy trail is very photogenic as well, both along the way and at the falls themselves. Spring flowers and the golds and reds of fall make for riots of color and beauty here, and in summer, the water cools a blast of greenery. This is a perfect hike to bookend a longer one in the area, tackle if you're staying at the nearby Sundance Resort, or simply choose for a casual but gorgeous jaunt to explore another classic example of northern Utah's natural charms.

Head southwest on the marked trail (#56, Stewart Cascades) just past the restrooms at the parking area. Within 100 yards you will turn

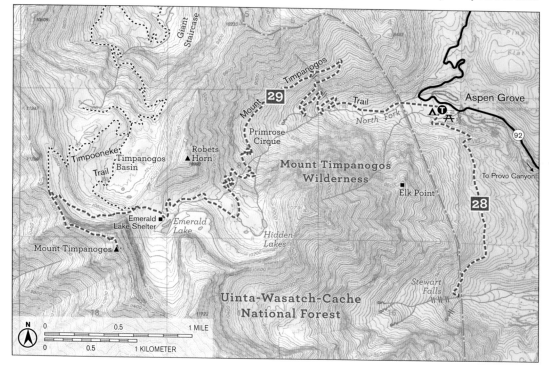

The bottom tier of Stewart Falls is a very pretty cascade.

sharply left, heading upward for 1 mile through a rustling grove of aspen trees. The smooth white trunks of the aspen, marked in spots with black knots and splotches, stretch up straight and tall, occasionally curving their branches into fantastical shapes. Leafy ferns and fragrant mint line the trail in season, making this an area of lush vegetation and beauty. Tall Douglas firs poke up here and there amid the aspen trees, adding the broad spread of their needled limbs overhead. Eventually the pine trees disappear, leaving you in a grove of solid aspen. The partial shade through this brief section can be welcome in the summertime. The path through this part is well trodden and easy to follow, which explains why you might encounter many other people on it as well. Despite any crowds, though, it is still a gorgeous hike. Shortly the trail exits into a treeless shrub area, although it is still quite beautiful with the steep mountain walls towering behind it.

Continue on through the clearing. The sound of the falls starts to beckon from where it roars over the cliffs and echoes against the walls. About 1.5 miles in, you will be able to see the falls from a nice angle. From here, the trail dips down to take you to the base of the falls. Here is where you will find places to take photos, sit and eat, or simply enjoy the water and the lovely views. Cascading over high, rocky mountain ledges, the water leaps down, its continual spray watering several small hanging gardens that dot the otherwise bland cliff face. Two tiers—three if the water is running high in spring—make this falls even more exceptional. Although it is possible to hike up to the base of the higher falls, this is not part of the official trail and can potentially be very dangerous, so it's not advised to do so. Looking downstream from the falls gives you a view of the stream running down the mountain and hillsides gently bumping off into the distance. To return to the parking area, simply take the same trail back down.

29 Mount Timpanogos

Roundtrip: 13.2 miles	**Map:** USGS Timpanogos Cave, Aspen Grove
Hiking time: 7–11 hours	
Elevation gain: 4580 feet	**Contact:** Uinta-Wasatch-Cache National Forest, Pleasant Grove Range District
Difficulty: strenuous	
Season: late spring–fall	

Getting there: From Orem, drive east up US Highway 189 (Provo Canyon) for 7 miles to State Route 92, the first left after the tunnel. Drive north on SR 92 and past Sundance Mountain Resort. Trailhead parking is immediately after the Forest Service fee booth on your left at 4.5 miles. **Notes:** Fee required. Maximum group size fifteen. Can be very crowded on weekends and holidays. Can be snow-covered November through midsummer.

Although it is only the second-highest peak in the Wasatch Range, Mount Timp, as it is often affectionately called, is the favorite peak of many native Utahns. To encourage his students to be physically active, Eugene Roberts, an athletics coach at Brigham Young University, started an annual summit event called the Mount Timpanogos Hike in 1912. The organized tradition

continued through the 1960s, and late in that decade an estimated more than 3500 hikers summited the peak in one day. Justifiably concerned about the serious erosion caused by this growing yearly display of foot-stomping love, the Forest Service requested the cessation of the hike in 1970. Timpanogos was designated a wilderness area in 1984 and has recovered quite nicely from

Mysterious atmosphere under the clouds as the Mount Timp Trail heads up (Photo by Sallie Shatz)

its earlier massive tramplings. Today, of course, hikers still tread the well-worn trail up, although in somewhat smaller groups. Regardless of the number of people you are likely to encounter on the way to Mount Timp, this is a classic peak experience that beautifully displays the alpine beauty of the area.

From the north (right) side of the parking area, head west onto the Aspen Grove Trail (a.k.a. the Timpanogos Trail). The ascent here is gentle, heading up through stands of aspen and Douglas firs before leading you to a lovely little waterfall at 1 mile, called First Falls by some and Timpanogos Falls by others. At this point the trail begins to climb more in earnest, winding you upward through switchbacks on the north side of a drainage. The views throughout this section are

astounding and help propel you along the trail and up its layers of switchbacks.

Another small waterfall greets you in another 0.5 mile, helping ease the climb, although you then must tackle a long switchback that takes you toward the Primrose Cirque. Cross a talus field below the cirque's rather forbidding headwall. By nature, the cirque is a rocky area and thus a good place to really watch your footing, particularly during springtime jaunts, when the trail may still have snowy or icy patches. At the top of the cirque, feel free to take a well-deserved breather: you've just conquered nearly 3000 feet of elevation gain.

From here, you have 1 more mile before reaching Emerald Lake, which is a definite highlight of this hike. At an elevation of 10,300 feet and a distance of 4.7 miles from the trailhead, you'll have ascended a breathless 3400 feet by this point. Lunch, camping, or even making this the final destination of a shorter hike are all great choices here. Keep an eye out around here for the unmistakable bright whiteness of the mountain goats that call this area home, as near the lake is where they are often spotted.

After leaving the lake, head west on the trail. It weaves around to the southwest of Timpanogos Basin, meeting up with the trail coming in from the Timpooneke trailhead in 0.5 mile. Once you have reached the ridge saddle in 0.8 mile—climbing another 1000 feet along the way—you see the brutal final bit of trail ascending to the Mount Timp summit. This last push is only 0.9 mile, but it directs you through a rocky, exposed section for another 450 feet in elevation gain. Switchbacks make the ascent somewhat easier, but the views as you head up the final part are what really encourage you to complete this hike.

From the 11,749-foot summit of Mount Timpanogos, you have striking, unparalleled vistas stretching out in every direction. The endless wash of mountains reaching to the east is truly staggering to comprehend, and the desert expanses sprawling out to the west are equally impressive—all of which helps explain why this particular Utah peak is so popular. From the summit, return back to the trailhead the same way.

30 Silver Lake (American Fork Canyon)

Roundtrip: 4.4 miles
Hiking time: 2–4 hours
Elevation gain: 1450 feet
Difficulty: moderate

Season: spring–fall
Map: USGS Dromedary Peak
Contact: Uinta-Wasatch-Cache National
Forest, Pleasant Grove Range District

Getting there: From Salt Lake City, drive south on I-15 to exit 284. Turn left onto State Route 92 and drive 12.6 miles to American Fork Canyon Road (State Route 144). Turn left and drive 2.5 miles to Tibble Fork Reservoir. In the parking lot, take the left toward Granite Flat Campground. Immediately before the campground, turn right onto dirt Silver Lake Road. Drive 3.2 miles to the Silver Lake Flat parking area. **Notes:** Fee required. Very end of access road may be difficult or impassable for low-clearance or non-4WD vehicles, depending on weather. May be crowded on weekends and holidays.

Set in a truly gorgeous mountainscape, Silver Lake in American Fork Canyon (not to be confused with the Silver Lake farther north off Big Cottonwood Canyon) gives you tremendous rewards for hiking its short length. In fact, just driving up the final bit of road to the trailhead provides a stunning view of an array of mountains in the distance, including Mount Timpanogos, giving you an idea of the unparalleled alpine scenery awaiting you on the actual trail. The possibility of seeing moose or bear is a tempting lure for

Amazing view to the south from the Silver Lake Trail

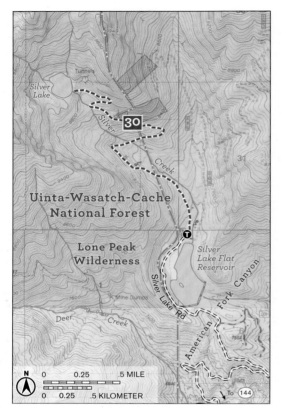

Head straight for the woods from the trail's starting point at the north end of the parking lot. Bristling with pines and aspens, the forest swallows up the trail as you head due north, with the occasional large boulder sitting with seeming incongruity in the midst of it all, having tumbled down eons ago from the high mountain flanks. In 0.5 mile you come across the Lone Peak Wilderness sign, signifying your entry into designated wildlands. As the trail angles to the northwest, small meadows here and there allow for views of the peaks, including White Baldy, the dominant one looming into the sky above your destination.

At 1 mile in, the trail bends sharply to the right (east) and soon casts you onto the mountain above the stream's drainage, offering more relatively unobstructed views. After following the contour of the hillside for a ways, the trail turns back toward the west, rising as it goes. You'll negotiate some switchbacks as they direct you higher up the mountain. Just before they cross into the basin that cradles Silver Lake, summer hikers may see a waterfall tumbling down the creek to the left, although by fall this may be less impressive in scope. In another 0.3 mile you top out into the cirque and behold the lake, 2.2 miles from the trailhead. Towering above the lake to the northwest is 11,321-foot-high White Baldy, a huge granite slab reminiscent of Italy's Dolomites. If you have keen eyes (or binoculars), you might even spot the beacon-bright white coats of mountain goats foraging above the lake. From here, simply return on the same trail to the parking area.

wildlife aficionados, but don't count on it. If you do happen to spot some creatures belonging to the *Alces alces* or *Ursus americanus* species, leave them be and don't cross their ramblings with yours—but do count yourself very lucky to have seen them in their singularly stunning home territory.

31 *Fifth Water Hot Springs/Diamond Fork Canyon*

Roundtrip: 4.5 miles
Hiking time: 3–5 hours
Elevation gain: 716 feet
Difficulty: easy

Season: spring–fall
Map: USGS Rays Valley
Contact: Uinta-Wasatch-Cache National Forest, Spanish Fork Ranger District

Getting there: From Salt Lake City, drive south on I-15 to exit 258 and head east (left) onto US Highway 6 toward Price/Manti. Drive east on US 6 for 11 miles to Diamond

Fork Road (Forest Service Road 029), which is signed for Diamond Fork CG. Turn left (north) onto this dirt road and drive 10 miles to the signed Three Forks trailhead parking area. **Notes:** May be crowded on weekends and holidays. Vault toilet at trailhead. Can be a great winter hike, but gate across the road is shut seasonally, adding 10 miles roundtrip. Bicycles and skis may be able to ascend past the gate. 4WD vehicle may be required in winter. Trail can be icy in winter. Bring plenty of water, preferably with electrolytes, as soaking in hot water can be dehydrating. People sometimes soak nude, although technically this isn't legal. Rattlesnakes may be along the trail during warmer months. Please do not leave trash at the springs.

Imagine this: you hike a forested trail along a burbling creek, gently meandering around boulders and beneath the shade of large pine trees. After just a few miles and a footbridge crossing, you come to a gorgeous little place: pretty waterfalls tumbling down over the rocks into several blue pools of hot spring water, just begging you to take a dip and relax in them for a while. This is the Fifth Water Springs up Diamond Fork Canyon, often referred to as Fifth Water/Diamond Fork. Not only is the trail quite scenic and relatively easy to ascend, the pools themselves are perfectly situated to make the setting very photogenic. The water ranges from hotter just beneath the falls to cooler in the pools farther away. Test each pool before committing to one, and enjoy your soak.

The springs are a remarkable place to visit in the wintertime, although that can add quite a distance to your trek since the gate on the road, well below the trailhead itself, is shut during the colder months. On the other hand, that means far fewer people visit then, which may ensure the hot springs will be your own personal playground for at least a little while. You can also camp overnight near the springs. You need to be very prepared for snowy or icy conditions, not to mention comfortable with winter trekking. But for those who have the requisite skills, it can be a blast; relaxing in hot springs while snow falls is definitely fun. Spring and fall are also excellent times to visit, and although summer might be warm, the trail is shaded much of the way. If you visit outside the winter season, be prepared for crowds on weekends. No matter how you slice it, though, these springs make the hike a memorable experience.

Head off along the well-marked trail, which meanders along the north (left) bank of Sixth Water Creek. Do not cross the footbridge to the right here. The trail dips and rises beside

A falls along Fifth Water Creek right by the soaking pools

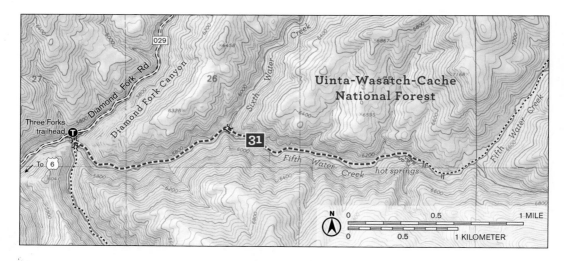

the stream, contouring with it as you steadily and easily gain elevation. Some exposed sections may be a little tricky if snow-covered but should be quite manageable if dry. About 1.25 miles in, you will come to another, fairly large footbridge that crosses over Sixth Water Creek just where Fifth Water Creek meets up with it. Continue now along Fifth Water, still staying on the north (left) side. Fifth Water Creek is noticeably smaller than Sixth Water Creek. In roughly 1 more mile, you'll know you are approaching the springs when the smell of sulphur starts to tickle at your nose, growing stronger the closer you get. The smell is not enough of a deterrent to keep you from enjoying the pools when you reach them, however.

The first pools appear at about 2.25 miles from the trailhead, on your right. The waterfall is another 50 yards or so up the stream. Here, you might notice a range of colors in the "hot pots." Some may appear creamy blue, some more muddied aquamarine, some quite clear. Over the years, artful hikers have arranged stones to make the pools more comfortable to soakers. Any nude bathers may be receptive to polite requests to cover up, particularly if you have children with you. If the area is crowded and the pools too full for your liking, try the stream itself, which can be delightfully warm as well since the pools simply run over directly into it. Above the waterfall are more soaking pools, but these can be exceptionally hot: the water can reach around 120 degrees Fahrenheit. Once you are done enjoying this natural hot springs experience, return to the parking area along the same trail.

32 *Mount Nebo*

Roundtrip: 10 miles
Hiking time: 7–10 hours
Elevation gain: 4100
Difficulty: strenuous

Season: spring–fall
Map: USGS Nebo Basin
Contact: Uinta-Wasatch-Cache National Forest, Pleasant Grove Ranger District

Getting there: From Salt Lake City, drive south on I-15 58 miles to Payson. Take exit 250 and head south on State Route 115/Main Street. Turn left (east) on 100 North, drive 6 blocks, and turn right (south) on 600 East. This eventually becomes Nebo Loop Road. From the canyon mouth, drive 28.2 miles on this road to the signed Monument trailhead parking on the right (west). Turn right here, then immediately turn right again onto dirt Mona Pole Road and drive north 0.4 mile to trailhead parking. **Note:** Vault toilet at Monument trailhead.

As the highest peak in the Wasatch Range, 11,928-foot Mount Nebo commands a lofty presence. Rather than a rugged granite pinnacle with imposing cirques and jagged edges, it actually sports rounded slopes and a seemingly gentle incline. Don't let appearances deceive you, though. This is definitely not the hike for anyone who has vertigo or is not in strong hiking shape. The trail to the top gains significant elevation during the final mile in particular, testing willpower as well as endurance. For your efforts, however, you can claim to have hiked the highest peak this range offers, gain phenomenal 360-degree views at the top, and pass through meadows of flowers or trees aflame with color, depending on the season you tackle it. Mount Nebo towers above busy towns in the valleys far below, and the wilderness experience you can have so close to human habitation is striking. The trail is well-defined from the start, despite the immediate climbing, but close to the top it goes through boulder fields replete with loose rock and exposure, which is actually more hazardous on the descent than the approach due to the possibility of loose footing. A well-planned journey, however, will make this hike one to remember.

Set off due west along the fence line from the Mona Pole trailhead. In just under 1 mile the trail departs the fence and continues slightly northwest, climbing gradually as it goes. Through this beautiful, not terribly demanding section, meadows ringed with pines greet you, and the views are generally open. Deer, moose, elk, and pikas with distinctive, chirruping cries all claim this area as home. In the summertime, you may notice an abundance of Indian paintbrush, columbine, lupine, primrose, and myriad other beautiful flowers keeping you company. The trail soon heads up the hillside, following a drainage and ascending a saddle to the ridgeline of Mount Nebo. Achieve this saddle in 2.3 miles. The trail starts to curve southward as it follows the ridgeline, offering glimpses of the sections still ahead.

Your next point of interest is 11,174-foot North Peak. A series of short, steep switchbacks make their way up a drainage on the north end before

Pippin scouts out the trail to Mount Nebo.

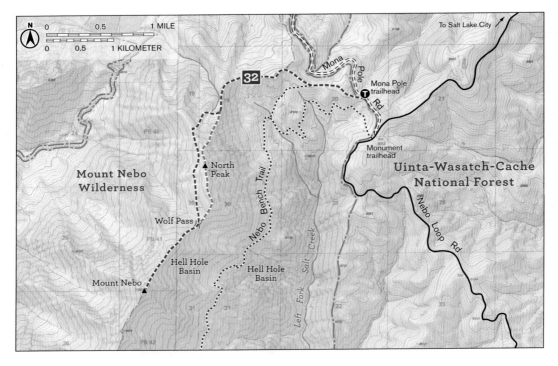

you reach the ridgeline. The trail will then skirt slightly below North Peak on its west side. For those who enjoy bagging as many peaks as they can, summiting that peak is fairly simple if you wish to take a slightly different route: as the trail heads toward the peak, simply veer off to the left to follow the ridgeline up to the summit. The summit is only about 300 feet off the trail, adding only negligible time and footwork to your day. If you're unsure of your overall stamina and time, however, sticking to the main trail is likely your best option.

As you skirt the side of North Peak, the saddle between it and Mount Nebo becomes visible. Known as Wolf Pass, it presents a drop in elevation and an easy walk along it before you are faced with the next significant challenge: what seems to be an almost completely vertical climb up to your destination. Although from Wolf Pass you are only about 0.75 mile away from the highest point in the Wasatch, that final ascent is truly brutal and will test your hiking

mettle. Stopping often to catch your breath is a great idea during the initial sustained climb that takes you up past the tree line and into a scree field.

Head up, up, up to a first little false summit and a ridge that roller coasters along as you still aim for the top. The final segment is basically trailless and demands scrambling over rocks and perhaps even needing to use your hands for support. When you finally make it to this section, Mount Nebo's actual summit awaits only a few hundred yards' walk away. From your vantage point on the rooftop of the Wasatch, views extend in every direction. You'll be able to see many other peaks in the range, as well as the Uinta National Forest, the Manti-La Sal National Forest, and, to the west, the dry expanse of the Great Basin. Once you've taken in the views and rested up, very carefully descend back down the loose rocks to Wolf Pass. From there it is a relatively easy return along the trail back to the parking area.

33 *Notch Peak*

Roundtrip: 8.5 miles
Hiking time: 5–6 hours
Elevation gain: 2800 feet
Difficulty: moderate

Season: all year
Map: USGS Notch Peak
Contact: Bureau of Land Management, Fillmore Field Office

Getting there: From Delta, drive west (the road will soon curve south) on US Highway 6/ US 50 for 36 miles. Turn right (north) on the dirt Notch Peak Loop Road shortly before mile marker 46. Drive 4.7 miles and turn left onto Miller Canyon Road. Drive 5.5 miles to the BLM picnic area. From here turn left and head southwest toward Sawtooth Canyon. After 2.8 miles pass an old wooden cabin now maintained by the BLM; continue another 0.75 mile to the trailhead. **Notes:** Summer can be extremely hot. High-clearance vehicle may be required to access trailhead. Dirt roads may be impassable if wet or snowy. Exposed sections. Map reading and routefinding skills necessary.

With a cliff face that rises nearly 4450 feet, Notch Peak (summit elevation: 9656 feet) has one of the highest cliffs in North America. Better known to rock climbers than to hikers, this is nevertheless a great hike that serves up the austere beauty typical in the center of the state's western half. Just as impressive as far more famous El Capitan in Yosemite, Notch Peak isn't on most people's radar due to its remote location in Utah's dry, barren West Desert. This is just as well, because it means you can enjoy this peak experience without fending off massive crowds. You also don't need to be a rock climber to tackle this one, as a wonderful hiker trail takes you right to the top and allows you to see the vast surrounding Great Basin area.

Notch Peak is an excellent hike for those craving solitude.

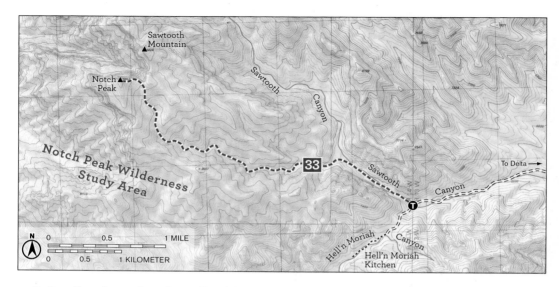

Strike off northwest from the trailhead. Just 0.5 mile in, veer left to stay in the main canyon. Narrow and fairly steep-sided, the canyon features pinyon and juniper, mountain mahogany, rock ledges, and the occasional bushwhacking episode. When you are 3.5 miles in you're at a saddle where a gigantic tree has fallen across the canyon. At this point, the views really open up and let you realize how high you've climbed. From here on to the final push, the trail isn't as well worn, but your destination ahead of you and to the left, the northwest, is obvious. Simply wind your way up the final 0.75 mile to the top here, being cautious of the insanely long drop-offs to your right. The white, gray, tan, and brown barrenness spreads out all around, making the desert seem otherworldly. A false summit may trick your eyes for a bit, but as you get closer to the top you will easily realize which one is the true summit.

As you continue up, also keep an eye out for gnarled, weather-worn trees clinging with proud, long-lasting tenacity to the east side of the saddle. A stand of ancient Great Basin bristlecone pines (*Pinus longaeva*) calls this place home. Considered to be among the oldest living things on the planet, the twisted bristlecones are beautiful, from the colors of their trunks and limbs to their contortionist bends and unique cones. Each cone is tipped with a claw-like bristle, which is where the name derives. At the top of Notch Peak, the surrounding views of the West Desert are magnificent, fully 360 degrees around. A clear day nets you views for hundreds of miles in any direction, demanding time to take it all in. When you have seen enough, return back down to the trailhead the way you came up.

Opposite, top: A young pronghorn antelope inspects the high country of Bryce Canyon.

Opposite, bottom: Sunlight illuminates a cottonwood tree deep within the Virgin River Narrows.

Southwest

With beautiful pine-covered mountains, fantastic red rock formations, the state's highest-elevation unit of the national park system, places famous the world over, and spots known only to locals, the southwest portion of Utah contains impressive hiking trails and stunning natural features. The most famous part of this area is Zion National Park, which is lauded for its gorgeous water-filled canyon known as The Narrows and the striking sandstone beauty of the main canyon. Since the park is on the world's radar, it sees about 3 million visitors per year. But the topography of southwest Utah ranges from these red canyons to snow-covered mountain peaks, deep gorges slashed through the earth, amphitheaters bristling with hoodoo spires, and sandstone twisted by wind and pushed apart by ice, wedging it into shapes that stir the imagination. The variety of hikes easily accessible within a day's drive is as astonishing as the differences in the landscape.

Little-known mountain areas such as the Pine Valley and Tushar Mountains offer cool experiences for summer visitors, while Snow Canyon State Park and Red Canyon in Dixie National Forest are smaller—but in many ways just as beautiful—versions of their more famous park-service cousins in terms of red-rock amphitheater beauty and colorful sandstone formations. Soaring summer temperatures in the very southwestern corner of the state are offset by unexpected high elevations at Bryce Canyon National Park and Cedar Breaks National Monument, both of which are known for red hoodoo formations that bring to mind more desert-like environs. But Bryce Canyon actually shuts some of its roads in the winter because elevations reaching over 9000 feet ensure that snow is a presence here every winter. The high point in Cedar Breaks is 10,662 feet, and it can get as much as 15 feet of snow in the winter, but its superb springtime flowers and fall foliage should not be missed.

34 Delano Peak

Roundtrip: 3.4 miles
Hiking time: 2–3 hours
Elevation gain: 1650 feet
Difficulty: easy/moderate
Season: all year

Map: USGS Shelly Baldy Peak, Delano Peak
Contact: Fishlake National Forest, Beaver Ranger District

Getting there: From Beaver, head east on State Route 153 for 16 miles to Forest Service Road 123 (Big John Flat Road). Turn left (north) and drive 5 miles on the dirt road, passing Big John Flat Campground. Continue another 0.5 mile to small trailhead parking pullout on the right. **Notes:** Vault toilets at campground. Access gates along Big John Flat Road may be closed in winter.

Never heard of the Tushar Mountains? That's a good thing if you're seeking solitude in a backcountry setting that easily rivals anything in the Wasatch Range farther north. The Tushars are the third-highest mountain range in Utah (the Uintas are first, followed by the La Sals

Beautiful views of the Tushar Mountains from the Delano Peak trail

outside Moab), and Delano Peak tops out at 12,179 feet, making it the highest point in two counties: Piute and Beaver. Although it certainly doesn't look it if you approach from I-15, Delano is higher than the highest mountaintop in the Wasatch (Mount Nebo, for those who like to keep track). This trail is matter-of-fact despite a fairly substantial elevation gain typical of most mountain hikes in Utah. A number of trails in the area also make the trailhead a good place to camp for a night or two and really explore the beautiful Tushars. The peak and the trail to it sport sweeping views, mountain goats, wild-flower-filled meadows in the summer, a relatively easy ascent even in the winter, and an overall abundance of lovely mountainous beauty. Happily, the Tushars are missing one thing: throngs of people. Not especially close to any of the state's major urban centers, the Tushars make a wonderful alpine playground for those who prefer to enjoy their wilderness with a generous amount of elbow room.

From the trailhead, walk up the two-track road toward the repeater tower. Angle east from the tower, ascending the obvious ridgeline toward your destination. Looking northeast from here, you can spot Bullion Canyon and Bullion Pasture. The mining history of the area is rich; for a short period, a gold-rush boom swelled the population with miners who had gold dust bedazzling their senses as they relentlessly panned the streams for nuggets of the precious stuff. Bullion Canyon, just north of Delano Peak, saw the bulk of the prospectors, and mining relics remain to this day.

Although the trail may seem to fade in and out, it's a very straightforward shot along the ridge, with Delano Peak always in your sights, so getting lost would take some effort. Cairns may also be in place to help you stay on the trail. Climbing the ridge's small peaks and valleys does require effort, though. The prospect of seeing a herd of snowy white mountain goats may distract you from the climb, and the views along the way should as well. Even with the elevation

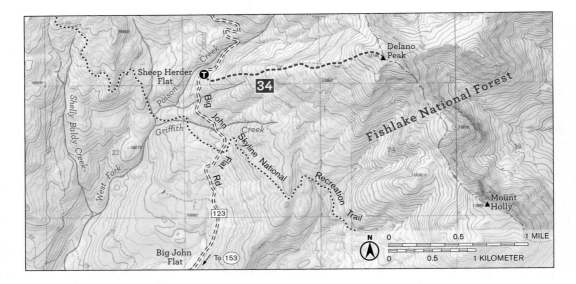

gain, this isn't nearly as rough a push as some other mountain trails in the state, so it can make for a more pleasant outing. Grassy slopes and the occasional volcanic boulder make up the scenery, and the way is delightfully free of the rocky scree fields that epitomize many high-mountain hikes elsewhere.

Immediately before the actual summit, there is a short, more rugged section, and then you hit the high point at 1.7 miles. A large sign informs you that you have achieved your destination, as if it wasn't clear. To the immediate north, you will see Mount Baldy (12,090 feet) and Mount Belknap (12,119 feet). Mount Holly to the south is shy of 12,000 feet by only one foot. Eagle Point ski resort also graces the view in that direction. Look toward the west to spy the Great Basin deserts far in the distance. When you're done soaking it all in, head back down the ridgeline to the parking area.

35 *Kanarra Creek Trail*

Roundtrip: 4.4 miles
Hiking time: 3–4 hours
Elevation gain: 700 feet
Difficulty: easy/moderate

Season: spring–fall
Map: USGS Kanarraville
Contact: Bureau of Land Management, Cedar City Office

Getting there: From Cedar City, drive 5.5 miles south on I-15 and take exit 51. Turn left and drive 4.7 miles south on Old US Highway 91 to Kanarraville. Turn left onto 100 North. Trailhead parking area is in 0.4 mile. Pay parking fee at self-serve kiosk, or park in town at Kanarraville Town Hall, 0.25 mile away, and walk from there to the trailhead.

From St. George, drive 33.3 miles north on I-15 to exit 42. Turn right onto State Route 144 and drive 100 yards to turn left onto Old US Highway 91. Drive north for 4.4 miles to 100 North and turn right. Parking area is in 0.4 mile. Pay parking fee at self-serve kiosk, or park 0.25 mile away at Kanarraville Town Hall and walk from there to the trailhead.

Notes: Flash flooding may occur in monsoon season (mid- to late summer). Walking through water required; some sections may be waist-deep. Canyon blockages and lack of ability to ascend rock wedges and waterfalls may shorten hike. No pets allowed; creek is water supply for Kanarraville. Fee for trailhead parking.

Like all slot canyons, the one that the Kanarra Creek Trail runs through is pretty cool. It is even more so than many because water flows through it, and it is less well known than the more famous ones in nearby Zion National Park, so your chances for a little solitude are greater. But this very nice hike with its showcase of classic slot scenery does indeed attract people, so be prepared to share. The presence of two waterfalls also helps to differentiate this slot canyon, making it memorable as well as potentially challenging to some. The trick to enjoying Kanarra Creek is to go up it as far as feels safe and doable for you and your party. If you only make it as far as the base of the first waterfall, rest assured that you have seen the best part of the canyon. The opportunities for outstanding photos are epic, so make sure you're ready to shoot. Part of the Spring Creek Wilderness Study Area (WSA), this gorgeous little canyon certainly falls squarely into the 73 percent of the WSA that is rated as outstanding for its scenic qualities.

From the parking area, proceed up the dirt road toward the water tank. The road drops, entering the Hurricane Cliffs and heading you toward Kanarra Creek Canyon proper. It crosses the creek, then continues on the north side of the creek until its terminus, at which point you begin to walk in the creek. The water level depends on the time of year and any recent weather events. When the weather has been calm for a bit, the stream can be clear as glass, allowing you to see every water-smoothed rock on the creek bottom as you make your way along it. Travel in or alongside the streambed here, getting your feet wet when necessary in what is usually cold water.

At 1.2 miles in you reach the slot part of the canyon, where the walls narrow in, zoom up, and tightly surround you. Although it can be rather dark through here, the light can also play on the cliffs, bouncing off the rock and stream bottom to create visual feasts. The rock walls curve up, around, and sometimes almost over you as sections bulge out, all carved by unassuming little Kanarra Creek flowing through. Beautiful photos are yours for the taking at virtually every turn.

Very shortly after entering the slot part, you encounter the first 15-foot-high waterfall. A

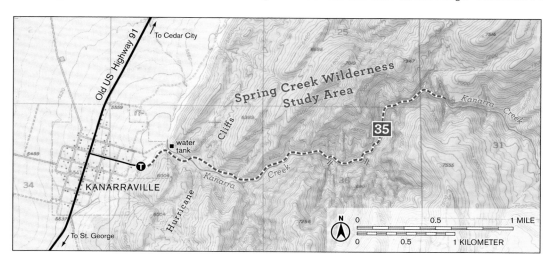

ladder constructed from a tree trunk should be at the side of it, but do not put your faith into the ladder either being there or being in good, safe condition. Do your own safety check before proceeding. Even if you only feel comfortable going this far, the beauty of this classic little slot canyon is worthwhile. If you do manage to clamber up and over the ladder—an endeavor assisted by a length of rope bolted into the rock wall beside the ladder, but again don't necessarily count on it being there or being in good shape—you will keep heading upcreek. Wedged-boulder creek obstacles may be in place; use your judgment to scramble up and over them.

Shortly after several more sinuous curves, you will encounter the second waterfall. This one may also have a crudely made ladder to the right side, as well as a rope hand-line, but once again don't count on it either being there or being in safe shape. If you make it past this second obstacle, keep going up the pretty creek. Several little areas to the side of the creek are somewhat flat and may make good picnic spots. Head up another 0.5 mile to experience more of the slot; going even farther is possible, but sometimes the vegetation can seem more prohibitive than is worthwhile. Return to your vehicle the same way, using care on the downclimbs over the waterfall sections.

The spectacular, unexpected slot canyon of Kanarra Creek

36 *Whipple Trail–Summit Trail Loop*

Loop: 17 miles
Hiking time: 8 hours–2 days
Elevation gain: 4400 feet
Difficulty: hard/strenuous

Season: fall–spring
Map: USGS Signal Peak, Grass Valley
Contact: Dixie National Forest, Pine Valley Ranger District

Getting there: From Cedar City, drive west on State Route 56 for 34.7 miles to Bench Road in Newcastle and turn left (southwest). Drive 9 miles to State Route 18 and turn left (south). Drive 25 miles to Central and turn left (east) on Forest Service Road 035. Drive 7.7 miles to Pine Valley. Turn left on Main Street and drive 3 miles to the Pine Valley Recreation Area and Whipple trailhead parking, at the end of the loop past the Ebenezer Bryce Campground.

From St. George, drive north on SR 18 for 27.2 miles to Central and turn right (east) on Forest Service Road 035. Drive 7.7 miles to Pine Valley. Turn left on Main Street and drive 3 miles to the Pine Valley Recreation Area and Whipple trailhead parking, at the end of the loop past the Ebenezer Bryce Campground. **Notes:** Can be very dry in summer. Seasonal campgrounds and water fountain nearby (May–September).

When most people think of southern Utah, green mountains don't usually come to mind. But the Pine Valley Mountains, rising with dramatic intensity northwest of St. George, are definitely mountains, and they are definitely green, at least once you're in them. The Whipple Trail (#31025) and Summit Trail (#31021) can be linked together to form a great loop hike that allows you to explore an area of the state that is not nearly as overrun as the ranges to the north and definitely nowhere near as jam-packed as nearby Zion National Park. The Pine Valley Mountains are truly beautiful, and enjoying them is even more fun because you don't have to share the space with many other people. Whipple Valley itself is an oasis of green, a truly charming mountain meadow that is delightfully inviting, particularly when the days are getting toasty on the valley floor below. The federally designated Pine Valley Mountain Wilderness area is legally considered to be "an area of undeveloped Federal land retaining its primeval character and influence without permanent improvements or human habitation, which is protected and managed so as to preserve its natural conditions." In other words, a lovely untrammeled wilderness in which to adventure.

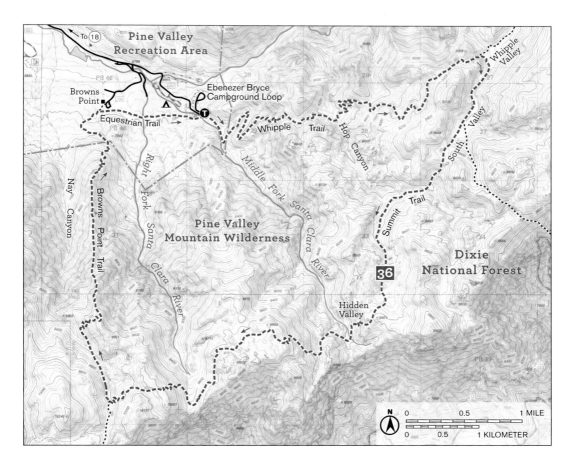

The Whipple Trail is lined with wildflowers in springtime.

interest to the geologically minded is that these mountains are formed from the Pine Valley Laccolith, the largest laccolith in the entire country, measuring over 18 miles long and nearly 7 miles wide. Igneous intrusions, laccoliths are formed when magma migrates up into the earth's crust and intrudes itself between two separate sedimentary rock layers, arcing the layers upward into a domelike shape. Volcanic activity made the very beautiful Pine Valley Mountains, and the Whipple Trail–Summit Trail loop hike is an excellent way to explore and enjoy them.

From the trailhead, jaunt eastward on the marked path, heading uphill as you walk. The first mile is relatively easy, but the elevation increases steadily over a series of switchbacks. As you ascend the snaking trail, you can catch glimpses of the remote Bull Valley Mountains to the west. In the fall, aspen trees along the way can cast an explosion of rustling golds and reds, adding even more beauty to the already engaging scenery. Your climb nets you over 1000 feet by the time you reach Hop Canyon and drop a few hundred feet into it. Climb back out of the canyon to the tune of another 1100 feet by the time you get to the sumptuous Whipple Valley at 5 miles in. The valley is a pleasant spot to rest up from your climb before you continue on. Here you meet the signed Summit Trail junction; turn right and head southwest into South Valley, which is also extremely enticing and pretty. Either one of these meadows can make for a great campsite, depending on your hike plan, but beware the mosquitoes during the warm months—they can be ferocious.

The trail jogs up and down by a few hundred feet here and there over the next several miles, using switchbacks again as it negotiates ridges and other earth contours while you continue to head south and west. Pass through Hop Canyon again, although this time at its southern end and higher in elevation. Pass through another small, very scenic meadow, Hidden Valley, which opens up abruptly 3 miles from the start of the Summit Trail. It offers another excellent campsite for those who are making a backpack out of this trip. Continue past the valley, where

A virtual oasis amid surrounding desert lands, these mountains are home to all the usual animals you think of—bears, marmots, deer, mountain lions, red squirrels, chipmunks. The vegetation runs the gamut from pinyon and juniper to the dignified Engelmann spruce. Of particular

Douglas fir, spruce, and aspen decorate the landscape, providing a good motivator as the trail ascends another 1000 feet en route to its junction with the Browns Point Trail, 11.5 miles into your hike.

Turn north at this junction in Nay Canyon for 3 miles in this section. You'll climb a small ridge,

finding yourself at nearly 10,000 feet. Ready yourself for a swift and rocky descent of 3000 feet as you drop down to the Browns Point trailhead in the Pine Valley Recreation Area. From there, turn right and head east for 1.5 miles along the Equestrian Trail to reach the Whipple trailhead and your parking area.

37 Snow Canyon

Roundtrip: 6.75 miles
Hiking time: 3–4 hours
Elevation gain: 445 feet
Difficulty: easy/moderate

Season: fall–spring
Map: USGS Veyo
Contact: Snow Canyon State Park

Getting there: From St. George, take exit 6 off I-15 and head north for 4 miles on Bluff Street. Turn left (west) onto Snow Canyon Parkway and drive 4 miles to Snow Canyon Drive. Turn right (north) and drive 0.7 mile to the fee station, then 1 mile to the parking area just south of the visitor center on the left side of the road. **Notes:** Fee required. Bring park trail map; trails crisscross, which can confuse hikers. Ranger on duty can provide more detailed trail information. Vault toilets in campground 0.1 mile from trailhead parking area. Tent and RV sites nearby. Can be very hot in summer. Sunrise and sunset offer the best light for photos.

The underrated Snow Canyon State Park is located southwest of its far more famous cousin, Zion National Park, and known more to locals than visitors. But Snow Canyon offers solitude, gorgeous views, and classic southern Utah canyon country for exploration, all of it accessible to most and far less crowded than Zion. Named for early pioneers Lorenzo and Erastus Snow, this is a truly stunning area that is overshadowed simply because it's in a state that has some of the world's most spectacular canyon-country geology. Located in the sprawling 62,000-acre Red Cliffs Desert Reserve, Snow Canyon's 7400 acres offer an especially good choice of trails and exploration for hikers traveling with children, or for those who want to experience red-rock landscapes with significantly less bustle and hustle than is usually found in more well-known outdoor areas such as Zion. There is a maze of trails in Snow Canyon, which allows you to connect them in order to enjoy longer hikes. It can be easy to miss some trail

turns or junctions, as not everything is marked, so be sure to take a park trail-guide brochure with you as you hike. Connecting the following hikes makes for a fun jaunt in this beautiful place.

From the parking area just south of the visitor center, go northwest up the initially paved Whiptail Trail. You quickly will come to a trailhead sign for Three Ponds Trail; turn left here. Head across slickrock, winding your way along the broad path over rocky shelves. Cactus and the hardy shrubs of desertscapes dot the surrounding area; pretty blooms are visible in springtime. Other lovely plants you can spy, depending on the time of year, include tall, skinny yucca; cholla cactus with its plump, cylindrical stems; the nodding orange blooms of globemallow; plentiful dusty-green sage bushes; and the beautiful white flowers of the sacred datura (also known as jimsonweed), a powerful hallucinogenic that you should definitely avoid ingesting.

Through a small sandy wash 0.75 mile in, watch carefully for the Three Ponds Trail sign,

Snow Canyon is a desert playground.

as it can be easy to get a little turned around. You should still be heading generally west and slightly north. The sandy section of the trail can be trying; slogging through deep sand makes for a great leg workout. Color-washed Navajo sandstone cliffs rise on either side, their red and orange hues making it very clear you're hiking through the southern Utah canyonlands. The walls, 400 feet high, are pocked by wind-blown holes, broken by vertical cracks, and banded with dark streaks of desert varnish from the passage of water during infrequent storms.

If you desire a slightly longer hike, jog left onto the Hidden Pinyon Trail and take that northward instead of immediately hitting the Three Ponds trail. Hidden Pinyon somewhat parallels Three Ponds for a short way. Sandy at first, the Hidden Pinyon Trail enters small canyons that offer minor scrambles over sandstone. This trail adds an additional 1.5 miles. Shortly after it rejoins the Three Ponds Trail on its north end, take the spur trail heading southwest for a very scenic overlook. Then return to the main Three Ponds Trail and continue hiking north and west.

Three Ponds is a hike whose name derives from the naturally formed potholes found in the sandstone. Filling up with water after rainstorms or from melting snow, potholes are an essential source of life-giving water in the desert, important to a variety of life forms from the tiniest microorganisms living right in them to the mammals who silently pad on careful paws to drink deeply late in the cool of night. The potholes can make for striking photos, particularly when they are full, although seeing them full can be rare. Summertime can be exceptionally hot and is not a recommended season for hiking this trail. Early springtime is best. Animals to keep an eye out for include kit foxes, quail, canyon tree frogs, and coyotes, although coyotes tend to be more nocturnal. Consider yourself extremely lucky if you spy graceful peregrine falcons, striking gila monsters, or slowly passing giant desert tortoise: these three less common species are all protected by law.

When you reach the potholes, the trail ends due to a steep pour-off. This section is an excellent choice for taking a break, eating lunch, or

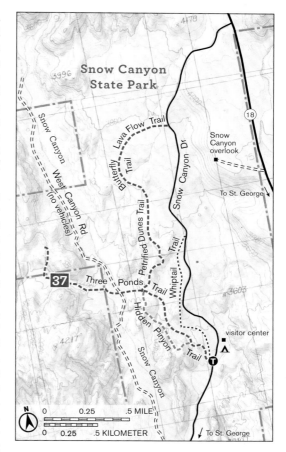

simply admiring the natural beauty of the potholes in the rippled, waving slickrock expanse. Return back down the trail toward the parking area until you come to the junction with the Petrified Dunes Trail and turn left. There isn't really much of a trail here, as the route takes you across the rugged slickrock dunes themselves, but most hikers shouldn't have too much problem finding their way. Sometimes cairns mark the way. After hiking through this picturesque section, you'll come to the junction with the Butterfly Trail to your left (west). Follow this pretty little trail now as it quickly curves northwest for 0.6 mile to its junction with the Lava Flow Trail. Turn right (northeast) here and walk 100 feet over a hard-packed trail to see lava tubes you can enter for a ways. From here, you can retrace your steps on the trails back to the parking area.

38 *Virgin River Narrows*

Roundtrip: 10 miles
Hiking time: 8 hours
Elevation gain: 334 feet
Difficulty: moderate/hard

Season: all year
Map: USGS Temple of Sinawava, Straight Canyon, Clear Creek Mountain
Contact: Zion National Park

Getting there: From St. George and I-15 northbound, take exit 16 onto State Route 9 east for 33 miles to La Verkin. (From I-15 southbound, use exit 27 for State Route 17 south.) Turn right to stay on SR 9 for another 20 miles to the park entrance in Springdale. From March–October, you must take a park shuttle unless you are a guest at Zion Lodge; exit at the Temple of Sinawava stop for this hike. **Notes:** Flash flooding may occur in mid- to late summer; Narrows access closed if flooding is expected. Fee required at park entrance. No permit necessary for day hikes. Walking through river required. Hiking poles and sturdy footwear that can get wet are highly recommended.

The famed Virgin River Narrows is very popular during the hot months.

The Narrows is one of Utah's most famous hikes, for good reason. The spectacular canyon walls, gorgeous slants of light, and unusual experience of mostly hiking in the actual river all conspire to create an unforgettable journey. Many people either venture into the river for just a few hundred yards or strap on their backpacks for an overnight trip. While both are fine options, perhaps the best way to take in this most classic hike is a full-day hike in which you get a real taste of these narrows yet can avoid the more challenging aspects of stream walking over hidden rocks while wearing a large, heavy pack.

From the Temple of Sinawava shuttle stop, head up the Riverside Walk for 1.1 miles to reach the entrance to The Narrows. This mostly paved part of the trail is a pleasant stroll through graceful trees, with several spots near the river for sitting and contemplating the beauty. Don't tarry long, though, for The Narrows ahead beckon. When you reach the river section, head right into the water and go upcanyon. The walls seem to stretch upward for an incredibly long distance, although this is not nearly the highest they get in this canyon. Streaks of desert varnish mingle with the russets and ambers and golds of the walls, which are most impressive when they bounce back the sunlight trying to reach down into the canyon. If the water flow is low, you may have sandbars to walk on here and there, but don't count on it. At 1.5 miles, watch for lovely Mystery Falls on your right (east) as they slide down the rocks. Consider yourself lucky if you spot folks rappelling down from the canyon into The Narrows.

As you continue upstream, the sculpted canyon walls curve around as you travel another 1.5 miles to reach the opening of Orderville Canyon, 3 miles from your starting point. Most people turn back here, which is certainly an option, but heading beyond and taking a gander into the canyon will provide you with an in-depth sense of The Narrows. At this point you will be utterly committed to walking in water regardless of how shallow it's been up till now. The canyon quickly tightens up for the remaining 2 miles to Big Spring, which is the required turnaround point for day hikers. The section between Orderville

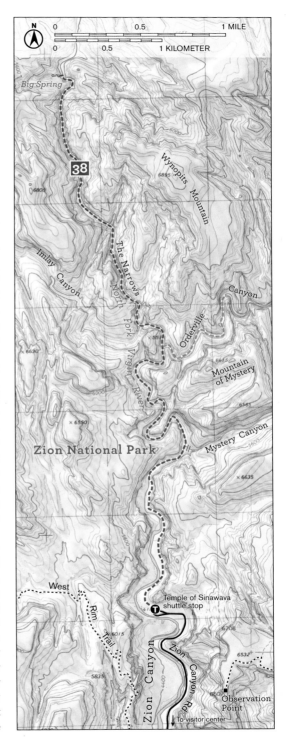

Canyon and Big Springs is known as Wall Street, and it is fair to say this is the most spectacular, most photographed area of The Narrows. Closely constricted walls swerve around, bending the light and the imagination. Return to the trailhead the same way, this time walking with the current.

Extending your hike: If you take a side trip into Orderville Canyon at the 3-mile mark, be prepared to enter a place even deeper and darker than The Narrows. Also be prepared to swim through some deep holes. The payoff is seeing a beautiful little canyon that few explore. Head in as far as feels comfortable, which generally is to the difficult-to-bypass but very pretty little Veiled Falls, then return the same way back to The Narrows.

39 Observation Point

Roundtrip: 8 miles	**Season:** all year
Hiking time: 4–6 hours	**Map:** USGS Temple of Sinawava
Elevation gain: 2150 feet	**Contact:** Zion National Park
Difficulty: hard	

Getting there: From St. George and I-15 northbound, take exit 16 onto State Route 9 east for 33 miles to La Verkin. (From I-15 southbound, use exit 27 for State Route 17 south.) Turn right to stay on SR 9 for another 20 miles to the park entrance in Springdale. From March–October, you must take a park shuttle unless you are a guest at Zion Lodge; exit at the Weeping Rock stop for this hike. **Notes:** Fee required at park entrance. Very hot in summer; may have snowy or icy areas in winter. Exposure and long drop-offs.

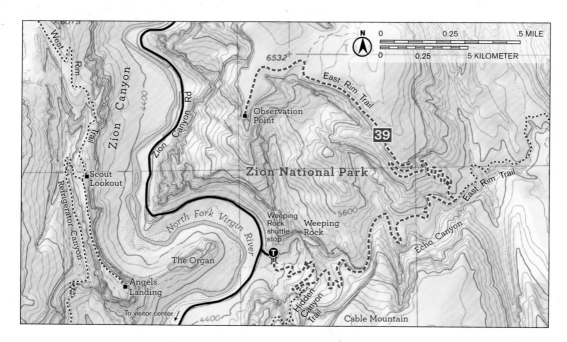

Although much of the Observation Point trail is paved in order to prevent erosion, it still isn't a casual walk in the park. Not for the faint-hearted, this hike with serious elevation gain is nonetheless a beautiful trail leading to a view that some think rivals that from more popular Angels Landing (which will actually seem puny by comparison when you gaze down upon it, far below you, from the top of Observation Point). Demanding that you ascend over 2000 feet in elevation, the trail will give you a workout. Nevertheless, this is a technically easy hike that most with lung- and willpower can accomplish. Stunning views at the top, interesting sections along the way, and a less common view of Zion from its eastern cliffs all serve to make this a hike to relish for those who tackle it. The imposing main Zion Canyon will be displayed for you, showing the massive cliff walls, the band of green running through it thanks to the Virgin River, and the overall extremely impressive, unique landscape of this national park to gorgeous advantage.

From the Weeping Rock trailhead parking lot, head out on the East Rim Trail as it leaves from the southwest corner of the lot and cross a small footbridge. You immediately begin to gain altitude as the trail inexorably heads upward, gaining 750 feet in the first mile, but the switchbacks make the grade not seem terribly severe. Originally a long Paiute Indian trail, the path was later expanded by pioneer ranchers, then turned into a daunting 18-miler before being shaped by the national park in the 1920s into the shorter trail it is today.

At 0.7 mile, you reach the junction with the Hidden Canyon Trail, which forks off to your right (south). Continue upward along the main trail, still climbing high above the valley floor. The trail levels out as you approach narrow, gorgeous Echo Canyon. At 2 miles, the East Rim Trail leads off to your right through Echo Canyon; stay on the main trail as it generally heads north in a sinuous pattern. No longer able to see the main canyon floor, and likely sharing the trail with far fewer people than you started it with, you wander through a mountainous sandstone wonderland, still ascending.

The lofty view from Observation Point

Continue up, up, up as the path spirals along the contours of the mountain, giving you breathtaking views and sometimes coming close to the edge of impressive drop-offs. Yellowish Kayenta rock adds to the already magnificent visual appeal. When you finally reach the top of the plateau, take heart in the fact the last 0.8 mile to the point itself is mostly level. The tremendous views from it are possibly incomparable in Zion as they sweep over the canyon and the folds and pockets of rumpled sandstone extending out all around you. If you look down you will also be able to see the zigzag switchbacks you ascended near the trail's start, which gives you great appreciation for the miles and ascent you covered to get here. Return to the parking area via the same route.

40 *Emerald Pools*

Roundtrip: 2.2 miles
Hiking time: 1–2 hours
Elevation gain: 400 feet
Difficulty: easy/moderate

Season: spring–fall
Map: USGS Temple of Sinawava
Contact: Zion National Park

Getting there: From St. George and I-15 northbound, take exit 16 onto State Route 9 east for 33 miles to La Verkin. (From I-15 southbound, use exit 27 for State Route 17 south.) Turn right to stay on SR 9 for another 20 miles to the park entrance in Springdale. From March–October, you must take a park shuttle unless you are a guest at Zion Lodge. Exit at Zion Lodge shuttle stop. **Notes:** Fee required at park entrance. Beware icy or slick conditions in winter and heat in summer. Exposed, potentially slippery edges with long drop-offs.

This incredibly popular trail is hiked often because it is short, sweet, and an excellent choice for families or those pressed for time. The three pools along the route—Lower, Middle, and Upper Emerald—showcase what a lush riparian area can look like in the desert, making this a welcome refuge on warm days. Summer days can find this trail outrageously bloated with visitors, so you might enjoy it more if you hike it in springtime or midweek. Each of the pools is lovely in its own way, and the lower pools are usually easily accessible for the very young or the less able, but hiking to each pool is recommended because each pool has its own charm, giving this trail a rightful place in the pantheon of classic Zion hikes.

Just across from Zion Lodge, the signed trail heads west across a little bridge over the Virgin River and turns right (north). Leafy green cottonwood, box elder, and willow trees provide

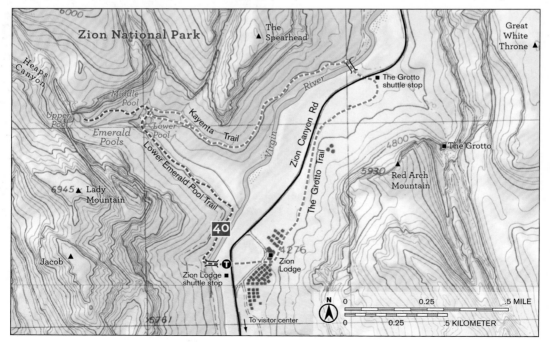

graceful shade and a sense of coolness in this canyon environment as you amble near the river. This first 0.6 mile of trail leading to the Lower Emerald Pool is paved, allowing ample access. The route soon heads west into Heaps Canyon, taking you to the lower pool first. The trail veers behind the waterfall that creates the pool, sometimes allowing a cooling mist to gently shower you as you walk. Water cascades over the desert-varnished ledge in a beautiful sliding sheet.

Now the trail heads uphill, becoming dirt and steeper, for the shorter distance from here to the Middle Emerald Pool. You will find yourself walking on top of the cliff you just passed under earlier, and the middle pool reflects the canyon walls near the rim. This is a gorgeous little section of the trail, often complete with chattering squirrels, trilling canyon wrens, and the quick movements of lizards on the rocks.

From here, head the final 0.25 mile up a sandy, exposed section to the Upper Emerald Pool, which is well worth the brief climb. The largest and deepest of the pools, the upper pool is created by water that either barely drips or merrily flows over the circular cliff to collect into a lovely oasis of green. The serenity of this little place—which depends partly on how many others decided to enjoy it along with you—displays some of the best Zion has to offer, with its mixing and matching of spring and seep water, lush plant growth, and leaping sandstone walls smoothed by the rush of water and wind. Return to the trailhead the same way, enjoying the views of the canyon as you descend.

The waterfall drops down to Lower Emerald Pool.

Extending your hike: The 2-mile roundtrip Kayenta Trail leads from the Grotto shuttle stop to the Emerald Pools and offers an alternative way to either reach or depart the Emerald Pools. Between the lower and middle pools, look for the small wooden sign saying "Grotto" and indicating a northward turn. Steep drops from this trail may discourage those with a fear of heights or with small children in tow, although the trail itself is fairly wide. It may be icy in the colder months. The Grotto Trail in the main canyon is a short 0.5-mile jaunt from the Grotto shuttle stop back to Zion Lodge.

41 Angels Landing

Roundtrip: 5 miles
Hiking time: 3–6 hours
Elevation gain: 1488 feet
Difficulty: hard

Season: all year
Map: USGS Temple of Sinawava
Contact: Zion National Park

Getting there: From St. George and I-15 northbound, take exit 16 onto State Route 9 east for 33 miles to La Verkin. (From I-15 southbound, use exit 27 for State Route 17 south.) Turn right to stay on SR 9 for another 20 miles to the park entrance in Springdale. From March–October, you must take a park shuttle unless you are a guest at Zion Lodge; exit at the Grotto stop. Otherwise, cars may park at the Grotto. **Notes:** Fee required at park entrance. Beware icy or slick conditions in winter and high heat in summer. Exercise extreme caution, know your limits, and yield to other people on the trail, particularly along the spine and at the very top. Do not hike final exposed section if there is rain, snow, ice, or lightning.

Without a doubt one of Zion's signature hikes as well as one known around the world, Angels Landing got its name in 1916 when an awestruck observer declared that only an angel could land on it. Soaring above the valley floor with a majestic air, Angels Landing beckons to thousands of hikers every year. While technically there are no major trail obstacles, the 1500-foot elevation gain, a chained area along the spine, and the dizzying height deter some. Many hikers will make it to Scout Lookout (also jokingly called Chicken-Out Point), about a half mile from the top, and call it a day once they see the narrow ridge that must be ascended in order to get to Angels Landing. Angels Landing has seen fatalities from falls, so know your limits. Those who take the challenge and make it all the way up are rewarded with spectacular views and a sense of accomplishment. With luck, you may even catch a glimpse of the endangered California condors who make their home in Zion and are sometimes spotted soaring over this trail.

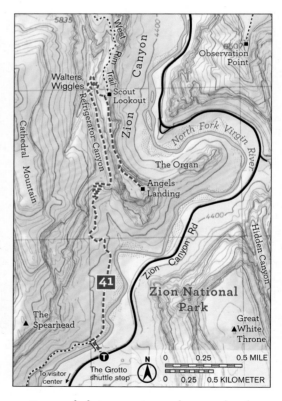

From the Grotto shuttle stop, take the footbridge west across the Virgin River. On the other side, you will see a trail sign to the right (north) for West Rim and Angels Landing; head that direction. The first 2 miles of the trail are paved and make for very easy walking, although you will notice the elevation gain. Once you pass the pretty, wooded river section and start to head up, gentle switchbacks make this a fairly easy ascent. At 1.4 miles in, you reach the cool of aptly named Refrigerator Canyon, which makes for a welcome

The final skinny spine hikers must ascend to get to Angels Landing

respite in the summer and a cold, often icy section in the winter.

When you reach Walters Wiggles, appreciate the trail-creation marvel that is a 250-foot ascent on twenty-one sharp switchbacks cut into an otherwise impassable canyon. Named after Walter Ruesch, Zion's first custodian, the wiggles are a marvel for not only the engineering feat they exemplify but also the fact that Ruesch had no engineering background. This is the part of the route where you will likely start to feel the burn as the climb sharpens.

At the top of the switchbacks, you soon will see a sign for Scout Lookout, and the valley floor will open up to the east. At this point, the trail diverges: to the left, or north, is the continuation of the West Rim Trail, and to your right, or south, is the steep, narrow incline of the final 0.4 mile to Angels Landing. This is the point at which hikers need to seriously assess their balance, stability, and fear of heights. Small children definitely have no place on this precarious section of the trail.

From this point on, the trail is chained in sections, offering handholds that are especially advisable during crowded moments. If some of the unchained, very exposed sections are particularly heavy with traffic, you might want to wait and tackle them after people pass. This section is not necessarily as frightening as it may first appear from afar; for most, the ascent over the ridge is a place to worry more about other people's actions than about falling into the abyss. This final approach over the knife edge of the monolith's spine has crests and valleys, with the very final part an easier stroll through a more flat, wooded sandy section.

Once you reach the top, take a gander at the stupendous views! Up here, there also is more room to spread out. Be aware of where the edges are and what others around you are doing. The scenery includes Observation Point, Echo Canyon, Cable Mountain, and the truly regal Great White Throne. This can be an excellent spot for lunch. From here, carefully return to the trailhead by the same route.

42 West Rim Trail

One-way: 15.4 miles
Hiking time: 1–2 days
Elevation gain: 2995 feet
Difficulty: hard

Season: spring–fall
Map: USGS Kolob Reservoir, The Guardian Angels, Temple of Sinawava
Contact: Zion National Park

Getting there: Starting point: From Springdale, drive 13.5 miles west to Kolob Terrace Road (Kolob Reservoir Road) in Virgin. Turn right (north) and drive 18.7 miles to signed turnoff for Lava Point. Turn right (east) and drive 4.3 miles to the West Rim trailhead. **Shuttle drop-off:** Park in Springdale or at the Zion Canyon Visitor Center. From March–October, you must take the park's mandatory shuttle system (unless you are a guest at Zion Lodge); exit at the Grotto stop. Cars may park at the Grotto during the rest of the year. **Notes:** Fee required at park entrance. Overnight permit required. Vehicle shuttle required. Road to trailhead may be inaccessible in winter or impassable for some vehicles, depending on weather.

Some of Zion's most amazing scenery is yours for the drinking in on this stout backcountry trail, which travels over a good section of the national park while showcasing to near perfection its sandstone monoliths, canyon-country topography, large ponderosa trees, and simply magnificent views that call for a great deal of awed appreciation. Fit hikers can finish this trail (north to south) in a day, but for deeper enjoyment and a more leisurely pace, plant your tent for the night at one of the excellent backcountry campsites along the way.

Begin high up at Lava Point, located at 7900 feet. Just 0.1 mile in, stay to the left at a fork in the trail, with the right option leading to the Wildcat Connector Trail. The first 4 miles wind through a tree-covered plateau known as Horse Pasture. This is very pleasant hiking through high-country meadows and tall ponderosa pines, hardy juniper trees, and Gambel oaks, although some like to zip through this section to more quickly reach views of Zion Canyon. If you are doing the overnight option, the nine designated backcountry campsites to choose from are all on this plateau. After leaving Horse Pasture, you begin the descent into Potato Hollow, which harbors a spring at the 5-mile mark and good views into rugged Imlay Canyon below.

Upon reaching a trail fork 6.5 miles in, you have a choice of heading left onto the Telephone

A slickrock portion of the West Rim Trail

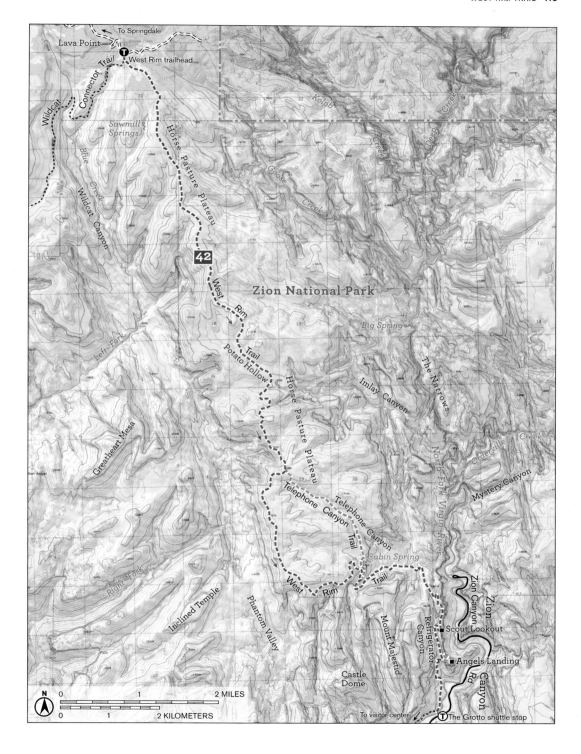

To Springdale
Lava Point
West Rim trailhead

Wildcat

Connector Trail

Sawmill Springs

Blue

Creek

Wildcat Canyon

Horse Pasture Plateau

Kolob

Creek

Goose

Creek

Deep Creek

42

Zion National Park

West

Rim

Trail

Potato Hollow

Big Spring

Imlay Canyon

The Narrows

Left Fork

Greenheart Mesa

Horse Pasture Plateau

Orderville Creek

Mystery Canyon

Telephone Canyon

Telephone Canyon

Trail

North Fork Virgin River

West

Rim

Cabin Spring

Trail

Right Fork

Inclined Temple

Phantom Valley

Mount Majestic

Refrigerator Canyon

Scout Lookout

Zion Canyon

Zion Canyon Rd

Angels Landing

Castle Dome

To visitor center

The Grotto shuttle stop

N

0   1   2 MILES

0   1   2 KILOMETERS

Canyon Trail or staying right on the West Rim Trail. The Telephone Canyon Trail is shorter by one mile, but the views aren't nearly as fantastic as those on the West Rim Trail, so consider your choice with your desired hiking experience in mind. To get the most out of this incredibly scenic hike, sticking to the West Rim Trail in this section is highly recommended. No matter which route you choose, you will hit Cabin Spring, which can make a nice place to take a break.

As soon as you leave Cabin Spring the trail immediately drops, descending 1800 feet in 2.8 miles. Mount Majestic and Cathedral Mountain tower to the south as you approach the spur trail, just south of Scout Lookout, to Angels Landing and usually a significant increase in foot traffic. From here you rapidly reach the twenty-one switchbacks of Walters Wiggles as well as the remaining 1.9 miles to the Zion Canyon floor and your terminus point at the Grotto shuttle stop. Through this section you can expect a large number of people day hiking to Angels Landing, but the views are still quite impressive as you wind your way down.

Extending your hike: Take the spur trail to Angels Landing (Hike 41) for an additional 1 mile roundtrip. Do not attempt this razor-thin, very exposed trail while wearing a backpack.

43 Canyon Overlook

Roundtrip: 1 mile
Hiking time: 1 hour
Elevation gain: 150 feet
Difficulty: easy/moderate

Season: all year
Map: USGS Springdale East
Contact: Zion National Park

Getting there: From St. George and I-15 northbound, take exit 16 onto State Route 9 east for 33 miles to La Verkin. (From I-15 southbound, use exit 27 for State Route 17 south.) Turn right to stay on SR 9 for another 20 miles to the park entrance in Springdale. From the Zion Canyon visitor center, head east on SR 9 for 5 miles, passing through the Zion-Mount Carmel Tunnel. Parking lot is immediately on your right; another one is a quarter mile farther on your left. **Notes:** Fee required at park entrance. Vault toilets available at parking lot.

Visitors coming into Zion from the east entrance often stop at Canyon Overlook for their first glimpse of the famed canyon, and this view does not disappoint. Accessible to many, this brief hike becomes an extraordinary experience when you reach the viewpoint and are presented with the jaw-dropping grandeur of Zion Canyon. The small ledges and rock tumbles to navigate along the way, along with an alcove section, can make it an interesting jaunt for younger hikers.

The trail starts on the north side of the road and immediately heads up a few carved stairs. This brief section brings you up 50 feet before the trail mostly levels out. Follow the sandstone ledge that skirts above the Pine Creek Narrows, enjoying the natural curving of the hike as it follows the path of least resistance. Glance down to your left and you will see the winding slice in the rock that is Pine Creek, a popular canyoneering destination. Your trail ducks beneath jutting overhangs, occasionally giving you the sensation of almost being in a cave. Although the path is clear, watch your footing. Large rocks must be negotiated here and there. Maidenhair fern adds its soft beauty as you wrap through the alcove.

In sections the trail veers back out toward the narrows drop-off. Railings help you mind the drop.

Hikers along the Canyon Overlook Trail in winter

The billowing canyon walls above and below are dotted with pinyon and juniper pines, although little of their shade will cover you on hot days. As you approach the viewpoint destination at 0.5 mile, bare slickrock meets your feet as you follow the curves and contours up small inclines to one of the most stunning views achieved for so little effort.

Zion Canyon opens up behind the sturdy railing that helps prevent long falls. The view that greets your eye consists of some of the canyon's most impressive rock monoliths, including Towers of the Virgin, the Streaked Wall, the Beehives, the Sundial, Bridge Mountain, the Sentinel, the West Temple, the East Temple, and the imaginatively named Altar of Sacrifice. Where you stand you are situated immediately above The Great Arch, which you cannot see from here but which can be glimpsed from the switchbacking highway to your left that descends into the canyon valley. The colors in the sandstone walls across the valley floor capture the eye with their myriad shades of rust, maroon, salmon, khaki, buff, and even shades of olive. After you've taken your fill of the splendor, return back down the same trail.

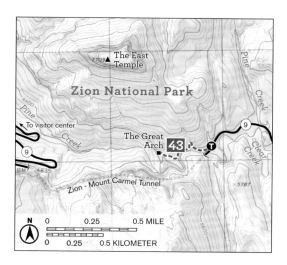

117

44 *Rattlesnake Creek/Ashdown Gorge*

***

One-way: 12 miles
Hiking time: 7–9 hours
Elevation loss: 3455 feet
Difficulty: moderate

Season: summer–fall
Map: USGS Flanigan Arch, Brian Head
Contact: Dixie National Forest, Cedar City
Ranger District

Getting there: Starting point: From Cedar City, head east on State Route 14. Drive 18 miles to State Route 148 and turn left (north). Pass the entrance to Cedar Breaks National Monument after 4 miles. After 1 more mile, find the large parking area on the west side of SR 143. *Shuttle vehicle drop:* From Cedar City, head east on SR14. Drive 8 miles to a large pullout on the left (north) side of the highway. The trailhead is at the west end of the parking area. **Notes:** Flash flooding may occur during mid- to late summer. Vehicle shuttle required (unless hiked as an out-and-back). Multiple water crossings required.

Lesser known than its more famous nearby cousins in Zion and Bryce Canyon national parks, Ashdown Gorge is nevertheless a spectacular example of Utah's canyon-country geography, featuring a deep, rocky gorge, carved from Wasatch Limestone, that is not nearly as crowded as other vicinity hikes. Miles of trail through the gorgeous gorge are usually vacant of other hikers, lending a deep sense of serenity and solitude to your adventure. Waterfalls, a natural bridge soaring far above one side of the gorge, bristlecone pines, stellar views of the red rims of the Cedar Breaks

National Monument amphitheater, and a sense of winding deep through a natural slice in the earth all conspire to make this hike one for the bucket list. Although the route described here is a one-way (east to west), with a vehicle shuttle, you also have the option of hiking it out and back from either end. If you decide to take this option starting from the western end, off State Route 14, note that you will be hiking uphill at the start. From this point, a roundtrip to the waterfall would be 6 miles.

From the parking area off SR 143, take the signed Rattlesnake Creek Trail heading due

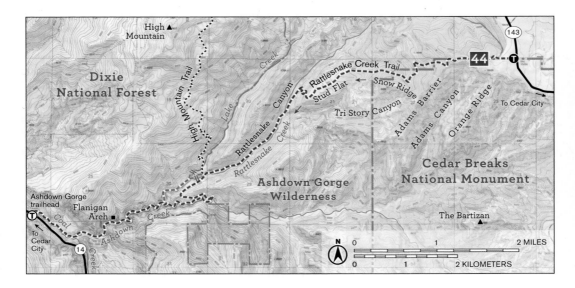

The forested eastern end start of the Rattlesnake Trail

west. Midsummer trips yield a spectacular car-pet of wildflowers here on the trail's high point, where you are breathing in refined air at 10,400 feet, as well as down in the gorge. Aspen-filled meadows line the trail during this first section, where the Cedar Breaks boundary fence keeps you company for a while. Just a little ways down, be sure to venture off the trail to the south by a hundred feet or so to see outstanding vistas over the monument's beautifully eroded rim;

viewpoints opening up through the trees are obvious.

The trail begins to descend more sharply at 1.7 miles, eventually dropping you down to Stud Flat 2.5 miles in. Views along this section are expansive, although the trail soon descends about 700 feet to the bottom of Rattlesnake Canyon, which is filled with ponderosa pines and other vegetation as the trail winds alongside and through the stream. From this point on, be prepared for plenty of stream walking, which may lead to cold feet if attempted early in the year.

The whitish, yellow, and dark-stained canyon walls almost immediately begin to rise above you as you head down the stream's courseway, tumbled with boulders small and large. Pines reach with mighty effort toward the sky as the canyon serpentines around, following its ancient water-cut path. You will encounter leaning rock alcoves, jutting ledges, shadowed nooks and sections exposed to full sunlight. When you are 5.5 miles from the trailhead, you will meet up with the junction of the High Mountain Trail to your right (north) and,

shortly thereafter, the confluence with Lake Creek. Head upstream here for 0.5 mile to see a lovely waterfall cascading down the cliff walls. Another waterfall awaits shortly up Rattlesnake Creek just above its junction with Lake Creek. From here, it is 1 mile to enter Ashdown Gorge itself.

After taking you sharply east before entering the gorge, the trail again turns to send you on a westerly path through the gorge. Evidence of past flash floods is high on the walls, and sometimes debris masses are caught in the canyon, awaiting the next huge flood to loosen them and send them hurtling downstream. Walk 2 miles through the twists of the canyon, much of which will find you in the water, to Flanigan Arch, which can be spotted high on the wall to the north as you pass through the deepest section of canyon. From here you have 1.5 miles to the parking area on SR 14. The trail was partially eaten up after a landslide in 2011, making the final passage somewhat less easy. Hiker-made trails curve around the landslide debris, or you can opt to simply scramble up to the highway.

45 *Spectra Point/Ramparts Overlook*

Roundtrip: 4 miles	**Season:** summer–fall
Hiking time: 3 hours	**Map:** USGS Cedar Breaks National
Elevation gain: 550 feet	Monument
Difficulty: moderate	**Contact:** Cedar Breaks National Monument

Getting there: From Cedar City, head east on State Route 14 (East Center Street) and drive 18 miles. Turn left (north) onto State Route 148 and drive 4 miles to the monument. Trailhead parking is at visitor center. **Notes:** Fee required. Heavy snow in winter closes this trail. Starting elevation is 10,200 feet. Cedar Breaks wildflower festival held in July. Abundant, excellent dark-sky star-viewing programs.

An undervisited scenic wonder, Cedar Breaks National Monument is a lovely example of the farthest western reaches of the Colorado Plateau's stunning geological beauty. Formed in order to protect "spectacular cliffs, canyons, and features of scenic, scientific, and educational interest," the monument is like the lesser-known little sibling of mighty Bryce Canyon. With its stunningly gorgeous, half-mile-deep limestone amphitheater, abundance of bristlecone pines as old as 1600 years, outrageous profusion of summertime wildflowers, views filled with hoodoos, and relative lack of crowds, this is the place to visit for gorgeous scenery that takes little effort other than some serious lung workouts to enjoy. Keep an eye out for colorful phlox, bluebells, buckwheat,

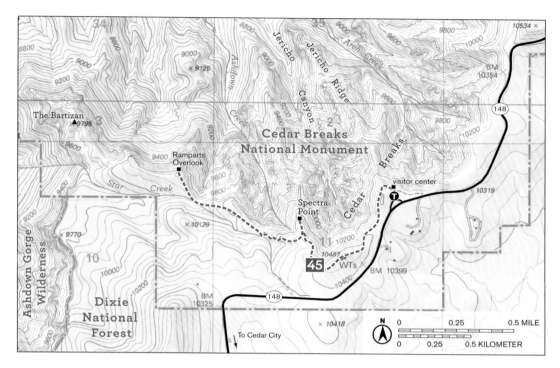

cinquefoil, elkweed, primrose, and other abundant flowers in the summertime months, when they can carpet the classic subalpine meadows. Although pines crowd the area, the trail itself is relatively unshaded, so it can still feel hot in the summertime, even at this elevation.

From the trailhead just south of the visitor center, head toward the rim and turn left as directed. As you weave along the rim from this trail, the views are spectacular the entire way. You will likely feel the elevation almost immediately, so slow down and enjoy the flowers as your heart strongly pumps along with your legs. Look down into the amphitheater as you walk—but pay close attention to your footing as well, as parts of the trail are very close to the edge—and observe the multihued beauty of the Claron Formation. You are also looking at the next "step" down of the Grand Staircase. Animals you may spy along the way include mule deer with their large ears, marmots, ground squirrels, chipmunks, Clark's nutcrackers, and even golden eagles catching the high wind currents.

From Spectra Point, you may return back to the parking lot to make this a 2-mile roundtrip hike or, when you reach the signed junction about 50 yards back down the trail, turn right toward the Ramparts Overlook another 1 mile on. To get to Ramparts you descend 300 feet along switchbacks. Fewer people choose to make the short additional trek to this overlook, so it's highly suggested if you want to experience a more peaceful, serene view of the beautiful amphitheater below. Ravens may call out as they

Delicate columbines in the morning light

Jaw-dropping view of Cedar Breaks from the Spectra Point Trail

circle far above the ground, their harsh caws bounding and echoing and lending a definite Southwest feel to this trail. On the return, look for the whitish, gnarled old trunks of bristlecone pines standing strong and determined in their high arid home.

46 Golden Wall–Castle Bridge Loop

Loop: 5 miles
Hiking time: 2–3 hours
Elevation gain: 500 feet
Difficulty: moderate

Season: spring–fall
Map: USGS Casto Canyon
Contact: Dixie National Forest, Red Canyon Visitor Center

Getting there: From Beaver and I-15 southbound, turn left (east) onto State Route 20 and drive 20.5 miles to meet US Highway 89 at Bear Valley Junction. Turn right (south) and drive 10 miles to Panguitch; here, US 89 takes a left (east) turn. Drive 7 miles to State Route 12 and turn left (east) at Bryce Canyon Junction. Drive 3.5 miles to Red Canyon Visitor Center. **Notes:** Vault toilet at trailhead. Snow can make winter and spring access challenging.

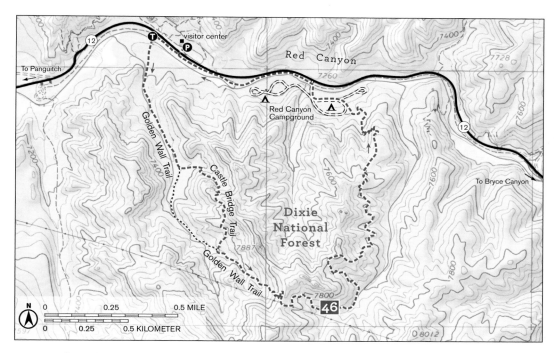

Many have described Red Canyon as a miniature version of nearby Bryce Canyon. While not as large or spectacular as the national park, Red Canyon certainly holds its own as a place that showcases golden-spired hoodoos, pink and red rock colorations, and sublime views that extend for miles. The Golden Wall Trail is a loop that offers some of the best views in Red Canyon, from inklings of the Old West to the otherworldly rock formations created over millennia by frost wedging, erosion, wildly whipping winds, and mad rushes of water in this usually dry country. The trail is rarely visited, so you have a high likelihood of having it much to yourself, which allows for an even greater enjoyment of the natural beauty surrounding you. Very hot in summer and potentially snow-covered in winter, this hike is a wonderful choice in late spring or in the fall. It connects two trails for a loop experience, covering more ground and more scenery than an out-and-back.

From the visitor center, cross State Route 12 and follow the dirt bike path in a westerly direction to the Golden Wall/Castle Bridge trailhead. Head south and begin slowly climbing as you walk in a wide wash. You will see pinyons, ponderosas, and other vegetation, including yellow rubber rabbitbrush in late summer. In 0.5 mile you will start to see hoodoos jutting out of the ground in all their colorful glory, and you'll likely wonder why so few other people share the trail with you. Here the Castle Bridge Trail intersects on your left; take it and enjoy the stunning rock formations and colors as you go along. As the trail travels over a ridge, you have ample views of the Golden Wall itself.

In another 0.6 mile, the Castle Bridge Trail rejoins the Golden Wall Trail and begins to climb in earnest. Along a knife-edge ridge, the trail's high point 2.5 miles in, watch your footing as you prepare for the most scenic portion of the trail to come. After a drop down, then another saddle, you ascend even more. The views from here are simply spectacular, with seemingly endless fluted walls of tightly packed hoodoos, undulating forests spreading out in the valleys

Spectacular scenery without the crowds on the Castle Bridge Trail

below, soft red hillsides bumping and rolling several deep in every direction, and far-off mountaintops teasing on the horizons. The trail descends and leads you to the Red Canyon Campground, from which it is a half mile back to the visitor center.

47 *Fairyland Loop*

Loop: 8.2 miles
Hiking time: 5–7 hours
Elevation gain: 1670 feet
Difficulty: moderate

Season: all year
Map: USGS Bryce Canyon
Contact: Bryce Canyon National Park

Getting there: From the junction of State Routes 12 and 63, drive 3 miles south on SR 63 to the Fairyland Point trailhead road. Turn left (east) here and drive 1 mile to trailhead parking. **Notes:** Fee required at park entrance. Road to trailhead is closed in winter, but may be snowshoed. Trail may be snow-covered in winter.

Not nearly as crowded as some of the shorter trails in Bryce Canyon, in part because of its length and in part because the shuttle system does not have a stop at its trailhead, the Fairyland Loop lives up to its name with spectacular groupings of orange- and cream-colored hoodoos that evoke images of an intricate, delicate home of bands of wild fairies. Making this a loop hike involves walking along the Rim Trail. Between dipping down into the hoodoo-speckled Bryce Amphitheater and traversing the rim with all its views, you get a full appreciation of this national

Eye-catching hoodoos along the Fairyland Loop Trail

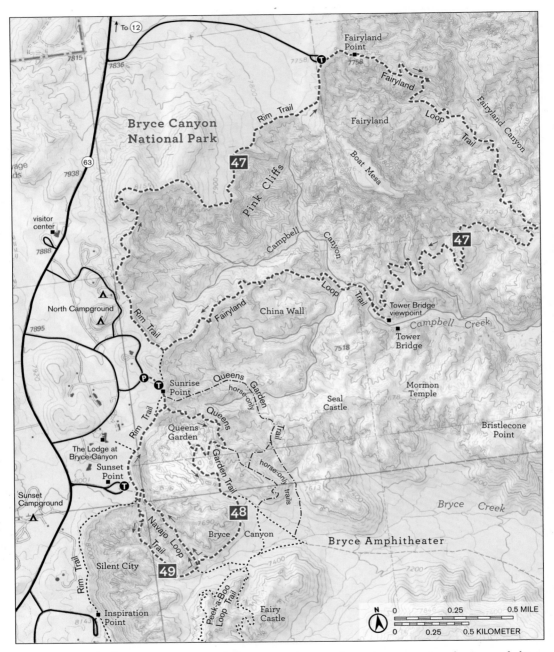

park's dazzling and unique scenery—and chances are you'll have it mostly to yourself.

Start at the wooded Fairyland Point trailhead, which offers a canopy of ponderosa pines, blue spruce, limber pines, well-named bristlecone pines, and an ever-present understory of shiny, red-barked manzanita bushes. The views from here are astounding, so take a moment to drink them in before descending the trail. Just below you will spy Boat Mesa, which does indeed somewhat resemble a sea-faring vessel stranded among the desert spires and buttes. Follow a slim ridge as it takes you down toward the spires and peaks of Fairyland.

Just 0.5 mile down you already begin to see the gnarly, tenacious juniper and pinyon trees of the more arid environment you have dropped into. These trees, found only in dry environments at certain elevations, are a testament to the rugged qualities needed by all life that seeks to plant roots in the spectacular yet dry climes of Bryce Canyon. The lowest part of the trail, Fairyland Canyon itself contains a proliferation of jaggedly shaped hoodoos that stir flights of fancy in even the most level-minded. The trail skirts Campbell Canyon; just past this, at the 4-mile point, is a slight spur trail to the east leading to a view of Tower Bridge that is worth the very brief 0.4-mile detour.

After returning to the main trail you pass China Wall to your south. Pocked with erosionally created windows, this long, white wall of fluted sandstone is the last main point of interest before you head out. Now you begin winding up toward the rim again, rising 770 feet in the last 1.5 miles of trail to the top. Once on the rim you are back in the forest canopy with incredible views to the east. Turn right to follow the winding Rim Trail the final 2.5 miles back to Fairyland Point.

48 *Queens Garden*

Loop: 3 miles
Hiking time: 2–3 hours
Elevation gain: 850 feet
Difficulty: easy/moderate

Season: all year
Map: USGS Bryce Canyon, Bryce Point
Contact: Bryce Canyon National Park

Getting there: From the Bryce Canyon Visitor Center, drive 0.4 mile south to the Sunrise Point turnoff. **Notes:** Fee required at park entrance. Trail may be snowy/icy in winter. Vault toilet located at trailhead.

The whimsically named Queens Garden Trail is a nod to playing "what shapes can I see?" in the fantastical hoodoos that make Bryce Canyon Amphitheater famous. Jutting up to the sky with a slowly ever-changing variety of shapes, the hoodoo for this particular trail is definitely in the eye of the beholder. Serving as an easy introduction to this national park, Queens Garden is ideal on its own or as part of a longer trail that ties in some of the others crisscrossing the amphitheater. This hike includes portions of the Navajo Loop and the Rim Trail, making it one loop beginning at Sunrise Point. Summer can find enormous crowds here, and fall is perhaps the best time of year for this hike. Winter, though, allows you the unique experience of white snow brightly contrasting

Her regal sandstone majesty surveys the Queens Garden.

The Queens Garden Trail winds through the Bryce Canyon amphitheater.

on the switchbacks, almost every corner of which offers yet another striking overlook from which to point your camera lens. The trail passes through some hoodoos via carved-out doorways and short tunnels, which gives you the feeling of passing through the earth itself.

Stay on the signed Queens Garden Trail until you reach the right-hand turn up the short spur trail to the "garden." At the end of the spur trail, your arrival is heralded by a grouping of hoodoos that fire up the speculative mind. Tall ponderosa trees incongruously shoot up from the otherwise barren hillsides, their dark green providing wonderful contrast with the creams, golds, umbers, and soft tangerine colors of the hoodoos and hillsides. The majestic form of "Queen Victoria" perches atop a hoodoo, surveying her realm with regal poise.

As you leave this natural garden of eroded shapes at 0.9 mile, you enter a forested area for a short, pleasant stroll. Then you are presented with the Navajo Loop Trail, at which point you want to turn right on it and head back up the bowl of the amphitheater. Although a fairly steep climb, this portion is again made with long switchbacks and is quite short at a mere 0.4 mile. Once at the top, you'll be at Sunset Point. Continue north along the aptly named Rim Trail, which has geologic trail kiosks along the way as it gently winds through the ponderosas back to your start at Sunrise Point, with the views over the amphitheater keeping you company to the east the entire 0.6 mile back to your vehicle.

with the hoodoos and, if the day is clear, a sky so deep blue it can boggle the mind.

From Sunrise Point, descend the Queens Garden Trail east along the ridgeline for a brief time before it drops down to line the slope instead. In the distance, you'll see seemingly endless views. Included in your panorama are natural creations with creative names such as Sinking Ship and Boat Mesa. Keep descending

49 Navajo Loop

Loop: 1.4 miles
Hiking time: 1–2 hours
Elevation gain: 550 feet
Difficulty: easy/moderate

Season: all year
Map: USGS Bryce Canyon, Bryce Point
Contact: Bryce Canyon National Park

Getting there: From the Bryce Canyon Visitor Center, drive 0.9 mile south to the Sunset Point parking area. **Notes:** Fee required at park entrance. Winter snow and rockfalls may prompt the park to close portions, usually the Wall Street section, but making it a roundtrip rather than a loop adds little mileage or time to this short hike.

Short and very sweet, Navajo Loop gives you perfect views of the chimerical hoodoos that put Bryce Canyon on the map. Although almost guaranteed to be crowded during peak season, this is one of the best trails in Bryce Canyon for its extremely rewarding display of the natural elements that draw people to this astounding area. From your starting point high up above the hoodoo-prickled Bryce Amphitheater, survey this section of the Colorado Plateau before you descend into the amphitheater to enjoy wandering near and through the slowly crumbling forms of colorful formations that capture the imagination of so many worldwide. The man for whom this park was named, Ebenezer Bryce, was a local cattle rancher in the late nineteenth century. His sole comment of record on the wild, hoodoo-filled landscape that would forever immortalize his name? "It's a hell of a place to lose a cow."

From the Sunset Point parking area, head east and quickly downward on long switchbacks, pausing every now and then to snap yet another photo of the unique rocks, shaped by frost-wedging during the wintertime, that line the trail and steeple upward in the distance. Squatty goblin shapes, long and elegant spires, and a color spectrum that ranges from bright orange to light buff to burnished brick red all serve to make this some of the most fantastic scenery on the planet.

A trail junction appears, splitting the Navajo Trail and the Wall Street section; take the right-hand turn to descend down the sharp switchbacks of narrow Wall Street. Notable for its

Sunlight practically makes the walls glow along the Wall Street section of the Navajo Loop Trail.

towering walls and equally towering ponderosa pine trees, this section was named for the financial district back East. This Wall Street, however, is leaps and bounds ahead as far as sheer beauty is concerned. The fluted sides of the hoodoos bend to create fascinating crinkles and allow the light to bounce in and around, to the photographer's delight.

At the bottom of the switchbacks, the trail curves left and east. At 0.6 mile you reach the junction with the Peek-a-Boo Loop. Here, you make a sharp left to once again ascend up switchbacks on the Navajo Loop Trail. Chute-like, it leads you back up to the rim via more switchbacks. You pop out at Sunset Point again to conclude this hike.

Extending your hike: You easily can add the Queens Garden (Hike 48) or Peek-a-Boo Loop Trail (Hike 50) to this one if you'd like a longer exploration.

50 *Peek-a-Boo Loop*

Loop: 5.5 miles
Hiking time: 3–4 hours
Elevation gain: 1555 feet
Difficulty: moderate

Season: all year
Map: USGS Bryce Point
Contact: Bryce Canyon National Park

Getting there: From the visitor center, drive 1.6 miles south to the turnoff for Bryce Point. Turn left for the trailhead parking. **Notes:** Fee required at park entrance. Trail may be icy/snowy in winter.

Tiny hikers approaching a trail junction on the Peek-a-Boo Loop Trail

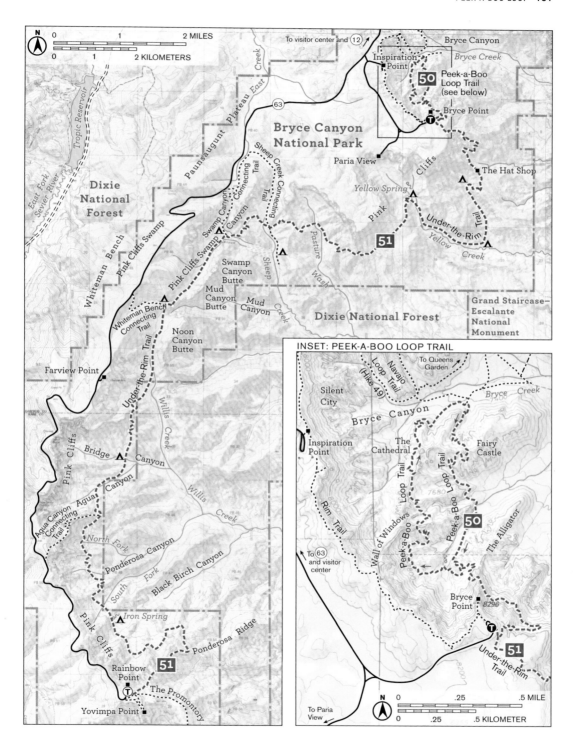

Main map labels:

N
0   1   2 MILES
0   1   2 KILOMETERS

To visitor center and (12)

Bryce Canyon

Bryce Creek

Inspiration Point

Peek-a-Boo Loop Trail (see below)

50

Bryce Point

Tropic Reservoir

East Fork Sevier River

Dixie National Forest

Paunsaugunt Plateau East Creek

63

Bryce Canyon National Park

Paria View

Cliffs

The Hat Shop

Yellow Spring

Pink Cliffs

Pink Cliffs Swamp

Swamp Canyon Connecting Trail

Canyon Connecting Trail

Sheep Creek Connecting Trail

Pasture Wash

Under-the-Rim Trail

Yellow Creek

51

Whiteman Bench

Swamp Canyon Butte

Sheep Creek

Mud Canyon Butte

Mud Canyon

Dixie National Forest

Grand Staircase–Escalante National Monument

Whiteman Bench Connecting Trail

Under-the-Rim Trail

Noon Canyon Butte

Farview Point

Willis Creek

Pink Cliffs

Bridge

Canyon

Agua Canyon

Agua Canyon Connecting Trail

North Fork

Willis Creek

Ponderosa Canyon

South Fork

Black Birch Canyon

Iron Spring

Ponderosa Ridge

51

Pink Cliffs

Rainbow Point

The Promontory

Yovimpa Point

Inset map:

INSET: PEEK-A-BOO LOOP TRAIL

To Queens Garden

8000

Navajo Loop Trail (Hike 49)

Silent City

Bryce Creek

Bryce Canyon

Inspiration Point

The Cathedral

Fairy Castle

Rim Trail

Wall of Windows

Peek-a-Boo Loop Trail

7680

Peek-a-Boo Loop Trail

50

The Alligator

To (63) and visitor center

Bryce Point   8296

51

Under-the-Rim Trail

To Paria View

8200

N
0   .25   .5 MILE
0   .25   .5 KILOMETER

The Peek-a-Boo Loop is named for the manner in which Bryce Canyon's famous natural hoodoos peek in and out along the trail, tantalizing with their bizarre shapes and beautiful colors that tumble together in a palette of apricot, rich rose, deep claret, and rust blending into olive blending into amber and softening into bleached ivory. The shapes of the ever-crumbling hoodoos allow your imagination to play a game of "what do I see?" while simultaneously encouraging a multitude of photos to capture memories of this unique hike. Although steep, this very worthwhile trail takes you right into the heart of the hoodoos as it winds you around and through them, serving up lovely views at every turn. This trail is the same one the park uses for guided horseback rides, which can be a fun option for those who'd rather have an equine do the walking.

From the Bryce Point trailhead, go east on the Under-the-Rim Trail. Quickly see the junction with the Peek-a-Boo trail, at which you will turn left. Keep an eye out for the ancient bristlecone pines, which are fairly easy to spot with branches that look like the fluffed-out tails of foxes and bear long cones tipped with claw-like bristles. As you drop down over the sides of beautiful badlands into the amphitheater, wind along the trail for 1 mile to the junction with the Peek-a-Boo Loop Trail. A forest of trees greets you, including large ponderosa pines, more bristlecones, and aptly named limber pines.

Take the left fork to approach the Wall of Windows, which will rise up to your north. The fluted hoodoo wall is slowly eroding due to natural forces, leaving behind many windows to the sky as well as the imagination. Pass through a short tunnel carved through the soft heart of a sandstone hoodoo and keep an eye out for the Cathedral, a collection of pointy-tipped hoodoos that do bear a resemblance to their namesake. Just half a mile from this point you reach the connector trail to Navajo Loop; bear sharp right here to head south along the Peek-a-Boo Loop Trail. As the trail sends you back to the starting point, it takes you just below the base of another droll formation called the Fairy Castle, and close to the sandstone jaws of the Alligator. At the end of the loop return the 1 mile back up the trail to Bryce Point and your vehicle.

51 Under-the-Rim Trail

One-way: 23 miles
Hiking time: 2–3 days
Elevation gain: 1500 feet
Difficulty: moderate/hard

Season: spring–fall
Map: USGS Bryce Point, Rainbow Point
Contact: Bryce Canyon National Park

Getting there: Starting point: From the Bryce Canyon Visitor Center, drive 1.6 miles south to the turnoff for Bryce Point. Turn left for trailhead parking. **Shuttle vehicle drop:** From the visitor center, drive 17 miles south to the Rainbow Point trailhead parking. **Notes:** Fee required at park entrance. Backcountry permit required. Shuttle vehicle required. Vault toilets at either end. Bring and know how to read USGS maps. Verify water availability in advance.

Backpacking Bryce Canyon just about ensures solitude as you traipse through the deep, hoodoo-filled amphitheater, benefitting from the less common view from below. Roughly a half circle, this trek allows you ample time to soak in the glory of seeing the unusual frost-wedged rock formations that draw people and cameras from around the world. Evergreen trees, including pointy Douglas firs, giant ponderosas, and bendy limber pines, dot the hillsides. Glimpse

Under-the-Rim Trail travels below the rim of impressive Bryce Canyon.

the pinnacles and spires that swirl up toward the sky, all fashioned into fantastical shapes that draw the eye and lend incredible diversity and beauty to this most excellent trek. Water may be found at these sites, but do not rely on it: Right Fork Yellow Creek, Yellow Creek Group Site, Yellow Creek, Sheep Creek, Iron Spring, and Yovimpa Point. Ask a park ranger about water availability along the trail before you go.

This describes the trail heading north to south. From the Bryce Point trailhead, walk southeast just 0.1 mile to the junction with the Peek-a-Boo Loop Trail. From there, turn right (south) onto the Under-the-Rim Trail. With a starting point at 8300 feet, you drop significantly in elevation almost immediately, possibly with chipmunks scolding you along. Half a mile into the hike you'll have sweeping views of the lovely Table Cliffs, the Paria River area, and even far south toward the Arizona border. After passing the Claron Formation, in 2 miles you'll reach

The Hat Shop, a fun collection of hoodoos that certainly seem fit to exist in a gigantic shop of sandstone "hats." The unique part about The Hat Shop is how it differs from the shapes most people see from right above the amphitheater walls; the spires in The Hat Shop are individual points topped with gray caprocks.

From here the trail drops a precipitous 650 feet into the Yellow Creek area, 3.4 miles in. This section is wooded, watered, and lovely. Three backcountry campsites make it a pleasant place to stay the night, although that means a short first hiking day. Barrel cactus found here may bloom in the spring, adding spots of color here and there. After you leave the more shaded valley, however, you'll encounter hotter and drier stretches as you continue southward. Views of the Pink Cliffs in the distance provide visual stimulation as the trail rises and drops along ridges and hillsides, winding through this far less trammeled section of Bryce Canyon.

The junction with the Sheep Creek Connecting Trail comes 9.5 miles in; continue ahead on the Under-the-Rim Trail as directed by the sign. The Sheep Creek area, however, is another excellent place to set camp for the night, especially if you're doing this trail in only two days. Just under 1 mile down the trail, the Swamp Canyon section also offers up campsites.

The Swamp Canyon area is well named, for it is the most lushly vegetated area in the park. Gambel oak, juniper, mountain mahogany, manzanita, and other plants decorate this section with an array of shades of green. Flowers also pop up in the spring and early summer months, nodding with colorful beauty as you make your way along the trail through here. It's a welcome mini-oasis in the otherwise orange and red rock-spire landscape. You'll pass the Whiteman Bench Connecting Trail 12.3 miles in. After dropping into the Willis Creek basin, then climbing up a little saddle, you'll descend again into Bridge Canyon. To the west is a natural bridge; if you don't see it as you descend, farther down in the canyon the dense vegetation can block your view.

Pass through a meadow, which can be flower-filled in the summer, to reach the junction with the Agua Canyon Connecting Trail 16.9 miles in. This one also drops in from the rim, so you may run into other hikers around this area. Meander up and down inclines, washes, and basins as you keep going south on the Under-the-Rim Trail. From a ridge you drop down into Iron Spring, 19.5 miles from the trailhead. From here you begin to climb steadily toward the rim and Rainbow Point, the terminus of this trail.

Opposite, top: Prickly pear cactus blooms throughout southern Utah in the spring.

Opposite, bottom: Colorful earth layers entice the eye.

South Central

Top: Beautiful colors and patterns on the rock walls of
the Willis Creek Trail

Bottom: Globemallow beside the Escalante River Trail

This part of Utah boasts a tremendous variety of natural attractions. Deep slot canyons beckon while canyon-country basins filled with outrageously colored and wildly shaped sandstone formations delight the eye. The state's largest natural mountain lake, a valley thicketed with little orangey-red hoodoos, and the geologic fascination of monoclines and upthrust land add to the allure. Cliffs eroded into startling beauty, soaring natural arches, and natural cathedrals carved out of the earth itself all define the landscapes here.

The nearly 2-million-acre Grand Staircase–Escalante National Monument draws visitors who are utterly absorbed by the huge river-carved canyons and the abundance of significant dinosaur fossils discovered on a regular basis. Other draws include the amazement of what some think is the world's longest slot canyon, the colorful whirls of sandstone that stun the eye and demand photographic worship, and the freedom of being able to explore in such a vast wilderness area that in some places seems virtually untouched by humans. Also tucked into this immense area are the bizarre sedimentary pipes of Kodachrome Basin State Park, where coppery-hued sandstone monoliths ring a basin and conjure images of Western movies played out against this dramatic natural background.

Not as well known as the other national parks in Utah, Capitol Reef is often viewed as a "drive-through" place by those traveling from Arches and Canyonlands to Bryce Canyon and Zion, or vice versa. But this landscape of geologic wonders just as beautiful and striking as the other parks' often pulls people back for future visits, eager to explore the 100-mile-long monocline called the Waterpocket Fold or roam through sandstone canyons on trails that, while sometimes busy, are still far less crowded than in Utah's other national parks. In the cool heights of Fishlake National Forest just to the north is Fish Lake, Utah's largest natural mountain lake and a sparkling gem that lures outdoor enthusiasts of all stripes to its shores and the surrounding forested mountainsides. Also found in this national forest is a "trembling giant" known as Pando, a massive 106-acre grove of genetically identical aspen trees that is one of the world's largest living organisms, if not the largest.

Rubbing shoulders with Capitol Reef's eastern edge is the San Rafael Swell, an area still little visited but getting more popular every year with its network of canyons draped and folded by the earth's massive geologic forces. Home to the eerily striking Goblin Valley, which contains a plethora of little hoodoos, as well as blissfully remote backcountry trails and hikes ranging from relatively easy to decidedly rugged, the Swell is a place to stop and explore for its spires, domes, buttes, slot canyons, high mesas, and a still-present sense of a vast, beautiful emptiness.

Ballerina Spire just ahead on the Panorama Trail

52 *Panorama Trail*

Loop: 5.9 miles
Hiking time: 3–4 hours
Elevation gain: 360 feet
Difficulty: easy

Season: spring, fall
Map: USGS Henrieville, Cannonville
Contact: Kodachrome Basin State Park

Getting there: From Escalante, drive 36 miles west on State Route 12 to Cottonwood Canyon Road in the town of Cannonville. Turn left (south) on Cottonwood Canyon Road. Drive 9 miles to the signed turnoff to Kodachrome Basin State Park. **Notes:** Fee required. Vault toilets, camping, information center.

Spires, chimneys, buttes, and walls of sandstone, all colored with alluring shades and shaped into engaging natural formations, keep hikers continually intrigued along the sandy red paths of this small state park. The Panorama Trail is precisely that: swept with panoramic vistas, it presents horizons poked with twisty red rock spires or rumpled with folding walls and flutes that create soft lines. Plus, you get to visit places with intriguing names such as The Hat Shop, Cool Cave, and Secret Passage. Not as ambitious a hike as many others in this book, the Panorama Trail is a satisfying enchantment for anyone who is young, less agile, pressed for time, or simply desiring to see some of southern Utah's

famously colorful landscape with less effort. Summer can be terrifically hot here, so springtime or fall jaunts are highly recommended. Wintertime offers the pleasure of billows of white snow draped over soft orange rocks, creating an enchanting playground that is particularly empty due to the cold. This makes the adventure all the more private, as you will usually have the trail to yourself at that time of year.

Just past the trailhead, you are immediately joined by the sandstone spires as they jut into the air. Walk 0.3 mile to the Panorama Point junction and turn right (north), passing graceful Ballerina Spire, Indian Cave, and The Hat Shop in quick succession within 1 mile. The

Intriguing sandstone formations on the Panorama Trail

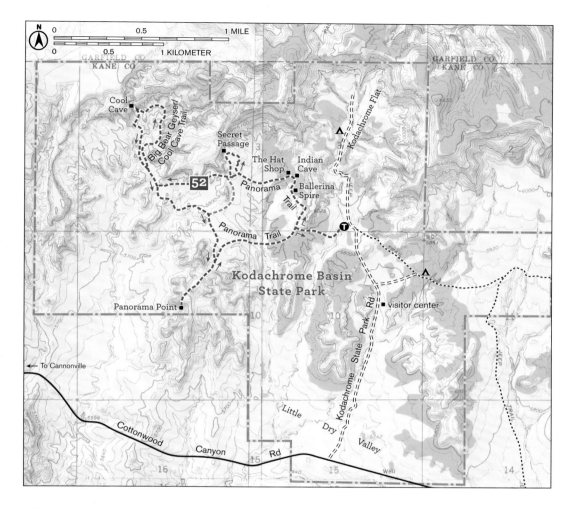

tall whitish sedimentary pipes that crop up are of primary interest to many who visit this trail. Close to seventy of the pipes dot the park and environs. Several theories exist as to the exact mechanism of their creation, from seismic activity or spring sedimentary buildup to wet slurry forced upward by deep pressures within the earth.

At 1.4 miles curve right to take the short Secret Passage spur, which swirls you around and through red walls and mini canyons that bring to mind old Western movies. When you return to the main trail you may choose to take a shortcut curving to the south if you wish to make this a shorter circuit; otherwise, continue west along the main Panorama Trail. Next up is the spur trail to Big Bear Geyser, then Cool Cave; turn right at the junction sign and walk down the red path, eventually into an increasingly narrow passageway that slots up toward its ending point at an alcove. The views along the trail here are long and lovely. Return to the Panorama Trail loop, turn right at the junction, and make sure to tackle the brief spur trail to Panorama Point, which offers a vista, as its name suggests. From here you can just glimpse the far-off line of Bryce Canyon, see the incredibly immense seep of Grand Staircase–Escalante National Monument, and catch sight of the 800-foot-high Gray Cliffs to your north. Finish the loop back to the trailhead.

53 *Willis Creek Narrows*

Roundtrip: 4.8 miles	*Season:* spring–fall
Hiking time: 2–3 hours	*Map:* USGS Bull Valley Gorge
Elevation gain: 280 feet	*Contact:* Grand Staircase–Escalante
Difficulty: easy	National Monument

Getting there: From Escalante, drive 36 miles west on State Route 12 to Cottonwood Canyon Road in the town of Cannonville. Turn left (south) on Cottonwood Canyon Road. Drive 2.8 miles to dirt Skutumpah Road, which is signed for Bull Valley and Kanab, and turn right (southwest). Drive 6.3 miles to the signed Willis Creek trailhead parking area on the right. **Notes:** Flash flooding may occur mid- to late summer; do not enter canyon if storms threaten. High-clearance 4WD may be required to access trailhead. Road may be impassable when wet. Multi-use trail; hikers must make way for horses.

Willis Creek is an ideal slot canyon for those who either don't have the experience or simply lack the desire to do some technical slot canyoneering. With all the amenities of a slot but with none of the more challenging aspects that stymie many, Willis Creek is a great way to check out the curves and swoops of stone that occur when persistent rushes of water inexorably force their way through the path of least resistance over time, leaving in their wake marvelous natural slices through the earth. Summertime can be quite hot, but the narrowest part of the canyon keeps you well shaded.

From the parking area and trail register, cross the road to enter the canyon, heading east. Ponderosas rise in stately height here and there during the beginning portions of the trail, along with junipers, pinyons, and single-leaf ash. Spring and summer hikes may find hardy desert wildflowers blooming, adding their color to the general beauty of the canyon. The wash becomes

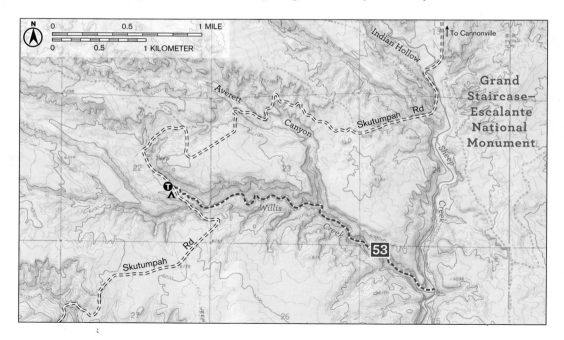

a narrows quite quickly, although the side walls are only about 25 feet high. But round a few more of the serpentine bends, and suddenly you're in a canyon with 100-foot cliffs soaring up overhead in sheer magnificence.

The deeper you go into the canyon, the higher and more sculpted the walls get, until they rise up to 300 feet high and it seems as if you're wandering through a natural Sistine Chapel. When golden light splashes onto the upper canyon walls, the sensuous curves stretching far above you are simply magnificent. Water usually flows through this little canyon, adding a sense of coolness along with the gently chiming sounds of the trickle passing over creek-smoothed cobblestones and sandy wash bottom. Cuts and curves and hollows and bulges play out in the walls, while the light, which sometimes reaches to the canyon bottom, gives almost perfect settings for even amateur photographers. A few pour-overs need to be negotiated around, but they are easily passable.

The best, tightest part of the canyon is all within the first 1.4 miles, right to where Averett Canyon heads off to your left (north). However, continue on through the canyon all the way to the junction with Sheep Creek to get a fuller picture of the natural contours and convolutions of this landscape. It's still a very pretty canyon here, just not as tight as the first part. Return the same way to the parking area.

The narrows of Willis Creek

54 *Lick Wash*

Roundtrip: 8 miles
Hiking time: 4 hours
Elevation gain: 335 feet
Difficulty: easy/moderate

Season: spring–fall
Map: USGS Deer Spring Point
Contact: Grand Staircase–Escalante National Monument

Getting there: From Escalante, drive 36 miles west on State Route 12 to Cottonwood Canyon Road in the town of Cannonville. Turn left (south) on Cottonwood Canyon Road. Drive 2.8 miles to dirt Skutumpah Road, which is signed for Bull Valley and Kanab, and turn right (southwest). Drive 19.8 miles and watch for the Lick Wash sign. The trailhead parking is a pullout on the left (east) side of the road. **Notes:** Flash flooding may occur mid- to late summer; do not enter if storms threaten. High-clearance 4WD may be required to access trailhead. Road may be impassable when wet.

Remote and lovely, Lick Wash is little visited and therefore quite the gem, since it features both beauty and solitude, a more and more rare combination in canyon country. Very exposed to sunlight, this hike is best in spring or fall, or at least best begun quite early in the day during the hotter months. Gentle enough for a stroll with children or the less able, this hike will still delight experienced canyon seekers who want to get a taste of the best trails through deep washes of sandstone. Fluted walls, interesting escarpments, and wide-ranging vistas around canyon bends all collaborate to make Lick Wash a memorable hike.

From the parking area, head southeast down the road into the wash. Filled with gravel and sandy, this is easy walking as you pass ponderosas and junipers along the way. Not particularly exciting at the start, rounded humps of layered Navajo sandstone gently thrust up not far ahead. Within 0.25 mile you are in a narrows, and within half a mile the walls are merely 10 feet apart. This slim corridor winds about, leading you farther southeast. The improbable sight of tall fir trees in the wash give even better understanding of how high the sandstone wall rims are, rising toward the sky as you follow their natural bends and curves. The cross-bedding of the sandstone continually draws the eye as the colors and light interchange over it depending on your angle and the time of day. At 1 mile in from the trailhead the canyon broadens somewhat as the walls rear 600 feet upward. The ivory and cream swells of Navajo sandstone enclose you from the left side, while cross-hatched walls draped in desert varnish and colorful mineral deposits grace your right-hand side.

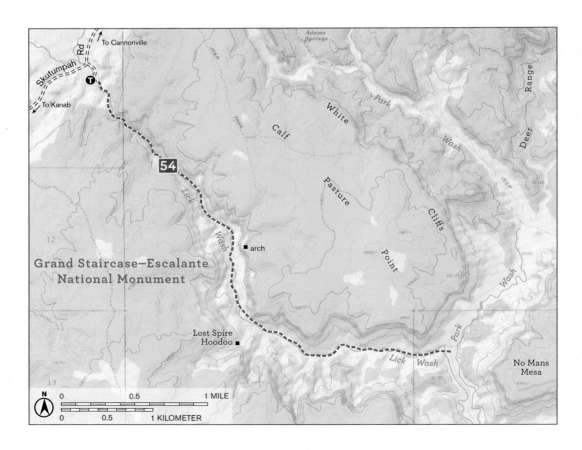

For the photographer, the round lumps and humps of sandstone cross-hatched and supremely colored make this a snap-happy place. Deep vermilion, toasty yellow, splashes of apricot and carrot, and varying streaks of darker shades dripping down white portions of sandstone can provide exceptional contrast against blue skies on clear days.

Side canyons and drainages invite exploration, so take the time to poke around them a little as you wander through this truly spectacular area. At 1.9 miles, look up to your left for a glimpse of a natural arch high on the cliff. A wash slips in on the right-hand side at 3.2 miles; explore up here for a scramble to Lost Spire Hoodoo, although some find this route too challenging. You meet Park Wash below No Mans Mesa at 4 miles in, where the surrounding cliffs walls rise to an impressive 800 feet above, encasing you in sheer canyon magic. From here return to the parking area.

Lick Wash is beautiful and remote.

55 Lower Hackberry Canyon

Roundtrip: 4 miles	**Season:** spring, fall
Hiking time: 3–4 hours	**Map:** USGS Slickrock Bench, Calico Peak
Elevation gain: 125 feet	**Contact:** Grand Staircase–Escalante
Difficulty: easy	National Monument

Getting there: From Kanab, drive 46.2 miles east on US Highway 89 to dirt Cottonwood Road. Turn left (north) and drive 14.4 miles to the trailhead parking area on your left (west). **From Cannonville,** turn right (south) onto Cottonwood Road. The first 8 miles are paved; the rest is dirt. Drive 31 miles total to the trailhead parking area on your right (west). **Notes:** Flash flooding may occur mid- to late summer; do not enter the canyon if storms threaten. High-clearance 4WD may be required to access trailhead. Road may be impassable when wet.

Well known for its beauty but not all that highly visited, Hackberry Canyon gets you deep into canyon country, surrounding you with towering rock walls, soft white domes of Navajo sandstone, cooling water for your feet, striking riparian lushness, and that typical beauty of a Utah canyon hike. Spring and fall are definitely the best times to do this hike, as summer can not only be quite warm but can leave you futilely warding off hordes of biting insects. This mostly gentle stroll is ideal for families or anyone who wants to experience a gorgeous canyon in a day. The most ambitious part of this hike is the road driving in, so strap on your boots and get out there.

From the trailhead, hike west and almost immediately drop into the wash of Cottonwood Creek, up which you head north (right). Walking in the wash usually involves wet feet, but if water

Cottonwoods grace the canyon.

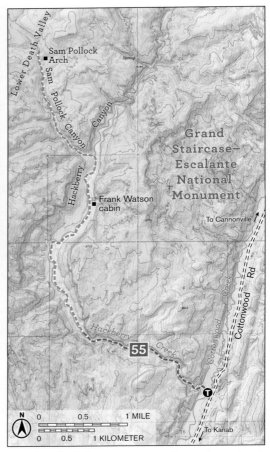

is there it probably won't be too deep. In a scant 0.2 mile you reach Hackberry Canyon; turn left into it and continue upstream to the northwest. Large cottonwoods and box elders rear up from the low banks of the creek, providing occasional shady spots as well as nice color contrast with the jutting rocks in their variegated color displays. Just past the entrance point you come upon a set of narrows that are deep and fun to wander through. For the next 1.4 miles your passage is bordered by a formation known as the Cockscomb, made up of high, striking Navajo sandstone domes and the layered conglomerate, siltstone, and sandstone of Kayenta, with each bend of the canyon revealing a new visual delight.

Wander another 0.5 mile, simply taking in the sights of Hackberry Canyon and enjoying the beautiful deep gorge and the very pleasant feeling of being in an oasis in the desert. When the canyon begins to broaden and the walls surrounding you get shorter, it is time to turn around and retrace your steps to the parking area.

Extending your hike: Continue to the Frank Watson cabin and Sam Pollock natural arch for a total roundtrip hike of 12.8 miles. From the mouth of Hackberry Canyon where it meets the Cottonwood Creek wash, it is 4.4 miles to the cabin and then an additional 2 miles to the arch, which is up a side canyon to the left (north). That route involves some scrambling over boulders. Hackberry Canyon also can be done as an overnight backpacking trip, which involves a car shuttle, an overnight permit, and a suggested 30-foot piece of rope or webbing to lower packs over dry falls. Its entire length, end to end, is 21.5 miles of relative seclusion.

56 *Wire Pass Trail/Buckskin Gulch*

Roundtrip: 5 miles
Hiking time: 3–4 hours
Elevation gain: 175 feet
Difficulty: moderate

Season: spring, fall
Map: USGS Pine Hollow Canyon
Contact: Vermilion Cliffs National
Monument (BLM)

Getting there: Wire Pass trailhead (starting point for overnight and day trips): From Kanab, drive east on US Highway 89 for 39.5 miles. Turn right (south) onto the dirt House Rock Valley Road. Drive 8.3 miles to the trailhead. **Notes:** Flash flooding may occur mid- to late summer; do not enter if storms threaten. Permit required for day hiking; pay at trailhead. Early morning departure highly recommended in summer. Wading may be necessary. Climbing up, around, and down large chockstones wedged into the canyon may be required. Free camping at trailhead and one mile south down the road. Vault toilet at trailhead. Road may be impassable when wet.

Considered by many to be the world's premier slot canyon, Buckskin Gulch is also its longest. Deep, sculpted cliffs reach as much as 500 feet overhead, in some places leaving the bottom of the canyon unlit because the sunlight can't reach down there. Patterned whirls and whorls slice into the sandstone walls, luring the eye as you wander down this deep cut through the earth. Dark stains drip down the walls, desert varnish painting the dark red and burnt orange canyon with a natural brush. The canyon's tremendous presence and striking beauty are sure to awe as you pass through this soaring natural chapel.

Starting from the Wire Pass trailhead means you can explore Buckskin Gulch as a day hike, since this is the closest entrance to the gulch itself. From the trailhead, hike east about 100 feet to drop into Coyote Wash. Just 0.3 mile from the trailhead, pass the signed Buckskin Gulch/Coyote Buttes trail junction and take the left (north) fork. Travel for 1.2 miles along the sandy streambed bottom. This very exposed section can be extremely unpleasant on hot days, which is why spring and fall are the recommended seasons for this hike. Low, salmon-colored cliffs soon tighten up to funnel you directly into a minor but very pretty slot section that is actually narrower than Buckskin

Obstacles in the gulch can be both daunting and fun.

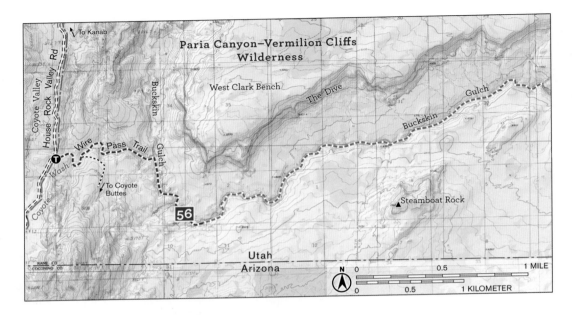

Gulch. After widening again, the route once again constricts into another slot section that is barely wide enough for the average person's shoulder width. These are classic Southwest slot canyons that expose you to the wonder of how the force of water cutting through relatively soft sandstone created such beautiful natural mazes you can explore.

The end of this slot section abruptly shoots you right into the confluence with Buckskin Gulch, at 1.7 miles from the trailhead. While the Wire Pass Trail is technically only 3.4 miles roundtrip, add a mile or even more to get a sense of Buckskin Gulch, exploring downstream into the world's longest, deepest slot canyon. The walls tower overhead, adding to the sense of wandering right through the earth's stony, sinuous belly. The canyon walls demand the close attention of your camera lens, as do the light and shadows playing with the russet and mahogany colors of the carved, curving cliffs. The sheer height of the canyon walls gives the distinct impression of a grand majesty, which certainly befits this most dramatic example of nature's path of least resistance when shaping the landscape. After sufficient exploration, return up the canyon and back through Wire Pass to the trailhead.

Extending your hike: To make an overnight out of Buckskin Gulch, obtain the required permits from the BLM first. A shuttle vehicle or a long roundtrip is required, as well as significant slot canyoneering knowledge and awareness of the weather forecast. The one-way mileage of 20.6 miles from the Wire Pass to the White House trailhead will showcase a major portion of Buckskin Gulch. Sucking mud pools, dankness, nose-pinching smells from standing water, and the threat of a flash flood can mark the full length of Buckskin Gulch as one for only those who are already experienced in canyon hiking. Be prepared for wading, swimming, scrambling, mud walking, and pure appreciation for this incredible canyon.

57 Pine Creek Box

One-way: 9.1 miles
Hiking time: 6–7 hours
Elevation loss: 1340 feet
Difficulty: moderate
Season: spring–fall

Map: USGS Posey Lake, Wide Hollow Reservoir
Contact: Box–Death Hollow Wilderness, Escalante Ranger District, Dixie National Forest

Getting there: *Upper Box:* From State Route 12 in Escalante, drive 18.2 miles north on Hell's Backbone Road, which starts out paved but soon becomes graded dirt. Drive to the signed Upper Box Access trailhead on the right (east) side of the road. Roadside parking. *Lower Box:* From SR 12 in Escalante, drive 8 miles north on Hell's Backbone Road, which soon becomes graded dirt. Turn right and park in the large area beside the road. There is a Road Closed sign just to the north of the parking area; the road to the actual trailhead is impassable to vehicles. **Notes:** Walking in water required. Shuttle vehicle necessary. Hiking from upper to lower is recommended in order to descend rather than gain elevation.

The Pine Creek Box is a gorgeous hike in the Box–Death Hollow Wilderness Area that drops you from the forested slopes of Boulder Mountain down into slickrock canyons near the town of Escalante. The changes in terrain make this an especially unique and interesting hike. From its pine-tree-strewn high end, the trail extends south all the way through a deeply carved canyon that reaches as much as 1400 feet above your head, the walls sometimes narrowing quite a bit as you head downstream. Showcasing a range of the area's stunning topography, the Box is fun and can be pleasant on hot days due to the presence of water, although it really is best in fall. Less known to visitors than many of the more famous nearby trails, the Box is nevertheless a spectacular example of southern Utah hiking at its finest. Best of all, its relatively unknown status

Desert scenery on the southern end of the Pine Creek Box

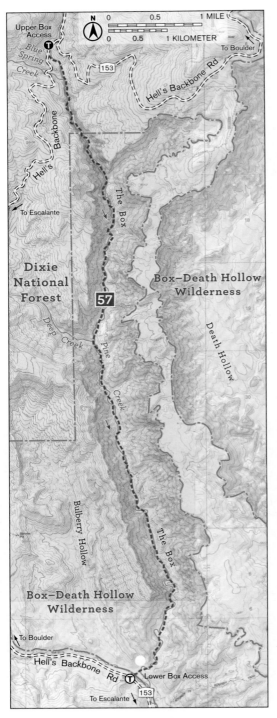

virtually ensures that you will have this trail mostly to yourself.

The creatively named Hell's Backbone Road was a Civilian Conservation Corps project, completed in 1933, that allowed the first auto access between the towns of Escalante and Boulder as well as into this remote area, although its original use focused more on local cattle interests than on recreation.

The following description is the north to south route. From the upper parking area, head due south beneath the towering pine trees, walking through a small meadow by a meandering creek as it naturally lazes itself downhill. Along your way ponderosa pines, Douglas firs, and even Engelmann spruce dot the banks and hillsides beside the trail, offering ample spots to take a break, eat lunch, or simply enjoy the forested traverse downstream. Spring flowers can scatter the grasses with spots of color. About 1 mile in, pass a simple wooden sign letting you know you have entered the Box–Death Hollow Wilderness. Along with the burble of the stream, it all makes for a charming start to your hike.

As the creek heads south, leading you along the twisting path that it carved into this deep gorge, typical sandstone colors decorate the walls. Hints of caramel, dashes of coral and tangerine and rose, billows of cream and russet, streaks of dark desert varnish, and even bands of pale green and lavender all mix into beautiful palettes that have attracted hikers and artists for decades now. Occasional sandstone pools capture water in small alcoves tucked along the drainage. The trail crisscrosses the creek now and then as needed, generally in places that are easy to ford or hop. The farther down the creek you descend, the higher the surrounding cliffs rise above you.

At 4.4 miles Deep Creek crosses Pine Creek from the west; here, the canyon walls leap nearly a thousand feet above you. Meander along downstream, crossing here and there as needed, sometimes skirting deep pools. The canyon will abruptly end, shoving you out onto an open, grassy flat, from where you reach your shuttle vehicle parked .03 mile southwest of the lower trailhead.

58 *Death Hollow*

One-way: 20.5 miles
Hiking time: 2–4 days
Elevation loss: 1540 feet
Difficulty: hard
Season: spring, fall

Map: USGS Boulder Town, Calf Creek, Escalante
Contact: Grand Staircase–Escalante National Monument

Getting there: Boulder Mail Trail: From Boulder, drive west on State Route 12 for 3 miles to Hell's Backbone Road. (From Escalante, drive 22.5 miles east on SR 12.) Turn north, passing a large sandy pullout with dumpsters on your right. At 0.2 mile a dirt road leads west; turn left here to reach the parking area in 0.5 mile and the trailhead in another 0.2 mile. *Escalante River Bridge trailhead:* From Escalante, drive 14.7 miles east along SR 12. (From Boulder, drive 12.8 miles west on SR 12.) Park at the Escalante River Bridge parking area on the west side of the highway, or in one of the overflow pullouts immediately to the south. **Notes:** Flash flooding may occur mid- to late summer; do not enter canyon if storms threaten. Walking in water required. Swimming may be required. Trekking poles recommended. Extremely hot in summer. Exposed slickrock descent. Shuttle vehicle required. Permit required for overnight use. Routefinding required; bring a topographical map.

Considered by many to be one of the premier hiking areas in the Grand Staircase–Escalante area, the ominously named Death Hollow (supposedly called thus due to the number of livestock that slipped or plunged to their deaths from the high, scrabbly slickrock sections over the years) contains sandstone beauty of staggering variety. While the entire

Looking over the sprawling sandstone canyons of the Death Hollow area

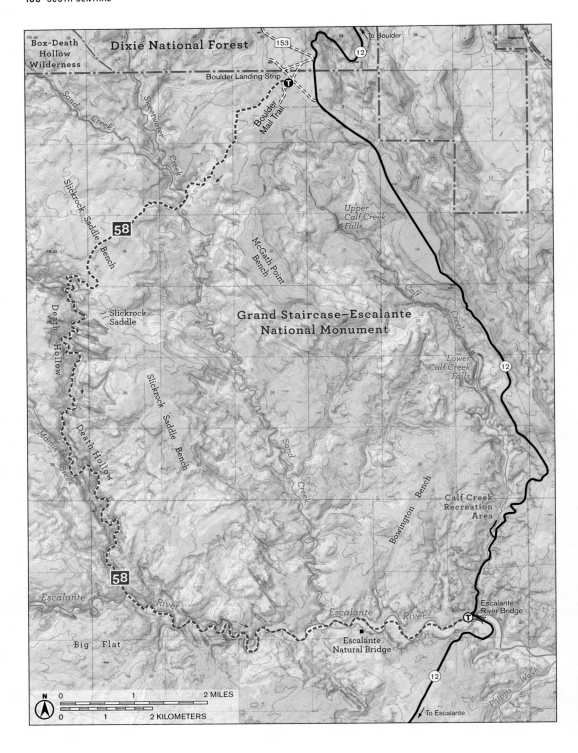

Box-Death
Hollow
Wilderness

Dixie National Forest

153

To Boulder

12

Boulder Landing Strip

Boulder
Mail Trail

Sand Creek

Sweetwater Creek

Slickrock Saddle Bench

58

Upper
Calf Creek
Falls

McGath Point Bench

Calf Creek

Grand Staircase–Escalante
National Monument

Death Hollow

Slickrock
Saddle

Lower
Calf Creek
Falls

12

Death Hollow

Mamie Creek

Slickrock Saddle Bench

Sand Creek

Bowington Bench

Calf Creek
Recreation
Area

58

Escalante

River

Escalante   River

Escalante
River Bridge

Big   Flat

Escalante
Natural Bridge

12

Phipps Wash

N

0   1   2 MILES

0   1   2 KILOMETERS

To Escalante

30-mile length of Death Hollow itself can be attempted, that is an epic journey containing hearty amounts of routefinding, non-trail slickrock walking, technical canyoneering, swimming in water-filled canyons, and required fitness. This less demanding yet still exceptional route offers a striking portion of trail with less significant effort involved and allows you to see why others wax poetic about the grandeur of Death Hollow.

Your journey heading north to south begins at the storied Boulder Mail Trail, drops down into Death Hollow, continues east along the Escalante River, and ends at State Route 12. The Boulder Mail Trail was the original route for bringing mail via pack train to the residents of Boulder Town. Boulder was the last town in the contiguous United States to receive its post by mule transport, which it did until the completion of SR 12 in 1940.

From the Boulder Mail Trail parking area, head roughly southwest past the well-signed trail register box. You'll be heading over the McGath Point Bench, which is high enough to give you outstanding views of the seemingly endless surrounding terrain of rumpled sandstone folds, juniper-prickled mesas and benches, and the alluring tangle of canyons into which you will enter. You drop into Sand Creek at 1.8 miles,

then climb back out to continue on the generally cairned route along Slickrock Saddle Bench for another 2.8 miles before finding the intersection with the deep, folded carving of Death Hollow itself. The descent here, usually marked by rock cairns, is not technically difficult, but it certainly is exposed and may give some hikers pause. Use caution if descending with large packs as you make your way down the slickrock wall, which is dotted here and there with tenacious shrubs. In the canyon, several river bends make fine places to camp.

As you head downstream, rounding bend after bend as the canyon walls soar above you, the views never become tiresome. Just 4 miles after the descent from the Boulder Mail Trail into Death Hollow itself, you pass Mamie Creek coming in from the west. After this point the canyon tightens into narrows, with several miniature waterfalls and sunken potholes to skirt or navigate. Another 3.8 miles on, you reach the Escalante River. Turn left to head east 7 miles to where it crosses beneath SR 12, being certain to keep an eye out for natural arches, ancient petroglyphs and pictographs, cliff dwellings, and generally an abundant continuation of the amazing scenery the entire way. The parking area is right at the highway.

59 *Wolverine Canyon*

Roundtrip: 10 miles
Hiking time: 8 hours
Elevation gain: 200 feet
Difficulty: moderate

Season: spring, fall
Map: USGS Pioneer Mesa, Kings Bench
Contact: Grand Staircase–Escalante National Monument

Getting there: From State Route 12 in Boulder, turn east on the Burr Trail and drive 18.5 miles to the signed turnoff for the Wolverine Loop Road. Turn right (south) and drive 11 miles on the dirt road to the Wolverine Canyon trailhead parking. **Notes:** Flash flooding may occur mid- to late summer; do not enter canyon if storms threaten. High-clearance 4WD may be required to access trailhead. Road may be impassable when wet. Map reading ability recommended. Can be very hot in summer.

Wolverine Canyon offers the beauty of redrock canyons without the twisty, windy bits of a slot canyon, making this a more casual stroll in an area that sees fewer people mostly

Pippin is eager to explore Wolverine Canyon.

because it can be an epic task to reach the trail-head, although it's certainly doable in the right vehicle and under the right weather conditions. Along with the high-rising red cliffs reaching skyward around you, chunks of petrified wood add visual appeal and particular interest on this hike. This general section is actually part of the Wolverine Petrified Wood Natural Area, and you quickly will find out why. Please resist any temptation to collect petrified wood here, or anywhere else for that matter, so that others may enjoy seeing it after you. Springtime trips also offer striking bits of color popping up here and there from flowering plants such as Indian paintbrush.

From the parking area, walk southwest along the drainage for 1.5 miles to meet with Wolverine Canyon. The pieces of petrified wood you begin to encounter are astounding, ranging from pieces that fit into the palm of a hand to enormous chunks as large as small cars. Petrified wood is commonly found in dry desert climes, the very nature of which served to preserve these remnants of ancient trees. Some positively enormous

pieces stick up out of the sandy bottoms here and there, giving rise to much speculation about what the landscape looked like millions of years ago. The colors on petrified wood are just as appealing, with the swirls of purples, mauves, lavenders, coppers, and of course the fascinating striations and circles that so clearly mark these heavy stones as being permutations of long-gone living wood.

This section is pretty wide open and exposed, making it a very hot process on warmer days. But from here you eventually head into the south arm of Wolverine, where the canyon walls swoop and curl around, the pale oranges and soft rose colors increasingly drawing the eye the farther in you go. Stone amphitheaters beckon, as do the irregular holes of wind-pocked solution cavities dotting the soft red walls in sections. Never creating any obstacles that might seem too ambitious to surmount, the canyon gradually heads southwest toward where it smacks into Horse Canyon about 5 miles in. This is your turnaround point. Return the same way back to the parking area.

Extending your hike: See the Little Death Hollow hike (Hike 60) for details on making Wolverine Canyon part of a longer, more challenging loop hike.

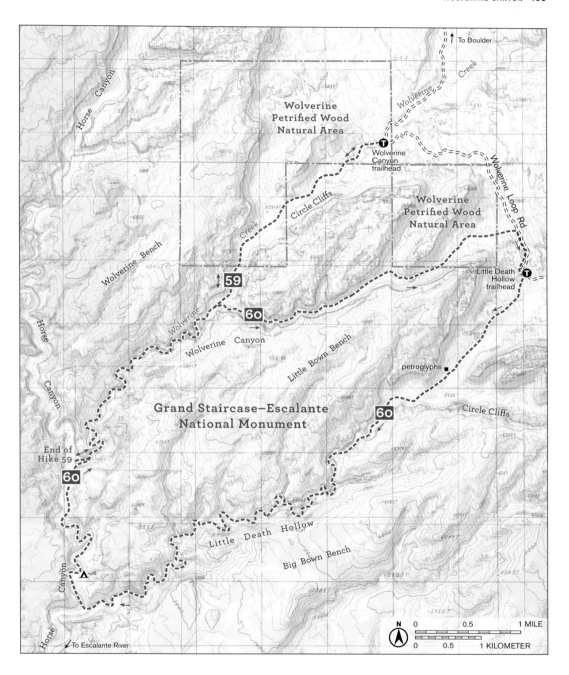

To Boulder

Wolverine Creek

Wolverine

Wolverine
Petrified Wood
Natural Area

Ⓣ Wolverine
Canyon
trailhead

Horse Canyon

Circle Cliffs

Creek

Wolverine Loop Rd

Wolverine
Petrified Wood
Natural Area

Wolverine Bench

↕ 59

60

Wolverine

Wolverine Canyon

Little Death
Hollow
trailhead Ⓣ

Little Bown Bench

petroglyphs ■

Grand Staircase–Escalante
National Monument

60

Circle Cliffs

End of
Hike 59

60

Horse Canyon

Little Death Hollow

Big Bown Bench

△

Horse Canyon

To Escalante River

N

0   0.5   1 MILE

0   0.5   1 KILOMETER

60 *Little Death Hollow*

Loop: 15 miles
Hiking time: 9 hours–2 days
Elevation gain: 650 feet
Difficulty: moderate
Season: spring, fall

Map: USGS Pioneer Mesa, Silver Falls Bench, Red Breaks, King Bench
Contact: Grand Staircase–Escalante National Monument

Getting there: From State Route 12 in Boulder, turn east on the Burr Trail and drive 18.5 miles to the signed turnoff for the Wolverine Loop Road. Drive 12.4 miles on the dirt road to the Little Death Hollow trailhead. **Notes:** Flash flooding may occur mid- to late summer; do not enter the canyon if storms threaten. High-clearance 4WD may be required to access trailhead. Road may be impassable when wet. Climbing over, under, around chockstones required. Free permit required for overnight camping.

Despite the rather forbidding name, Little Death Hollow is a very scenic, up-close-and-personal experience of the area's stunning, unique topography. Although the beginning of the hike does not elicit much of a wow factor with its flat, sagebrush dotted plains, the eventual destination is well worth the initial slog. Winding through impressive narrows at its slimmest point, this long loop brings you the opportunity to scramble, slither, slide, scale, twist, and shove yourself through beautiful red-rock sandstone passages that curve and twine around in that classic form found throughout the spectacular canyons and drainages of this vast area. The fact that you have to work to reach the slot canyon makes your time in it all the sweeter for having truly earned the experience. Although this canyon is passable by those who are fit and agile, flash flood events can change its makeup in a heartbeat.

From the parking area, set off southwest, keeping to the wash's north side for somewhat easier walking. This section is flat and uninspiring and can be quite hot, but trek on with the knowledge you will soon arrive at far greater beauty. The red cliffs widely set to either side promise more interesting views to come while also hiding an arch you might spot as you hike on. A mile in, keep your eyes peeled for a large boulder with petroglyphs on it, situated in the sand on the

A simple beginning to an amazing canyon

right-hand (northwest) side of the trail. Knowing the ancients wandered this area as well, and most likely explored down the canyon as you are about to, adds a nearly tangible connection with those long-gone people. At 1.5 miles a small side canyon tempts, but continue heading along your path. Just over 2 miles in, the walls narrow in on you, presenting a vision of the far more spectacular slot to come ahead. At 4.7 miles in, you hit the narrowest part of the canyon.

The narrows section here is spectacular, as slim as a mere two feet across in some portions. The slickrock weaves and twists around, with entering light making it even more fascinating as you slowly meander through its curves. This is a section where you are likely to encounter chockstones and pools of water, depending on recent weather events, and you will have to be able to negotiate both boulders and tight spots. This may also be where the canyon becomes impassable to those who are not prepared for the possibility of deep water or for descending down a steep drop; it is far better to simply turn back here if the effort to continue proves too challenging for your group. Even if this is a turnaround point, what you have seen of the canyon thus far will not have disappointed, and ending here can still make for a good day hike.

When you are 6.5 miles in, you come to the junction with Horse Canyon. Between here and the junction with Wolverine Canyon you will find campsites useful if you are spending the night. At Horse Canyon, head north for 2 miles until you reach Wolverine Canyon, which opens to your right, or northeast. Wolverine is also a lovely canyon, and the wider passageway means easier, faster walking through it. Although it does not sport the narrows of Little Death Hollow, winding sandstone meanders through Wolverine, making it a lovely 3.3 mile return route back to the Wolverine Loop Road (see Hike 59 for more details). After you reach the road, it is another 0.5 mile to the parking area.

61 *Lower Calf Creek Falls*

Roundtrip: 5.5 miles	***Season:*** all year
Hiking time: 3–4 hours	***Map:*** USGS Calf Creek
Elevation gain: 175 feet	***Contact:*** Grand Staircase–Escalante
Difficulty: easy	National Monument

Getting there: Fifteen miles east of Escalante or 11.4 miles west of Boulder on State Route 12, a well-marked turnoff to Calf Creek Recreation Area heads west. Turn here into the parking lot. If it is full, as it often is spring through fall and on weekends, there are pullouts on either side of the highway to both the north and south. Use caution when walking from any of these pullouts down into the parking area. **Notes:** Pay at self-serve kiosk for parking (no fee for walk-ins or cyclists) and camping. Picnic area, toilets, potable water, playground, volleyball courts. Early morning start recommended in summer. Can be crowded on weekends and holidays.

The tallest waterfall in southern Utah at 126 feet, and easily accessible from State Route 12, Lower Calf Creek Falls gets a good amount of traffic. Regardless, Lower Calf Creek is highly recommended due to the beauty of both the trail and the falls, as well as viewable ancient ruins and rock art along the way (binoculars are useful, as they are well off the trail). Trail brochures are available here, and you should pick one up, as its details will add depth to your enjoyment of the hike. Small wooden signposts along the way indicate the information stops in the trail brochure, which points out various flora and the otherwise difficult-to-spot ruins across the canyon.

Although the trail is relatively easy, sections with deep sand and short climbs can feel very taxing on particularly hot days.

The well-marked trailhead starts at the north end of the parking lot. Head north along the trail, which remains on the west side of Calf Creek the entire way. You are hiking through a beautiful canyon with towering Navajo sandstone walls rising up on either side all the way. Many small social trails lead off at various points, but please stay on the main trail to help avoid degrading the canyon further. Pinyon and juniper trees, cottonwoods and box elder, Gambel oak and willow, and plenty of greenery such as the jointed horsetail and waving cattail scatter over the canyon floor, well watered by the perennial stream. In the springtime, red Indian paintbrush, orange globemallow, yellow rubber rabbitbrush, and other plants sprinkle over the canyon to create startling bursts of color. Fall hikes yield stunning changing colors on the box elders and cottonwoods.

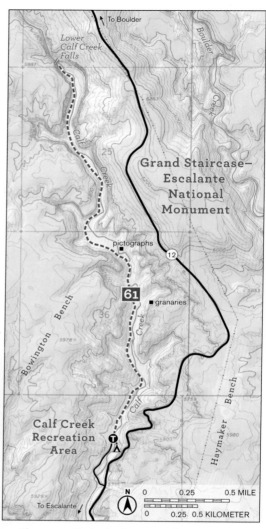

Trail's end at the stunning falls

About 1 mile in, look across the river to near the top rim of the canyon cliff on the east side. Binoculars may help you spot the small stone granaries left behind by Fremont Indians many centuries ago. Keep heading upstream, and in 0.5 mile more you can see the red pictographs of rock art, also on the opposite canyon side. Three figures in the classic triangular Fremont rock art shape guard the canyon wall in a wide but shallow alcove.

There is little shade until 1.9 miles in, when you round a corner and the trail veers a little more west. At this point the canyon narrows. You can see several sections of gorgeous desert varnish streaking down the cliff. At 2.75 miles, you round a corner and suddenly see the waterfall first plummeting off a high shelf, then dropping onto another shelf before tripping off that one and sliding down the sheer, smooth cliff face to the large pool below. It is a jaw-dropping sight after the pleasant meander of the canyon, particularly if you hit it midmorning when full sunlight illuminates the clear water, the green moss, and the desert varnish clearly visible right under the slim curtain of the falls.

There is a white sandy beach (yes, really) and plenty of little areas to sit and eat lunch or snacks while taking in the falls. Swimming can be refreshing on a very hot day, but beware—that water is cold enough to steal your breath, even on the hottest days in July. When it's finally time to pull yourself away from this little slice of paradise, simply retrace your steps back along the trail to the parking area.

62 Escalante Natural Bridge

Roundtrip: 4 miles
Hiking time: 2–3 hours
Elevation gain: 67 feet
Difficulty: easy

Season: spring–fall
Map: USGS Calf Creek
Contact: Grand Staircase–Escalante National Monument

Getting there: From Escalante, drive 14.7 miles east along State Route 12 (from Boulder, drive 12.8 miles west on SR 12). Park at the Escalante River trailhead on the west side of the highway or in one of the overflow pullouts immediately to the south. **Note:** Walking through river required.

This is the perfect short introduction to the Escalante River area, and despite its brevity it offers up an amazing array of the area's beauty: a riparian river canyon, soaring sandstone canyon walls, ancient petroglyphs to spot, a natural bridge, and the very pleasant gurgle of water slipping through its course along the entire length of the trail. This charming hike takes you alongside and through the river, offers the occasional shady shelter of draping greenery, and drenches you with the beauty of canyon country because of the huge sandstone walls and domes and buttes you encounter along the way, culminating in the graceful leap of the slender natural bridge. Easy to access right from the highway, this trail can see heavy activity on holidays and weekends, although it usually is less crowded than the popular Lower Calf Creek Falls just up the road. Very family

Escalante River Natural Bridge

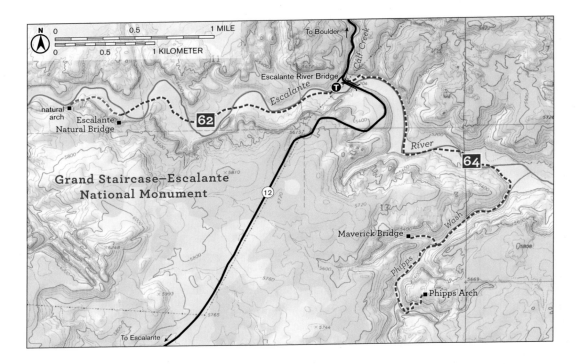

friendly, this is a beautiful hike on a hot day due to the river's constant proximity as well as several river crossings.

From the parking area, head southwest toward the river and take the right (west) fork at the signed junction. Continue alongside the river, ambling through the sandy trail and enjoying the shade of overhanging trees. The trail crosses the river a few times; the crossings are typically shallow and not too difficult in the warmer months unless there's been a recent storm. Large cottonwoods (which may rain down their white "cotton" on you in the springtime, often making patches of the ground appear snow-covered); non-native Russian olive trees, with their thorny spikes; small, dusty green clumps of sage dotted everywhere; and other riparian vegetation make this a surprisingly lush hike in an otherwise mostly barren landscape.

The dark red and pale yellow walls of sandstone rise to your left as you walk, with smooth-domed Navajo sandstone piling here and there on your right. The colors of canyon country are what bedazzle many, along with the fantastical shapes, and this hike does not disappoint in the slightest as far as those scenes.

Before you reach the natural bridge, you will first spy an arch pushing out from high up the cliff walls, even though it is actually farther down from the bridge. Keep an eye out for it looping out from the left-hand (west) side of bulging sandstone ahead, well above the tree line. Then, just 2 miles in, you reach Escalante Natural Bridge—which technically is an arch, as it was created via erosion rather than water. At 130 feet high, it soars overhead, making for fantastic photos. After soaking in the beauty of the area, return the same way back to the trailhead.

Extending your hike: Explore as far up the river as desired to continue the inundation of stunning natural beauty just about everywhere you look.

63 *Escalante River*

One-way: 14.2 miles
Hiking time: 10 hours–2 days
Elevation gain: 750 feet
Difficulty: moderate

Season: spring–fall
Map: USGS Escalante, Calf Creek
Contact: Grand Staircase–Escalante National Monument

Getting there: *Starting point:* From State Route 12 on the east side of Escalante, at 0.25 mile east of the high school turn north at the Escalante River Access sign. Just before the road reaches the cemetery, it turns sharply east and becomes dirt. In 0.4 mile take a left-hand (northwest) turn at the road fork. After another 0.5 mile park in the lot near the trailhead register. *Ending point:* From Escalante, drive 14.7 miles east along SR 12 (from Boulder, drive 12.8 miles west on SR 12). Park at the Escalante River Bridge parking area on the west side of the highway or in one of the overflow pullouts immediately to the south. **Notes:** Be prepared for significant river walking. Shuttle vehicle necessary.

The last major river to be discovered in the contiguous United States, the 85-mile long Escalante River is beloved by those who enjoy hiking this area for its cool, riparian beauty in the midst of the canyon-country scramble of sandstone walls, canyons, buttes, spires, arches, and general dryness. An oasis in the hot seasons, the Escalante is often hiked in summertime, although that is not always the best choice. Swarms of insects in late spring and early summer, frightening thunder and deluges of rain during the summer monsoon season, and of course major heat can all conspire to make it more challenging in the hottest months. Regardless, the Escalante River corridor is spectacular any way you slice it, and spending a good amount of time wandering its curving lengths and exploring the surrounding beauty is an excellent way to experience some of southern Utah's most classic scenery. Although hiking the entire length of the river is a feat some hikers happily attempt, one of the most popular and scenic stretches winds between the town of Escalante and where the river crosses beneath State Route 12. While ambitious and fit hikers can cover this ground in one long day, an overnight trip allows you to experience the striking beauty of this river canyon at a more leisurely pace.

This route is west to east. From the Escalante River trailhead parking area, head north on the

Escalante River Trail sports cottonwoods and canyon walls.

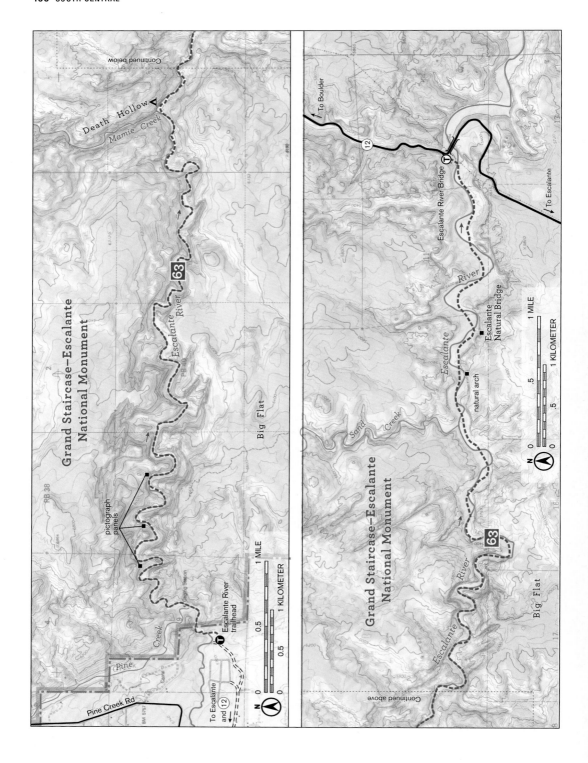

Grand Staircase–Escalante
National Monument

Death Hollow

Mamie Creek

Continued below

Escalante River

63

Big Flat

pictograph panels

RB 38

Pine Creek

Pine

Escalante River trailhead

To Escalante
and (12)

Pine Creek Rd

BM 5767

N

0   0.5   1 MILE

0   0.5   1 KILOMETER

To Boulder

(12)

Escalante River Bridge

To Escalante

Escalante River

Escalante Natural Bridge

natural arch

Sand Creek

Escalante River

63

Big Flat

Grand Staircase–Escalante
National Monument

Continued above

N

0   .5   1 MILE

0   .5   1 KILOMETER

trail as it winds downhill. Cross the river and follow the trail east alongside it. Large, domed Navajo sandstone walls rise above the river as you near the confluence with Pine Creek at 0.8 mile. Keep an eye out for ancient pictograph panels on the cliff walls by the river within the first 2 miles. The trail crosses the river multiple times as it curves and winds with the natural sinuousness of the water's passage through the landscape, each bend bringing more visual delights. Cottonwoods, willows, and box elders shade the way here and there as the thirsty trees grow up right on the banks of the river.

For those wishing to camp for a night, about 7 miles in, near the junction with Death Hollow

(Hike 58), is a good choice for both halfway mileage as well as locations from which to choose. Death Hollow is also a gorgeous side canyon that can invite further exploration if you build in the time for it, whether by camping for the night or simply adding more time to an already long day. Downstream 5 miles from Death Hollow you reach the confluence with Sand Creek, the rising cliff walls above you heralding its approach. Another 0.4 mile from Sand Creek you will spot the first of two natural features, an arch and then the graceful rise of Escalante Natural Bridge leaping skyward. The final 1.8 miles will bring you to the Escalante River Bridge trailhead and the end of the hike.

64 *Phipps Arch*

Roundtrip: 5.7 miles	**Season:** all year
Hiking time: 5–7 hours	**Map:** USGS Calf Creek
Elevation gain: 400 feet	**Contact:** Grand Staircase–Escalante
Difficulty: moderate	National Monument

Getting there: From Escalante, drive 14.7 miles east on State Route 12 (from Boulder, drive 12.8 miles west on SR 12). Park at the Escalante River Bridge parking area on the west side of the highway or in one of the overflow pullouts immediately to the south.
Notes: Be prepared for river walking (or bushwhacking if you'd rather not walk in the water). Routefinding may be necessary. Some exposure involving sandstone friction hiking at final section to reach arch. Early morning start recommended during summer.

Phipps Arch is a particularly interesting arch due to its oddly thick shape. Part of the Phipps–Death Hollow Wilderness Study Area (WSA), the arch is apparently named for Washington Phipps, a nineteenth-century friend or business partner of John Boynton. The somewhat murky story says things went terribly awry over either a business deal or a woman, leading to the murder of Phipps and the subsequent fleeing of Boynton. Whatever the truth of the tale, the unfortunate Phipps posthumously enjoys an eponymous legacy throughout the area. From this particular trailhead to the arch, you get to start by hiking along (and through) the riparian Escalante River area, so it's a double bang for your buck.

Be prepared to hike through the water in at least some sections, and also to do some routefinding, as the arch itself is not visible from the canyon below and you must scramble up sandstone ledges to access it. From the arch, the tumble of rocks and canyons and hole-pocked sandstone walls and domes you can see gives you perspective on the wildness and beauty of the area.

From the parking area, cross to the east side of the highway and the gated entrance to the river. A sign tells you private property is beyond the fences, so please respect this boundary. Once you reach the canyon, the trail heads to your left (east) across the water and up a little sandbank. If you don't see anything resembling a trail, just

View of Phipps Arch from the trail

turn east into the canyon, keeping an eye on the slickrock ledges on the left (north) side. There you will see a path snaking back and around, first up through scrub brush, then into and over the pale yellow ledges themselves.

Continue downstream to reach Phipps Wash, which opens to your right (west) in 1.6 miles. Head up the wash, which may involve negotiating a small stream or waterpockets. Sand walking occurs as well, although the views, with the canyon walls rising around you, are lovely. About 0.6 mile into the wash, a small canyon opens up on your right with a hiker-made trail leading in. Head up it about an eighth of a mile to see Maverick Bridge, a very small but interesting natural bridge (the true location of which is mislabeled on topo maps). Return back out to the main Phipps Wash and turn right to continue heading south.

After 2.8 miles, with cottonwood trees and other greenery still present, the wash opens up with a large draw to your left (east). Look for hiker trails heading over the water and up sandy banks in that direction; if none are present, just make

your way east and slowly up, passing rugged little junipers along the way. Although Phipps Arch is not visible from this vantage point, it is just above you on your left (north), hidden behind the sandstone ledges and slopes you must ascend for 0.3 mile in order to reach it. Here you must pick your way up through the usually cairned sandstone, skirting along ledges that almost naturally seem to switchback. One section demands some scrambling up, and this may be the area that deters those with fears of heights or exposure, although it likely won't faze most. Once you pass this section, head up through a small sandstone bowl, at which point you can begin to see the arch framed against the sky above you.

Thick and sinuous, the leaping sandstone wall from which the arch is carved is draped in black desert varnish streaks and rounded and smoothed along its top. Explore under and behind the arch, admiring the canyon views that extend in several directions. Carefully pick your way back down the sandstone slopes and ledges and return to the parking area the same way you entered.

65 *Devils Garden (Escalante)*

Loop: 0.5 mile
Hiking time: 1 hour
Elevation gain: 0 feet
Difficulty: easy

Season: all year
Map: USGS Seep Flat
Contact: Grand Staircase–Escalante
National Monument

Getting there: From Escalante, go 5 miles east on State Route 12 to the signed Hole-in-the-Rock Road heading southeast (from Boulder, it is 25.7 miles west on SR 12; signs point you in from either direction). Drive 13 miles on the dirt Hole-in-the-Rock Road to the signed Devils Garden turnoff to your right. Head 0.5 mile to the parking area.

Notes: Vault toilets, picnic tables, fire pits, and grills by parking lot. No camping allowed. Roads may be impassable when wet. Can be very hot during summer.

A playground of wildly intriguing hoodoos and even small natural arches, Devils Garden is a sandstone delight filled with the most outrageously shaped formations, fantastically colored and fit for exploring and photographing. Taken as either a first introduction to the Hole-in-the-Rock Road area, or as a stopping point after longer hiking jaunts farther down the road, Devils Garden may be small but it utterly exemplifies the fascinating yet sometimes bizarre natural topography of this part of southern Utah. Its brevity in scope and nearness to the trailhead makes it especially perfect for children or those who want to see some amazing natural

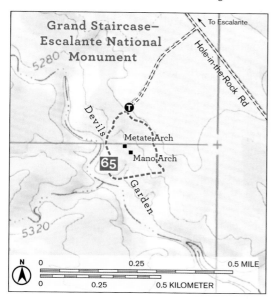

Metate Arch in Devils Garden

beauty but would have a difficult time tackling a more challenging trail. Overlooked by many, this truly is a classic example of canyon country features, and best of all it is easily accessible to nearly all who wish to see it.

From the parking lot, go straight due south into the garden. From hoodoos that resemble anything from howling coyotes to avian sentinels to giant stone guardians à la those on Easter Island, this is a wonderful little place to wander for a while. Here there is no specific trail; instead, this physically small but imaginatively rich natural rock garden invites a meandering exploration that can start and end at any point, dipping into, behind, around, on, over, and through the fanciful shapes.

Slickrock traverses, small dips and scrambles down rough boulders, and well-beaten sandy footpaths leading and crisscrossing in every direction allow you to play choose-your-own-adventure as you wander among the rocks. Like a miniature version of the area's larger-scale natural attractions, Devils Garden still proudly displays its small rounded domes, layered and multicolored hoodoos jutting up at irregular angles and with intriguing moldings, small dry washes racing through the rocks, and mushroom-headed spires.

One particular feature here that attracts many shutterbugs is the small, very graceful arch crossing from a large rock to a smaller yet very sturdy outcropping. You can easily walk beneath it, and many find it manageable to scramble up onto the rock from which the arch springs. Known as Metate Arch, this is a beautiful example of the natural erosional processes that create the stunning, unique beauty that draws so many hikers to these places. Mano Arch, lower-slung and bulkier than Metate, is tucked around a corner nearby. After having explored this fun little playground, return to the parking area.

66 Zebra Slot and Tunnel Slot

Roundtrip: 5.7 miles
Hiking time: 3–4 hours
Elevation gain: 380 feet
Difficulty: easy/moderate
Season: all year
Map: USGS Tenmile Flat
Contact: Grand Staircase–Escalante National Monument

Getting there: From Escalante, go 5 miles east on State Route 12 to the signed Hole-in-the-Rock Road heading southeast (from Boulder, it is 25.7 miles west on SR 12; signs point you in from either direction). Drive 8.2 miles south on the dirt road to park at Halfway Hollow; the unsigned parking area will be on your right just after a cattle guard.
Notes: Map reading skills helpful. Roads may be impassable when wet. Walking through deep water may be required in Tunnel Slot. Very hot in summer.

Once upon a time, there were two very short but very striking slot canyons somewhere out in the vast, forbidding desertscape below a long, low-slung plateau. Some knew of these slots, but neither sign nor trail led to them, so they were semi-guarded secrets. But as is the way with people and technology, these beautiful little slot canyons became heavily photographed, mapped, discussed, and referenced, leading more and more people to them. These two little canyons, now called Zebra and Tunnel, are still gorgeous, and still not marked on either maps or signs, but their secret is long since out, and therefore they can be included in this book. Although they are short, they typify the perfect slot canyon in terms of simple splendor. Zebra easily rivals famed Antelope Canyon in beauty if not in scope, and Tunnel is just a heck of a lot of fun to wander through.

From the parking area, head northeast across Hole-in-the-Rock Road and follow the

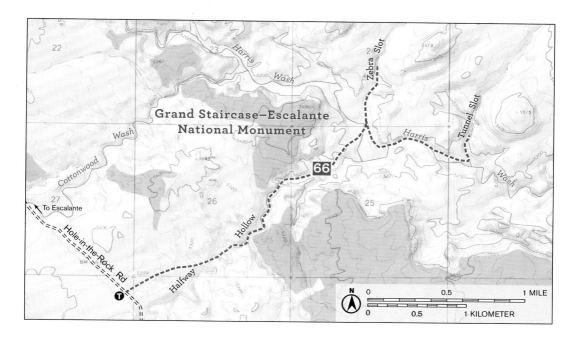

well-trodden footpath. The low rolling hills, covered by sagebrush, do not seem to indicate anything exciting ahead, but know you are heading the right way, especially with the cairns and bootprints along the path. In 0.6 mile you will begin to see slickrock, heralding the approach of the slot canyons. Along the dry streambed bottom, tracks of cattle and humans mark the ground, but you can cut short some of the meandering turns by following paths over the benches on either side. Wooden fencing suspended from a heavy cable stretching across the canyon is sectioned off and relatively easy to push open so you can pass through. After 1.5 miles, Harris Wash comes in from your right, wide and open. Turn left and head north to Zebra Slot. In a mere 0.2 mile a canyon shoots off directly in front of you. Enter this northwest canyon, which is at first fairly wide and dull gray but very soon narrows into the spectacularly striped and colorful Zebra Slot.

Thin, delicate bands of Creamsicle orange layer with bands of creamy white, all smooth and rounded as the canyon walls narrow in, creating

Gorgeous stripes in Zebra Slot

a spectacle of natural beauty that dazzles the eye. These layered, undulating walls are close together but wide enough for most people to pass through. Fine sand on the bottom nestles in hollows between the rounded rock lumps, each little turn inviting further exploration. At the end of the all-too-brief canyon, a dryfall brings you up short. Turn back here to retrace your footsteps out into the main wash.

Hike back out the way you came in; this time you are walking south. Back in wide Harris Wash, turn left and head 0.25 mile northeast to the first side canyon at your left. Walk up this large, rather dull-seeming canyon for another 0.25 mile to get to an abrupt narrowing. The very aptly named Tunnel Slot seems dark and forbidding as you approach it, but it really is quite short at only about 125 feet in length. It may contain deep, cold water—recent storms usually leave water in the canyons—but it also might be utterly dry. Once you have gone through Tunnel Slot, return the way you came and retrace your steps back to the parking area.

67 Spooky Gulch and Peek-a-Boo Gulch

Loop: 3.5 miles
Hiking time: 3–4 hours
Elevation gain: 380 feet
Difficulty: moderate

Season: all year
Map: USGS Big Hollow Wash
Contact: Grand Staircase–Escalante National Monument

Getting there: From Escalante, go 5 miles east on State Route 12 to the signed Hole-in-the-Rock Road heading southeast (from Boulder, it is 25.7 miles west on SR 12; signs point you in from either direction). Drive 26.2 miles down the dirt road and turn left (you may see a small wooden sign that says Dry Fork Trailhead). Continue another 1.7 miles along the very bumpy two-track road to the parking area. During spring and fall, weekends, and holidays the parking lot can be full, but there are pullout spots before you get to the main lot. **Notes:** Flash flooding may occur mid- to late summer. Roads can be impassable when wet. Can be very hot in summer. Very tight slot through Spooky Gulch; larger people may not fit. No camping allowed near trailhead. Routefinding, topographical map reading, and navigation skills required.

Spooky and Peek-a-Boo were long-held secrets of canyon country, but they have exploded in popularity over the last decade or so with the help of some national attention from articles in big publications. These are considered two of the best true slot canyons in southern Utah—particularly the aptly named deep and sometimes dark Spooky—accessible without the use of technical gear. Be aware that a section in each one demands either down-scrambling or up-scrambling. Also, these slots are in no way meant for larger people. Even the skinniest person will need to turn sideways and slither through like an awkward lizard in Spooky's narrowest section.

Traffic jams can and do occur when the canyons are full of visitors. Keep an ear out for the noise of people approaching you, as each canyon can be hiked in either direction, and wait for them to pass if it seems the canyon is getting tighter. The recommended route is hiking up (north) Peek-a-Boo, east across the connecting desert hills and washes, and then down (south) Spooky before returning west along the Dry Fork wash to the parking lot.

The parking area is on the south rim above Dry Fork Coyote Gulch. From this high vantage point you can see across the washes and hills of the desert, but you can't tell there are slot

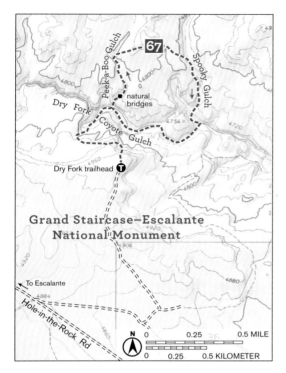

abruptly open up in a wide east-west running wash, which is Dry Fork. At this point, turn east (right). The wide, sandy wash has pockets of large, pretty white flowers known as jimsonweed or datura, which is a potentially fatal hallucinogenic. Take pictures but nothing else of this photogenic plant.

One hundred yards down the wash, the seemingly improbable south entrance to Peek-a-Boo rises to your left in a recess in the cliff wall, about 20 feet above the wash floor. There is often a large pool of water immediately below, which can hamper efforts to climb up and enter here. Footholds have been pecked into the rock, and it isn't that difficult for those who are agile and unafraid of heights. However, if the area below is indeed filled with water, ascending the sandstone with wet soles can be so challenging as to be nearly impossible. Often groups of people will help one another up by providing hands or shoulders or even legs to grab on to. Use your best judgment.

An alternative here is to take a bypass route to the west; it ascends up a long, sandy hill that is easy to walk but can be enervating on hot days. This is routefinding and is not a designated trail. Just to the west of Peek-a-Boo's entrance, head north uphill along what is generally a footpath, although social (and probably some just confused) trails may lead you slightly astray. You can't get too off course here if at any point you simply veer sharply right (east), as you'll reach the canyon drop-off into Peek-a-Boo and thus be able to track it to its easily accessible northern mouth. From that entrance, you can head down it, remembering that at the end you will have to scramble or slide down the southern rock opening to the wash below.

Heading either up or down Peek-a-Boo, you will find thin natural bridges delightfully arcing overhead near the south end, some deeper but quite short sections that may be filled with water, and fun spots to wiggle through or over where water has carved the sandstone into holes and curves. The south end is chamber-like, gradually narrowing as you head north, then opening and widening again into more of a wash.

canyons and may in fact be wondering what all the fuss is about. From the trail register, the marked footpath heads east and north through the low pinyon and juniper trees. Follow it and remember to keep to it as much as you can so new social trails aren't developed. The trail skirts along sandstone ledges, heading east before switchbacking down. It is easy to lose the trail in this section, although you can't really get lost here; follow the cairns down if you see any, or simply look for the marked trail cutting through the sandy section below and aim for it. Once down on this section, the trail heads more north and across a wide, flat area dotted by scrub brush.

When the trail comes to what seems to be a straight wash down, follow it very carefully, as loose scree can make the sandstone path tricky. You will see trails going through sand around the sandstone areas, which can make for better footing. At the bottom of this slide, the trail meanders more easterly through a wash punctuated by very large juniper trees. The path will

Spooky Gulch gets so narrow you cannot pass another human being.

along the Dry Fork wash to the south entrance of Spooky.) Rock formations to the north stand sentry-like over your passage. In 0.5 mile you reach a wide, sandy wash. Here, a trail cuts down the hillside into it. The north entrance to Spooky is to the south, straight down the wash.

Spooky is an amazing slot canyon that tightens and twists and deepens as it heads south. Longer than Peek-a-Boo, it absolutely demands a slimmer physique. Those with bigger builds or chests may need to get down on the ground in some sections, as it is actually slightly wider on the bottom, or forego this hike altogether. It is literally impossible to pass another human being in the narrowest serpentine section, so make sure to wait for others heading in the opposite direction to pass before you continue. You will also need to take off your daypack and either push it before you or tug it along behind. Sometimes people leave their packs at the entrance to either canyon and retrieve them afterward.

Once the wash narrows into the actual slot section, you will encounter the most technical aspect of the canyon and the reason it is best to hike it north to south. Going upcanyon can make this a much more serious challenge than many hikers will be prepared for; coming down is somewhat easier. Large, tightly wedged boulders demand scrambling, wedging, and dropping down about 10 feet to the canyon floor in two different sections. There are some hand- and footholds that can help. A fear of heights or a short stature can make this section tricky, although people are usually able to help one another through it.

After this part the fun really begins when the slot tightens. Wavy lines on the canyon walls fascinate the eyes, and sharp little bumps on the sandstone may shred your clothing or skin if you're not careful. You know you are nearing the end when the slot opens up and you can walk normally again. After you tumble back out into Dry Fork Coyote Gulch wash, blinking from the sudden sunlight, make your way back west up the wash, keeping an eye out for the wooden sign to your left (south) about 100 yards past the opening to Peek-a-Boo that will direct you back uphill to the parking area.

Once you exit Peek-a-Boo's north end when it opens up at about 0.65 mile in, you should notice a path leading generally east across the sandy hills and dips. (It can be easy to miss this or lose the trail on the way over to Spooky. If you do, return back down Peek-a-Boo, then walk east

68 *Coyote Gulch*

Roundtrip: 26.4 miles
Hiking time: 2–4 days
Elevation gain: 900 feet
Difficulty: moderate
Season: all year

Map: USGS Big Hollow Wash, King Mesa, Stevens Canyon South
Contact: Grand Staircase–Escalante National Monument

Getting there: From Escalante, head east on State Route 12 for 5 miles to Hole-in-the-Rock Road. Turn south and drive 34 miles on this dirt road to Hurricane Wash, which is marked by a wooden sign. Parking is on the right-hand side (west) of the road, although 4WD vehicles may make it in an additional 0.3 mile to the trail register and smaller parking area. **Notes:** Flash flooding may occur mid- to late summer; do not enter canyon if storms threaten. An early start is highly recommended in summer. Wading through water in sections is necessary. Free overnight permit required. Free camping allowed at trailheads. Roads may be impassable when wet. 4WD recommended, especially for last 0.3 mile of road to trailhead register, although parking before then is also available. No pets allowed. Although vault toilets are in the canyon, visitors are required to pack out solid waste.

Surprisingly riparian canyon floor in Coyote Gulch (Photo by Kay Luther)

Stunning and grand, Coyote Gulch is considered by many to be the pinnacle of southern Utah hiking. A massive, breathtaking arch, gracefully towering sandstone canyon walls, a lush riparian area winding through the desert, small waterfalls, and smaller but still impressive arches all adorn this large, popular gulch. Find your way here midweek if possible to avoid crowds and to be able to choose the best campsites in the gulch. Coyote Gulch serves as an excellent ambassador for Grand Staircase–Escalante hikes, and parts can be done as day hikes, but at least a one-night backpack is recommended in order to more fully experience this gorgeous landscape.

From the Hurricane Wash trailhead register, go east and down into the wash. Although this initial sandy traverse can seem long and rather barren, not to mention hot and dry, it also makes the approach easy for children and those uncomfortable with the slickrock heights at some other entry points. Leave early enough in the morning to be sure the heat of the day will occur when you're down in the gulch itself, with access to the cool waters of the stream. This dry section of Hurricane Wash actually follows an old two-track road, leading you to a hiker's maze fence that will allow humans but not cows to pass through and continue on.

After 1.8 miles, continue to head right (east) to follow the drainage for another 2 miles. Eventually you will spot the giant walls of Navajo sandstone that herald the goal of this hike: Coyote Gulch. Keep your beautiful destination in mind as you push through the shadeless deep sand. Close to the water-bearing gulch, cottonwood trees and willows start to make a welcome appearance, adding delightful green contrast to the amber and gold hues of the wash bed and rock walls. You reach the actual confluence with Coyote Gulch 5.1 miles from the trailhead, and here the lovelier part of the hike is finally revealed. Head down the canyon (upstream) to the right (south). At this point you may start to spend significant time walking in the stream itself, whether by choice or necessity, so bringing

along a pair of shoes you don't mind getting wet can be a help. Ample shade is now available as well, slanted down by the canyon walls.

The desert-varnished cliffs soar to tremendous heights around you as you continue toward the heart of Coyote Gulch. At 6.5 miles, you will have your first jaw-dropping view of Jacob Hamblin Arch, what might be called the granddaddy of arches for its scale, width, and soaring beauty. Spanning 102 feet across, with the bottom part of the arch rising 80 feet above the stream floor, it's a treasure for photographers.

Originally known as Lobo Arch for an ill-fated wolf who suffered the typical fatal consequences of meeting thoughtless and decidedly non-conservationist ranchers, the arch was renamed after a converted Latter-day Saint missionary sent to similarly convert Native Americans in southern Utah in the 1850s. Perfect campsites are located near this arch, which is 7 miles in from your starting point. Immediately beyond the arch are springs that seep from the canyon wall on your left (north), which also makes this area a good choice for spending the night. However, if you're here on a weekend or over spring break, be aware that many other hikers may have the same idea.

Copper-hued Kayenta ledges catch the eye as you meander down through the canyon. When you are 1.7 miles from Jacob Hamblin Arch, stream water cascades over slickrock ledges. Nine miles in, Coyote Natural Bridge presents itself. Nearly as spectacular as Jacob Hamblin Arch, the bridge is beautifully framed by well-watered greenery. Another spring dribbles down the north wall just past the bridge. As you amble along and through the stream, small, pretty waterfalls drop over the ledges just below another arch known as Cliff Arch, although many also know it as Jug Handle Arch, located 11 miles into your hike. The falls are passable through careful downclimbing.

The walls overhead begin to squeeze in now, rising over 600 feet above your head. A trail leading out of the gulch, known as Crack in the Wall for literal reasons, rises above at the 13-mile mark. In just another 0.2 mile you will tumble

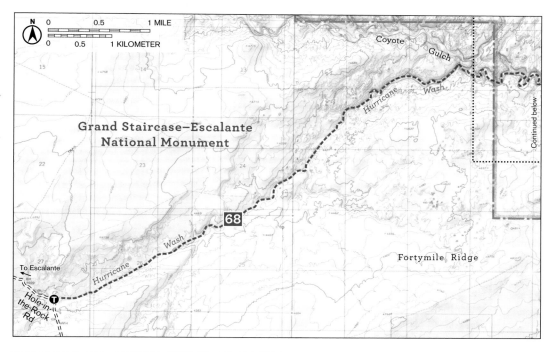

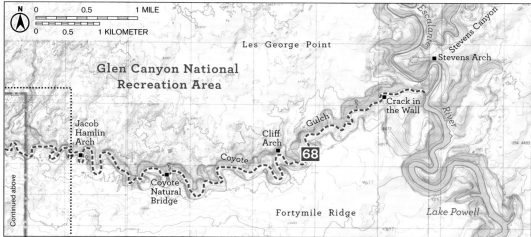

into the confluence with the Escalante River, which is marked by an abundance of riparian life and the classic features of whitish Navajo sandstone domes swelling up toward the sky. Depending on water levels, the river here can be high, although in recent years it has hovered at the shallower side. Stevens Arch is visible just a ways upstream. Return to the Hurricane Wash trailhead the same way, enjoying the views from the other direction.

69 *Willow Gulch–Broken Bow Arch*

Roundtrip: 4.7 miles
Hiking time: 2–3 hours
Elevation gain: 900 feet
Difficulty: easy
Season: all year

Map: USGS Sooner Bench, Davis Gulch
Contact: Grand Staircase–Escalante National Monument, Glen Canyon National Recreation Area

Getting there: From Escalante, head east on State Route 12 for 5 miles to Hole-in-the-Rock Road. Turn south on this dirt road. You will pass well-marked Dance Hall Rock on your left at 37.9 miles, then signed Carcass Wash at 40.5 miles. At 43 miles (1 mile south of Sooner Wash), look for a dirt road to your left (east), which should be signed County Road 276. Drive east on this spur road for 1.4 miles to the trailhead register and parking area. **Notes:** Free overnight permit required. An early start is highly recommended during hotter months. Walking through water may be required. Free camping allowed at trailheads. 4WD recommended. Roads may be impassable when wet.

Although just driving to the Willow Gulch trailhead can be a significant endeavor in itself, it is a trip well worth making to see the gorgeous Navajo sandstone domes, walls, and arches of this canyon, particularly distinguished Broken Bow Arch. Making for a perfect day hike, Willow Gulch displays some of the best scenery this part of southern Utah has to offer, helping you understand why so many love the Grand Staircase–Escalante area and extol the virtues of hiking here.

From the trailhead, strike off northeast and head down a sloping, sandy hillside toward the canyon below, enjoying the intriguing shapes of hoodoos and domes as you descend. Once in Cottonwood Wash you continue generally east, through the usually dry, wide area. A brief narrows section is fun to walk through, although it

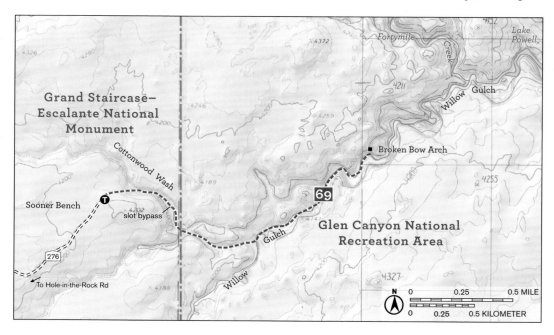

can be bypassed to the south as well. The canyon opens up again and soon you pass the boundary into Glen Canyon National Recreation Area about 0.5 mile in. One mile in is the confluence with Willow Gulch; turn left to continue eastward along the gulch. A thin riparian area stretches along the watercourse through here, supporting the growth of willows and invasive yet hardy tamarisk.

When you round a corner and the massive Broken Bow Arch comes into view, it really is breathtaking. Soaring at a sharp angle 170 feet into the air, this large arch is fascinating not only for its beauty but for the improbability that anything could have carved through its thickness to create such a beautiful piece of natural architecture. Intermittent yet persistent water flow through the many years ensured this arch's formation. Its stature is such that many who see it consider it one of the finest examples of natural arches in the area. Standing directly beneath this behemoth gives a strong idea of its scale and scope as it rises far above.

After taking in your fill of the scenery, return to the parking area the same way, being sure to turn slightly right (west) at Cottonwood Wash rather than erroneously continuing up Willow Gulch.

Huge, impressive Broken Bow Arch

70 *Pelican Canyon–Fishlake Hightop*

Roundtrip: 11 miles
Hiking time: 5–6 hours
Elevation gain: 2513 feet
Difficulty: moderate

Season: spring–fall
Map: USGS Fish Lake
Contact: Fishlake National Forest, Fremont River Ranger District

Getting there: From the intersection of I-70 and State Route 24 near Richfield, drive 34.3 miles south on SR 24 to the turnoff for State Route 25. Turn left (east) and drive 10 miles to the signed Pelican Overlook turnoff. Turn left (west) here and drive 1 rough dirt mile to the trailhead parking. Alternatively, from Torrey, drive 22 miles west and north on SR 24 to the turnoff for SR 25. Turn right (east) and drive 10 miles to the signed Pelican Overlook turnoff. Turn left (west) here and drive 1 mile to the trailhead parking. **Notes:** Seasonal campgrounds, RV hookup sites, lodges, cabins, restaurant, general store all accessible before the trailhead. Routefinding and map reading skills useful. May be impassable in winter due to snow and road closure.

Covering 2500 acres, gorgeous Fish Lake is Utah's largest natural mountain lake, situated in a beautiful setting with rolling hills covered in aspen trees and tall pines. One hundred ninety-one miles south of Salt Lake City and only 42 miles northwest of Capitol Reef National Park, the Fish Lake area is accessible but not overrun with crowds, even during the busier summer season. Settled centuries ago by Fremont Indians, the area was also a passageway along the epic Old Spanish Trail. Modern markers and interpretive signs mark some of the old route. The Pelican Canyon Trail winds you through the green hillsides, offering views of shimmering Fish Lake and beckoning you toward the heights of the mountain for beautiful vistas. In the summer, the trail, on the west side of the lake, sports wildflowers and the soft rustle of the breeze through aspen leaves. In the fall, the changing colors are utterly spectacular and not to be missed if you plan a trip to the general area.

From the trailhead, go west along the trail. Sagebrush hills first greet you, eventually undulating their way into a glacial valley with aspens. At 0.25 mile in, you will encounter a trail fork with a sign indicating Pelican Canyon Trail, Rock Spring and Gahew Spring; continue along the left fork, slightly uphill and still west. Follow the signs indicating Fishlake Hightop and Tasha Springs so as not to get confused by other social trails heading off in different directions. The

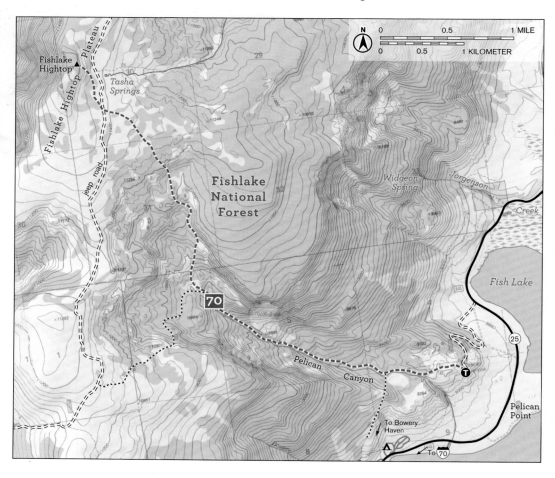

Perfect mountain stream rolling through an aspen-filled meadow on the Pelican Canyon Trail

aspen trees here are not part of Pando, an aspen colony farther south near the Doctor Creek campground area that is considered to be among the largest living organisms in the world because all trees in it are genetically identical clones. Nevertheless, the aspens here are still beautiful as you tackle the hike upward.

At 2 miles in you will see a set of signs. Follow the one that says "Right Fork Pelican Canyon Trail #4368," indicating another 2 miles to Fishlake Hightop. The landscape flattens out into a plateau, then into aspens again, then into plateau. Be sure to look behind you at some points to see the view spreading out to the east. On the plateau sections it can sometimes be easy to lose the trail; cairns might be present, but keep heading north toward a rocky finger, which is your destination. Once at the rise of volcanic boulders officially called Osiris trachyte, clamber up and around them to find the 11,633-foot high point of Fishlake Hightop. The views roll on in every direction from here. Once done taking in your fill of the sights, return to the trailhead via the same trail.

71 Spring Canyon

One-way: 10 miles
Hiking time: 6–7 hours
Elevation gain: 290 feet
Difficulty: moderate

Season: all year
Map: USGS Fruita
Contact: Capitol Reef National Park

Getting there: *Chimney Rock trailhead:* From the Capitol Reef visitor center, drive 3 miles west on State Route 24 to the marked Chimney Rock parking area on the right (east) side of the highway. *Spring Canyon shuttle vehicle parking:* From the visitor center, drive 4 miles east on SR 24 to mile marker 83. Park in the large pullout to the right (south) immediately east of the mile marker, or in the one directly across the highway. **Notes:** Flash flooding may occur mid- to late summer; do not enter if storms threaten. An early start is highly recommended in summer. Walking through water required. Be sure Fremont River is not flowing too high, as crossing it is necessary. Shuttle vehicle necessary. Vault toilet in Chimney Rock trailhead parking lot. No fee required.

Spring Canyon is a beautiful, relatively easy hike with soaring red cliffs, a brief narrows section, pockets of fabulous wildflower displays in late spring and summer, and the sense of a remote backcountry experience that is easily accessible from the highway. The trail winds through patches of scrubby vegetation including the hardy pinyon and juniper trees found extensively throughout the Colorado Plateau. Dusty gray-green clumps of roundleaf buffaloberry also make an appearance, as do intriguing delicate desert trumpet plants. Along the initial section, keep an eye out for petrified wood chunks both on and alongside the trail. If you look carefully,

Prickly pear cactus shows off its stunning bloom in Spring Canyon.

you can see chunks laid out in the fallen, broken form of the living trees they once were. Please remember to only take pictures.

The starting point for this west to east hike is the Chimney Rock trailhead, from which you first notice the dramatic geologic forces that have slowly worked over millennia to create the jagged outlines of cliffs, monoliths, and land upthrusts that fascinate visitors. From the parking lot, the trail leaves northeast across the red Moenkopi layer, although it almost immediately begins to wind southward. It soon ascends a series of switchbacks, through a grayish-white bentonitic sandstone layer known as Chinle, that quickly exercise your lungs. As you climb, the red Wingate walls that lead into Spring Canyon become visible to the southeast. Just 1.3 miles from the parking area you reach the trail junction that splits between Chimney Rock and Spring Canyon. Take the left fork as directed.

The trail descends into a wash leading into wide Chimney Rock Canyon, which runs southwest to northeast. Tall cliff walls on either side highlight the very easy walking through this canyon; in places they are pockmarked with wind-created solution cavities and sometimes painted with desert varnish. Bighorn sheep have been spotted in the canyon here, so be on the lookout for them. It is far more likely that they will see you than that you will ever glimpse these curious yet shy creatures, however. In 3 miles you will come across a trail sign. To your left is Upper Spring Canyon, while your route heads south and east. From this open, grassy area, which in the springtime can have bobbing patches of soft orange globemallow plants, it is 6.5 miles to Spring Canyon's terminus at State Route 24.

The red walls of the canyon soon spread out as you continue down, revealing Kayenta ledges

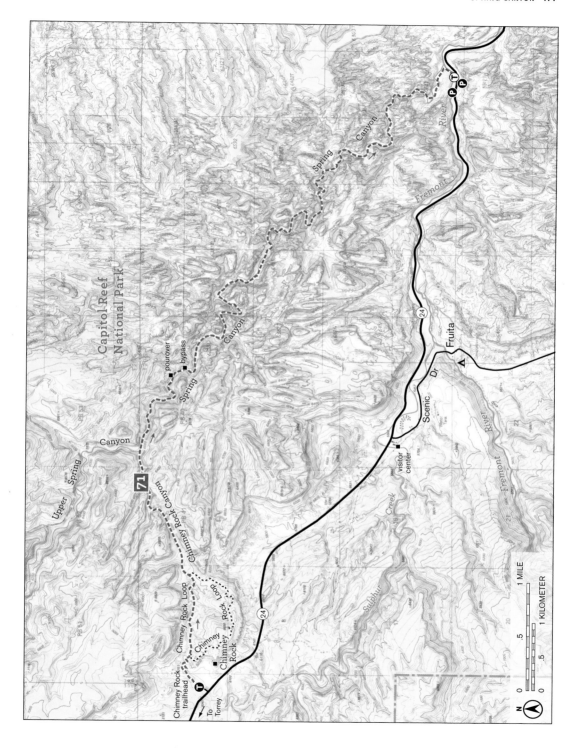

Capitol Reef
National Park

Spring   Canyon

Fremont   River

P T
P

Spring   Canyon

Canyon

pourover bypass

Spring

Upper Spring   Canyon

71

Chimney Rock Canyon

Chimney Rock Loop

Chimney Rock Loop

Chimney Rock Loop

Chimney Rock

Chimney Rock

Chimney Rock
trailhead

T

To
Torrey

24

24

Fruita

Scenic Dr.

visitor
center

Sulphur Creek

Fremont   River

N

0
0

.5
.5

1 MILE

1 KILOMETER

and black volcanic boulders scattered here and there. From here until the end the hike can generally be exposed to sun, which makes this trip far more pleasant from April through May or from late September through early November than during summer months, when heat can be brutal. After rounding a gentle corner that then steers you more south, the wash constricts into a brief narrows section that can be fun to amble through. Earlier-spring trips can mean there are water pools through this section, however, which you may want to avoid by taking the bypass on your left-hand side. You will have to do this anyway after a few minutes of narrows navigation, as that part of it abruptly ends at a steep, impassable pourover.

Just past the pourover on the bypass trail you will traverse a fairly narrow section close to the edge. While safe as long as hikers carefully watch their footing, this might cause anyone with vertigo to look determinedly away from the drop-off to the right! The trail skirts the canyon below for a short ways before coming to another steep section on which the trail might seem extremely narrow or perilous, depending on your comfort with heights. During weather events this portion of the trail can easily be wiped out as well; if that has happened, it could mean the end of this hike for the day. After navigating this brief part the trail swiftly drops back to the wash below and a wide, flat surface for walking. At this point you could choose to walk back up the narrows for a ways to explore the small canyon you just passed above.

Once headed back down, the trail ambles pleasantly through the wash. Sandstone walls rise on both sides, and small stream-smoothed boulders and rocks litter the sandy wash. Farther downstream green box elder and cottonwood trees start to appear in small clumps. These provide great little spots for rests, particularly if the day is warm. About 6 miles in there may be a pool of water to negotiate, depending on what time of year you do this hike, but it is passable. Past this point benches rise now and again on either side of the wash; in the spring months, colorful flower riots can make this an exceptionally lovely section. Prickly pear, rough mules ears, and globemallow may dot or even carpet small areas.

When the wash widens again, you are getting close to the Fremont River. A huge overhang on the right makes for cool walking under its varnished leaning wall. Just past the overhang you will suddenly be presented with what seems like a jungle of tamarisk and willows. Bushwhacking is pretty much a necessity here, although social trails exist and you can't get lost. In 0.4 mile you'll reach the Fremont River; finding places to cross is usually fairly straightforward. Head 0.2 mile west along SR 24 to the shuttle vehicle.

72 Cohab Canyon–Frying Pan–Cassidy Arch

One-way: 5.6 miles
Hiking time: 4–6 hours
Elevation gain: 1020 feet
Difficulty: moderate

Season: spring–fall
Map: USGS Fruita
Contact: Capitol Reef National Park

Getting there: *Cohab Canyon trailhead:* From the Capitol Reef visitor center, turn south onto Scenic Drive and proceed 1.2 miles. You will see a large wooden barn on the right (west); park in the pullout area across from it to the east. The trailhead is just to the southwest down the road, on the south side of the road. Even more parking spots are available 200 yards north of the trailhead at the picnic area on the east side of Scenic Drive *Shuttle vehicle parking at Grand Wash trailhead:* Drive 2.2 miles south from the Cohab Canyon trailhead on the paved Scenic Drive to the graded dirt Grand Wash Road; turn left (east) and drive another 1.3 miles to the parking area. **Notes:** Pay fee for Scenic Drive (Cassidy Arch trailhead) at self-serve kiosk just south of the campground along the drive. Shuttle vehicle necessary, unless willing to retrace steps. Can be very hot in summer. Lightning exposure during thunderstorms. Flush toilets in campground; vault toilets at Grand Wash parking area off Scenic Drive.

This stunning combination of three trails offers a trip right into the sandstone heart of Capitol Reef National Park. There are two choices of starting point for Cohab Canyon: a trailhead on State Route 24 or the one on the Scenic Drive, just by the campground. This route starts from the Scenic Drive trailhead for less driving time, and the stroll down the canyon itself is more breathtaking from its western end. Additionally, if you are staying at the campground the trailhead is a mere 100 yards away down the paved road, just across from and slightly southwest of the imposing barn.

From the Cohab Canyon trailhead, you will immediately begin to head uphill. The initial 22 switchbacks are perhaps the most strenuous part of the hike, and it's nice to conquer them right away. If you pause for breathers along the way, the views become only more stunning the higher you go. At the top, the trail meanders southward before a sharp turn left (east) into Cohab Canyon itself. Supposedly named after "cohabitation," the moniker is a nod to the polygamist-settler history of the area.

Once you enter the canyon, cliff walls soar up on either side. To the north the yellow-red walls are pocked with holes rather unappealingly known as solution cavities. Scoured out by millennia of winds whipping sand particles, these holes add fascinating texture to photos and intrigue the imagination. During the spring months, you will usually see many wildflowers through here, including dusty red Indian paintbrush, soft orange globemallow, and crystal red penstemon. As you head deeper into the canyon, drainages open up to the south. Called the Wives, these drainages present seven slot canyons that can be attempted by those with the proper gear and knowledge. Otherwise, simply explore as far into any one of them as you are able before turning back to the main trail. These little side canyons also offer shady spots to rest during the hot months.

Cassidy Arch as seen from the trail

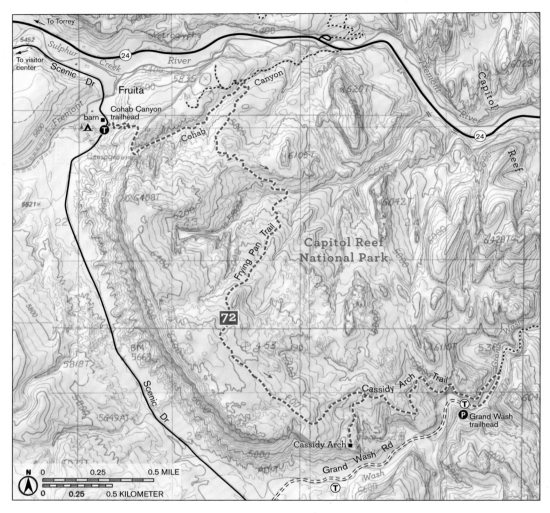

At 0.9 mile in, a wooden sign alerts you to the fact that the trail will follow the wash below. Here you get to walk along red and cream-colored slickrock, peering down into water-pockets that may hold water, depending on the season. Black volcanic boulders scatter across the russet-colored sandstone. Cairns should direct you down and around, although you won't get lost without them. Just past 1 mile there is a sign for the Fruita Orchard Overlook to the north, which is a pleasant but not essential view. Just 100 yards past this sign the trail turns to the right (south) and uphill. A few yards into the ascent there will be two more wooden signs indicating that you can either head left (east) toward SR 24, or south (right and uphill) to the Frying Pan Trail. Go south here.

After curving around a bit, the trail lands on top of the ridge above the canyon you just came through, offering an excellent view of Navajo sandstone domes and spires, to the north, and the rounded tangerine dollops of sandstone that top Cohab Canyon. The trail then really opens up, taking you through low juniper and pinyon scrub and revealing the rocky benches and turns and canyons you will pass. On this section of the hike, the Frying Pan, you are fairly unlikely to run into other people, since most do either Cohab

Canyon or Cassidy Arch and not this connector. The serenity and silence can be deeply peaceful as you head deeper in the heart of the park.

Meander up and down small inclines and some flatter sections, enjoying the views and solitude along the way. You will reach the highest section of the trail in 2 miles, at which point you might catch a glimpse of the La Sal Mountains far to the east if the day is clear enough. Keep heading south for 1 mile to where the trail diverges. A sign indicates it is 0.5 mile south to Cassidy Arch. Head in that direction as your trail swiftly turns to slickrock, with many rock cairns along the way to help you find the route.

Cassidy Arch is unusual in that you will be somewhat above it upon when you view it, rather than standing below it as with most arches. There is plenty of space stretching around the arch to sit and look at it, take pictures, or gaze into the rocky jumble of sandstone to the east. The arch is named after one of the west's most well-known outlaws, Butch Cassidy; legend holds that he visited the area back in his heyday.

After enjoying the arch, return north along the spur trail to the junction point with the Frying Pan Trail and head south and down along what is now officially the Cassidy Arch Trail. The remaining 1 mile to the canyon floor of Grand Wash winds alongside Wingate cliffs and Kayenta ledges, offering up a pleasant descent. Once at the sandy wash bottom, turn right and head west about 0.25 mile to the Grand Wash parking area.

73 *Hickman Bridge*

Roundtrip: 1.8 miles
Hiking time: 1–2 hours
Elevation gain: 400 feet
Difficulty: easy

Season: all year
Map: USGS Fruita
Contact: Capitol Reef National Park

Getting there: From the Capitol Reef visitor center, drive 2 miles east on State Route 24 to the large Hickman Bridge parking area on the left (north) side of the highway. **Notes:** An early start is recommended in summer. Vault toilets at parking lot.

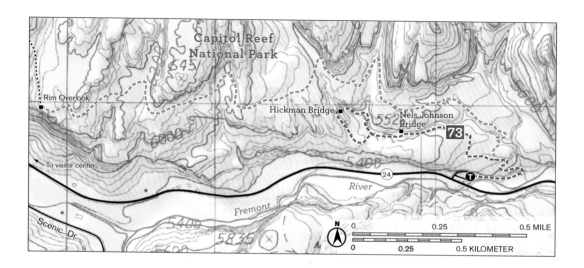

View of Hickman Bridge

While short, the Hickman Bridge Trail pro- vides classic examples of Capitol Reef geology and ancient Native American history. The natural bridge is actually quite spectacular and offers fantastic vantages for photos or sim- ply taking in its beauty. The brevity and relative ease of this hike make this an excellent choice for children, those with limited time, and those less sure of their hiking ability. The bridge is named after local settler and educator Joseph Hickman, a visionary of the tourist industry who played a large part in creating what would eventually become Capitol Reef National Park.

From the parking lot, head east toward the trail and pick up a trail guide if you desire. Pass alongside the river and head up switchbacked rock ledges onto sloping hillsides, where the openness allows for expanding views of the large rock walls and monoliths surrounding you. Less than half a mile from the trailhead you will come across a wooden sign indicating a trail split. Take the left- hand route to Hickman Bridge, 0.7 mile away. At this point you have a stellar view of Navajo Dome, which rises majestically directly behind the sign.

The trail skirts a wash, then drops down into it. After rising out again, keep an eye out on the north wall for a Fremont Indian granary tucked into a little alcove above the trail. Just 100 yards past this remnant of long-gone local inhabitants you will find a small bridge spanning the wash. Named the Nels Johnson Bridge, it is a lasting, if little-known, homage to one of the more recent pioneer settlers in the area.

After coming back up out of the wash again, you will find a fork in the trail. For a more impres- sive first view of Hickman Bridge, choose the right fork, which will lead you directly under the bridge itself. Here is where you'll realize the actual scope of the natural formation, which mea- sures 133 feet from end to end and soars 125 feet above the ground you stand upon. Streaked with dark desert varnish, the thick bridge gracefully rises up to provide a nice contrast with the sky above. You'll notice the tumble of huge rocks beneath it, which are testament to the significant and ongoing natural processes that created and will continue to shape the bridge. Head uphill on the marked path to reach a point somewhat behind the bridge so you can turn around and admire the view to the east through it.

From here the trail winds south and then east, gently descending in a small loop to return you to where the path forked above the wash. Return back to the parking lot along the same trail, being certain to appreciate the views going in the opposite direction.

Extending your hike: For those seeking a longer, more strenuous, yet extremely rewarding hike, return to the initial trail split and hike 2 miles west to the Rim Overlook (also described in Hike 74), for an added roundtrip mileage of 4 miles and elevation gain of 1100 feet. It offers a spectacular view of Capitol Reef orchards and the winding Fremont River far below.

74 *Navajo Knobs*

Roundtrip: 9.3 miles
Hiking time: 5–6 hours
Elevation gain: 2400 feet
Difficulty: hard

Season: all year
Map: USGS Fruita
Contact: Capitol Reef National Park

Getting there: From the visitor center, drive 2 miles east on State Route 24 to the large Hickman Bridge parking area on the left (north) side of the highway. **Notes:** Can be very hot in summer. Lightning danger during thunderstorms due to exposure. Vault toilet at parking area.

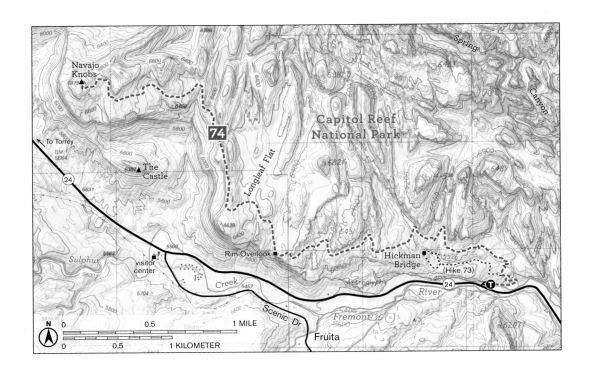

Heading up the Navajo Knobs Trail

Hickman Bridge Trail, Hike 73), the crowds sharply dissipate as you continue toward the knobs, making this hike one of the more tranquil of the trails directly accessible from the highway.

From the Hickman Bridge parking lot, set out eastward on the trail, which follows the base of the red cliffs on its north side, paralleling the sweet gurgle of the Fremont River for a few minutes. In the fall months, swaths of yellow rubber rabbitbrush and changing leaves on the cottonwood trees make this little section a visual feast. Soon, the trail turns up and away, heading northward. Basalt boulders dot the sandstone ledges, giving rise to visions of ancient volcanoes erupting and tossing chunks of lava for miles. In reality, the lava flow cap of nearby Boulder Mountain merely boiled over from the pressures beneath it, sending rivers of molten rocks down the slopes to be carried out to the surrounding desert and canyon lands via stream action and floods. The black rocks do provide great contrast to the buff and brick colors of sandstone layers, however, and also make for an excellent backdrop to the spring flowers that sometimes crop up right in front of them. Prickly pear and claret cup cacti can provide especially showy blooms that are a photographer's delight. In 0.4 mile you reach the junction with the Hickman Bridge Trail; continue to the north (right) for Navajo Knobs.

After briefly dropping into a wash, the trail continues on slickrock, circling the cliffs, moving with the bend of the land, and continually rising. Flat areas relieve the climb, which is not particularly arduous at this point. At 2 miles you've reached the Rim Overlook, which does indeed provide a dramatic vista to the west over the rim. From here, you can spy down into the orchards and the visitor center and other buildings, and observe the tilting rise of the land toward the western horizon, as well as see the gorgeous sweeps of rocky landscapes to the south and east.

Continue upward for the next 2.5 miles to Navajo Knobs. The trail dips down, curves around the natural sandstone wall concavities and convexities, and eventually leads you up a long, broad sandstone ramp, which due to its shadeless exposure can be exceptionally hot on

You will feel every inch of this sublime hike due to its significant elevation gain. But the reward for it is just as vast in terms of the incredible views that await you along the way and at the very top. The scenery from the Navajo Knobs is more than spectacular as it stretches out in every direction, from Thousand Lake Mountain to the northwest to Boulder Mountain to the southwest and the Henry Mountains to the southeast. The rumpled, rippling canyon country of Capitol Reef is exposed to your bird's-eye view, making the scope of this park truly visible and even more impressive as you realize how much vast wilderness surrounds you. Although you will likely encounter an abundance of other hikers during the first mile or so of this trail (since it coincides with the start of the popular but far shorter sunny summer days. As you approach the knobs themselves—which will be visible above you to your north during the last half mile—watch for the trail to sharply bend right, inviting you to scramble up the side of the knobs for the last hundred-odd feet. Perched on top of the knobs (this may not be feasible for those with any fear of heights), you can scan the 360-degree outlook for as long as you want. These views are unparalleled and worth a long time observing. When you're done, head back down the same route to the parking area.

75 Golden Throne

Roundtrip: 4 miles
Hiking time: 2–3 hours
Elevation gain: 730 feet
Difficulty: moderate

Season: all year
Map: USGS Golden Throne
Contact: Capitol Reef National Park

Getting there: From the Capitol Reef visitor center, turn south onto the Scenic Drive for 7.8 miles to the end of the pavement. Turn left (east) onto the graded dirt Capitol Gorge Road and drive another 2.2 miles to the road's terminus in a parking area.
Notes: Fee required for Scenic Drive. An early start is recommended during the hotter summer months. Scenic Drive may be closed if there is flood potential.

Like a stately buttress rising into the sky, the Golden Throne is a majestic piece of natural architecture that is truly eye-catching. A giant piece of Navajo sandstone, it is somewhat unusual due its regal yellow color, which isn't often found in the more commonly whitish Navajo formation. The shape intrigues as well, being large and roughly circular as its sits in its position high on the reef, commanding quite the view of the park. Canyons, sandstone walls, and beautiful views of the Henry Mountains to the east all collaborate to make this hike incredibly scenic the entire way. Its location well down the Scenic Drive, then down the dirt Capitol Gorge Road, also ensures that fewer people tackle it, which generally means more solitude for the hiker in which to enjoy the sensational natural contours, designs, and views of Capitol Reef.

The trail begins in the northwest corner of the parking area, almost immediately rising up past the sandstone

The Golden Throne

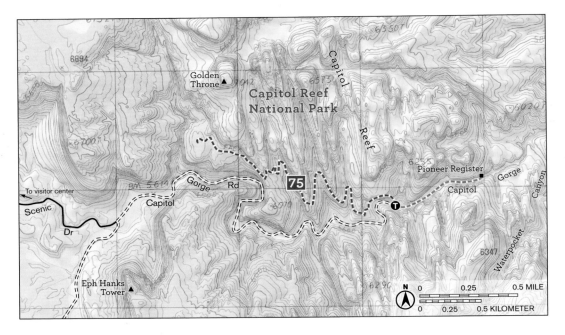

walls. It circumnavigates deep grooves of natural drainages as it winds high above Capitol Gorge. First in a westerly direction, you swiftly climb above the canyon floor. You'll be able to see along the Capitol Gorge Road you entered on and get a sense of the massive canyon walls curving through this area. The trail bends a bit, then generally heads north, fairly soon veering away from the road below and drawing you deeper into the canyons. Flattening along shrubby sections, then winding against the cliffs again, then widening once more, the trail curves through the landscape, where rugged plants firmly settle themselves into the dry earth. Pinyon, juniper, the spiny fingers of Mormon tea, prickly pear cactus, and other plants all seem to thrive in their high desert home, decorating the flat sections as the trail climbs, then flattens several more times.

Fins and slabs of sandstone rise around as the path follows through a canyon. Individual rocks may be cerise in color, or streaked and splotched with mauve, cantaloupe, or citron. The sheer beauty of the area lies in the meeting of slickrock and sky, the dusty green buffaloberry bushes against the red sand dirt, and the sense of being set loose in a jungle of sandstone. Once in the flatter juniper- and pinyon-dotted section, turn around to see the bulk of the Henry Mountains lifting up behind the sandstone canyon walls to your east. This is a spectacular view with its beautiful juxtaposition of alpine mountains in the distance and slickrock canyon country in your foreground—and, in fact, surrounding you on all sides.

Eventually you reach a ragged slickrock bowl where a sign proclaims that you are at trail's end. The Golden Throne rises in all its grandeur to the north, dominating the view as it juts up behind a valley of creamy sandstone. Although you can continue on from here if you'd like to try to get closer to the sandstone monolith, there is no trail and you'd be heading cross-country, which is only advisable if you have a good map and understand how to read it. From here, simply return to the parking area via the same route, which allows you to enjoy the stellar views of the distant mountains behind the sandstone along a portion of the way.

Extending your hike: From the Golden Throne trailhead, walk east along the main canyon to reach the Pioneer Register. At 0.6 mile in, look up on the left-hand side of the canyon walls to see, scratched into the rock, the names and dates of people who passed through here in the 1800s. The thick, dark substance that makes up some of the names was presumably axle grease from wagon wheels. These intriguing signatures are protected by law, and it is illegal to add anything to this panel.

76 Upper Muley Twist Canyon/Strike Valley Overlook

Loop: 9 miles (15 if entrance road is impassable or if in a low-clearance vehicle)
Hiking time: 6–9 hours
Elevation gain: 1100 feet
Difficulty: hard

Season: spring, fall
Map: USGS Bitter Creek Divide, Wagon Box Mesa
Contact: Capitol Reef National Park

Getting there: From the Capitol Reef visitor center, drive 9.3 miles east on State Route 24 to the Notom Road turnoff and turn right (south). The first 10 miles of Notom Road are paved; after that the road is graded dirt. Continue south on the Notom-Bullfrog Road for 32.5 miles to the Burr Trail turnoff. Turn right (west) and drive up the switchbacks for 3.1 miles to the signed Upper Muley Twist Canyon turnoff on your right (north). Alternatively, from Boulder, just where SR 12 sharply curves west by the Burr Trail Grill, the signed Burr Trail heads east. Turn east here and drive 30.5 miles on paved road through Grand Staircase–Escalante National Monument. At the Capitol Reef boundary, the road becomes graded dirt. From there it is 2.2 miles to the signed Upper Muley Twist Canyon turnoff on your left (north). Drive 3 miles in a wash to the trailhead parking area. Low-clearance vehicles may have to park at the turnoff; doing this would make the roundtrip hike 15 miles.
Notes: Roads may be impassable when wet. Vehicle type and clearance will dictate trail mileage; a high-clearance 4WD vehicle is likely needed to access trailhead. However, road goes through a beautiful wash, so don't let walking it deter you. No fee necessary.

The warm lower elevations of Capitol Reef's southern half beckon in early spring and again in fall. Fairly exposed most of the way, Upper Muley Twist is an excellent choice when the weather is cooler. The unusual, memorable name comes from a legend about nearby Lower Muley Twist Canyon, which was called "narrow enough to twist a mule." As you approach the trailhead from the Burr Trail, look for Peek-a-Boo Arch in a sandstone wall to the east. Framed against that deep blue southern Utah sky, the white sandstone of this thick, unusual-looking arch contrasts with the leaping spines of red sandstone curving out of the landscape in front of it like the back of some ancient dinosaur.

The Upper Muley Twist loop has a low canyon-bottom section and a high canyon-rim section. The suggested route starts in the canyon and circles around to the rim in a clockwise direction. Going this way, the elevation gain is less pronounced, and the rock scrambling sections are mostly uphill, which tends to be more appealing than facing them downhill. From the Strike Valley parking area, head north through the canyon up the wash. Almost immediately, you are surrounded by burnt umber and cream-colored cliffs pocked with solution cavities (holes carved out by years of wind-tossed sand particles that wear away at the rock), dark streaks of desert varnish sliding down the walls, and desert flora

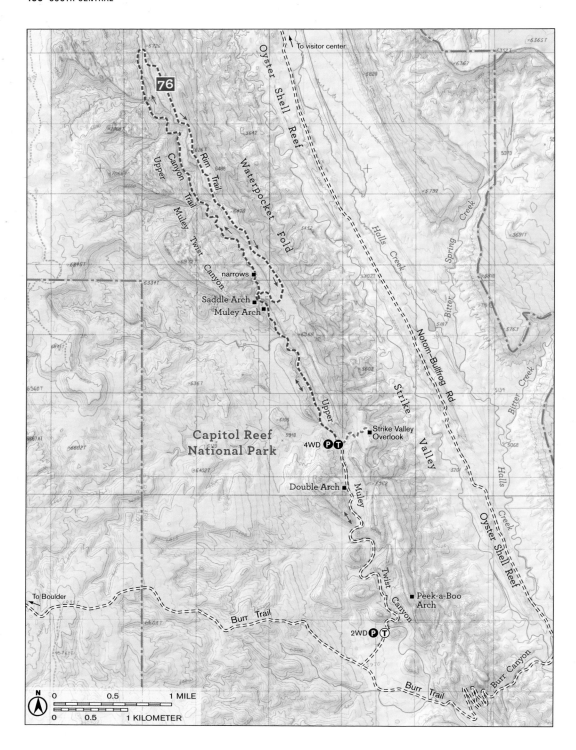

To visitor center

Oyster Shell Reef

Waterpocket Fold

Upper Canyon Trail

Rim Trail

Muley Twist Canyon

narrows

Saddle Arch

Muley Arch

Halls Creek

Spring Creek

Bitter Creek

Notom-Bullfrog Rd

Upper

Strike Valley

Strike Valley Overlook

Capitol Reef National Park

4WD

Double Arch

Muley

Bitter Creek

Oyster Shell Reef

To Boulder

Twist Canyon

Peek-a-Boo Arch

Burr Trail

2WD

Halls Creek

Burr Trail

Burr Canyon

N

0   0.5   1 MILE

0   0.5   1 KILOMETER

Spectacular views of the monocline as seen from the Strike Valley Overlook

such as serviceberry bush, prickly pear cactus, manzanita, the ubiquitous pinyon and juniper trees, and cliffrose in the springtime.

For 4 miles you wander through the wash (which mostly makes up the trail), keeping an eye out for more of those arches, including the distinctive Double Arch to your left early on. At 1.5 miles in, Muley Arch rises from the western sandstone walls. Barely a quarter mile later Saddle Arch also rises to the west, easily distinguished by its resemblance to the narrow gullet of a saddle. Across from Saddle Arch at 1.7 miles, a well-cairned route heading uphill marks the turnoff for the rim hike. Stay on the canyon bottom and walk through the wash. With the trail here framed on either side by russet-orange Wingate sandstone walls, you're rambling directly through the water-carved belly of Utah canyon country.

Amble along the canyon floor, enjoying the sections where the rounded orange slickrock reaches right to the wash while you walk on sand. When you reach 2.3 miles, another set of cairns will show you a bypass route to your right (east), which traverses above an eventually impassable section of tight narrows and slots. Consider taking time to first explore the narrows to the west,

because they're quite fascinating. Ancient native hand- and toeholds are grooved into the rocks in this narrows section, testifying to the long-ago presence of humans as well as our timelessly curious and determined nature.

Returning from the narrows to the cairned bypass, make the ascent and then maneuver 0.5 mile along the thin rims and benches of the eastern wall as it curves above and along the narrows below. Some sections here might involve minor scrambling and backtracking to find the best way through; keeping an eye out for cairns and referring to the USGS map is a good idea for those unfamiliar with crossing canyon country. While getting very lost in this section would be a feat, the footpath itself isn't necessarily straightforward. The bypass trail ends with a drop back into a wash. About 200 yards north up the wash, the rim trail heads up to the east, marked by a sign. Ascending here, the trail skirts north and east over the sandstone, rising and rising.

When you reach the top, the views over the Strike Valley seem endless, and you'll realize what a beautifully empty wild playground surrounds you. From a sign indicating the descent you just came up, the trail meanders south just over 2 miles across the top of this Navajo sandstone ridge. Although sections are cairned, heading too far either west or east yields impassable drops, so there is nowhere to go but south. Watch for blooming cacti in the springtime, including prickly pear and fishhook.

After the first 0.75 mile a few saddles to drop into and then climb out of necessitate sharper attention to the trail. The eventual descent back into the canyon should be cairned, although it is also obvious. Watch for small loose rocks on the descent and take foot placement very seriously in this section. Although this isn't an extremely perilous downclimb unless the rock is slick or icy, for anyone with vertigo or exposure issues, this might be a deal breaker. After you reach the canyon floor, it's an easy and pretty 2-mile walk back along the wash to the trailhead.

Extending your hike: The Strike Valley Overlook is 0.5 mile to the east from the parking area. Take this short jaunt for a spectacular overlook of the Strike Valley, particularly if you choose to not make the entire Upper Muley Twist loop hike.

77 Horseshoe Canyon

Roundtrip: 7.5 miles	**Season:** all year
Hiking time: 4–5 hours	**Map:** USGS Sugarloaf Butte
Elevation gain: 700 feet	**Contact:** Canyonlands National Park
Difficulty: easy	

Getting there: From the junction of I-70 and State Route 24, 11 miles west of Green River or 109 miles east of Richfield, turn south on SR 24 and drive 25 miles. Just 0.6 mile past the turnoff for Goblin Valley State Park, turn left on a dirt road, marked for Hans Flat Ranger Station, that curves east. (From Hanksville, drive SR 24 north 18.4 miles to the dirt road and turn right.) Drive 24.2 miles to a fork in the road, which is marked right for Hans Flat Ranger Station and left for Horseshoe Canyon. Turn left and continue 5.1 miles to another two-track dirt road marked Horseshoe Canyon Foot Trail. Follow this road 1.8 miles to the trailhead parking. The long dirt-road approach may deter those in 2WD vehicles, although it is certainly passable by lower-slung vehicles under optimal weather and road conditions. **Notes:** Flash flooding may occur mid- to late summer; do not enter canyon if storms threaten. An early start is highly recommended in summer. Primitive camping, information kiosk, and pit toilet at trailhead. Roads may be impassable when wet. 4WD recommended.

Located north of the remote Maze District of Canyonlands, the Horseshoe Canyon Unit is separated geographically from the park's main area. But it is well worth the trip out, particularly if you are doing a tour of the region's national parks, as the trailhead is accessible en route either to or from Capitol Reef and Canyonlands. Horseshoe Canyon is mostly known for its famed Great Gallery, a naturally protected petroglyph site high up on the canyon wall. The history of the people who left their Barrier Canyon-style artwork here is murky at best, since it can be gleaned solely from the very distinctive markings they left on the rocks, but their culture is estimated to have existed anywhere from 1500 to nearly 10,000 years ago. The beauty of this canyon is just as stunning as the human-created artwork within it.

The trail starts on the southwest end of the parking area and is somewhat level before it

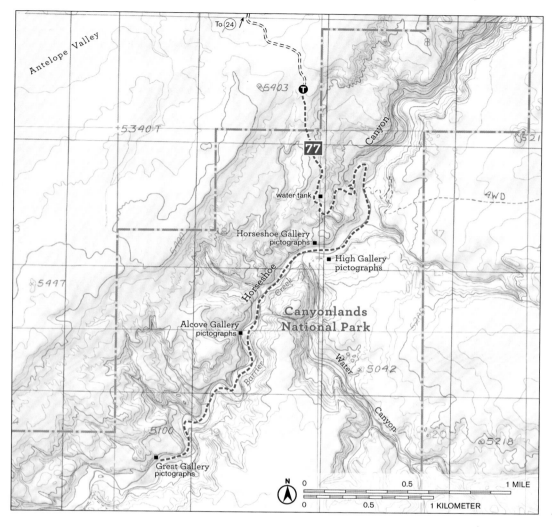

begins to switchback and descend into the canyon. At 0.4 mile you pass an old water tank and watering troughs erected by long-gone area cowboys. At this point you are following an old road originally built to facilitate oil extraction on the plateau across the canyon. A locked gate prevents cattle from passing through, but hikers can navigate the turnstile-type gateway to continue down the trail. Long switchbacks lead you to the canyon floor at 1.5 miles.

From here, travel due south along the canyon, which is wide and very pleasant. Spring through fall, keep an eye out for evening primrose clinging to the ground, offering up delicate blooms that unfurl early and late in the day. During the late summer and early fall months, yellow rubber rabbitbrush flowers add a splash of color, and you may also spot purple thistle. Cottonwood trees grace the area, offering shade on warm days as well as lovely contrast with the desert-varnished cliff walls jutting skyward. At 2 miles you will see a spur trail on your left, leading to the High Gallery pictograph panel. This is a nice little panel to behold, although it really doesn't

Claret cup cactus

hold a candle to the main attraction still ahead. Another smaller panel, Horseshoe Gallery, is almost immediately past this site, on the west side of the canyon. Multiple social trails lead to viewing points here.

At 2.5 miles you come across the impressively soaring walls of Alcove Gallery on your right (west). If it's a warm day, this is a great spot to sit in the shade, explore the already heavily explored site, and take in the combination of damaged ancient pictographs along with evidence of century-old cowboy and/or oil driller "archeology" that effectively destroyed much of the ancient rock art. This vandalized site is, unfortunately, more impressive for its natural grandeur than for the lingering presence of the people who lived and traveled through here many centuries ago.

Another 1.2 meandering miles through the canyon from here you reach the Great Gallery. The huge figures painted onto the west canyon walls do not seem that big as you approach, mostly because they are so high up that it is not easy to visually assess their scale at first. Wander right beneath the walls, though, and the impressive scale becomes more clear. If you have binoculars or a good camera zoom, you will more easily appreciate the artistic nuances of the figures, many of which have been described as ghostly by previous modern viewers. Usually from May through mid-October, park rangers are present to answer questions, give background history, and make sure this site stays untouched so that future generations may also enjoy it. Big metal ammo boxes set by benches in a shaded viewing area hold large binoculars and pamphlets of information on the Great Gallery. This makes for an excellent lunch spot. From here, most people simply return north along the canyon to the parking area, although some keep venturing down the canyon for more exploration.

78 *The Chute of Muddy Creek*

One-way: 15 miles
Hiking time: 10 hours–2 days
Elevation gain: 550 feet
Difficulty: hard

Season: all year
Map: USGS Tomsich Butte, Hunt Draw
Contact: Bureau of Land Management,
Price Field Office

Getting there: *Tomsich Butte parking:* From Green River, drive west on I-70 for 30 miles to exit 131. From here drive west and south 5.6 miles on the dirt Temple Mountain Road to a junction and keep left. Drive 5 miles to another junction and again stay left. In another 5 miles come to the signed Reds Canyon/Tan Seep junction; turn right. Drive 4 miles to another junction and turn right. In 0.9 mile come to the Reds Canyon/McKay Flat junction; turn left to McKay Flat. In 8.5 miles come to the signed Hidden Splendor Junction and turn right. Drive 6 miles to Tomsich Butte, passing the butte on your right as the road descends to a large parking area. *Hidden Splendor Mine parking:* Follow directions above to Hidden Splendor Junction; turn left. In 2 miles reach the Hidden Splendor airstrip. Drive over the airstrip (which is still used, so watch for small aircraft) to the large parking lot. **Notes:** Flash flooding may occur mid- to late summer; do not enter canyon if rain threatens. Roads may be impassable when wet. High-clearance 4WD vehicle may be necessary. Walking through water required. Check with BLM for current water flows; high flow may make walking difficult or dangerous. Wetsuits or drysuits advisable during shoulder seasons. Overnight camping near either trailhead parking; no camping inside canyon itself. Vehicle shuttle required.

Although a dull name like Muddy Creek may not stir the imagination, this hike is an epic adventure in a ruggedly scenic canyon. Tall sandstone walls lean in, splashed with dark desert varnish and stippled with cross-hatchings and layers, rising far above the waters of Muddy Creek. Although not always flowing, when it does the Muddy slips through The Chute from wall to wall in some sections, requiring you to walk directly through it. Spectacular high walls, sinuous narrows in some sections, and the sensation of walking through the carved belly of the earth are all part of the "Chute of the Muddy" experience. Be prepared to meet up with flowing liquid or shoe-sucking mud, depending on overall conditions. Before ever entering this canyon, be very certain about the weather. There is little to no escape throughout most of it should a flash flood strike. Slicing

Hondu Arch marking the start of the Chute of Muddy Creek

right through the desert landscape of the San Rafael Swell, the Muddy presents an ambitious, beautiful hike that is well worth the effort. Those who either cannot arrange a shuttle vehicle or don't desire a long hike can simply enter the canyon, hike as long as they wish, and then return the same way.

This hike description is north to south. From the Tomsich Butte parking area, first admire the intriguing shape of Hondu Arch to the southwest. Then point yourself downstream on the Muddy and start walking. For the first several miles the canyon is broad, and you may find yourself skirting the side of the stream or fighting your way through tangled brush that seems determined to impede progress. A little over 2 miles in, the canyon begins to narrow and deepen to ever more impressive beauty, each corner of the Coconino formation delivering high walls and a greater sense of being very small in the midst of this deep gash in the rock. Ripples of mud, piled-up sand banks, or pools of water may present new obstacles or new objects of beauty to behold.

As you continue south downstream, the canyon walls widen, narrow, widen, and finally begin to narrow in earnest as you approach the 6-mile mark. A number of canyons intersect along the way, Music (7 miles into the hike) being one you might consider poking up a little bit for its loveliness. From this point, you will be traveling through the narrowest, grandest part of The Chute, a 4-mile section that rivals the beauty of any canyon in the southwest. The deepest canyon in the San Rafael Swell, the Chute of the Muddy slips and slides you through twisting turns, small dryfalls, potholes, shelves and ledges, alcoves, and boulder-strewn runs. At its narrowest point, logjams far overhead indicate the substantial power of flash floods that rip through the canyon. Once you are through the narrows and reach Chimney Canyon coming in from the west, a milder, wider 4 miles remain before you reach the exit point and labor slightly uphill to get to the shuttle vehicle parked at Hidden Splendor Mine.

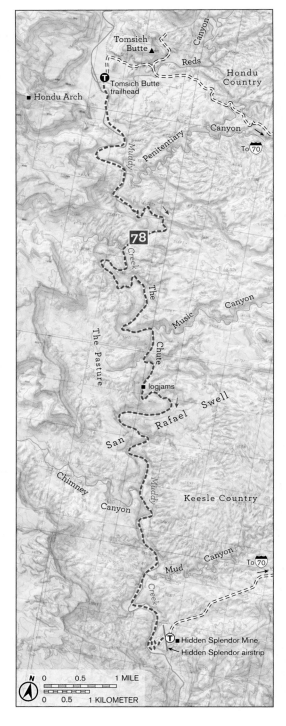

79 Crack Canyon

Roundtrip: 6 miles
Hiking time: 2–4 hours
Elevation gain: 290 feet
Difficulty: easy/moderate

Season: all year
Map: USGS Temple Mountain
Contact: Bureau of Land Management, Price Field Office

Getting there: From the junction of I-70 and State Route 24, 11 miles west of Green River or 109 miles east of Richfield, go south for 24 miles on SR 24. (From Hanksville, go north on SR 24 for 19.5 miles.) Turn west onto Temple Mountain Road, which is signed for Goblin Valley. At 5.2 miles in the road splits, with the left fork leading to Goblin Valley. Continue driving west on Temple Mountain Road for 2.2 miles to a junction with Behind the Reef Road. Drive south 4.2 miles to the signed parking area for Crack Canyon on your left. Park here; if in a high-clearance 4WD vehicle, you may attempt to drive in another 0.7 mile to the actual trailhead, although this section is through a wash that may be in terrible condition. **Notes:** Flash flooding may occur mid- to late summer; do not enter canyon if rain threatens. Use of ropes may be required. Scrambling up, over, and down wedged chockstones required. Wading through water may be required. Overnight camping available near trailhead parking and other close-by areas.

Uncrowded yet still gorgeous, filled with an abundance of natural cracks in walls, pocked with wind-blown holes, and home of slot slithering and downclimbs, Crack Canyon is an awfully fun canyon that is off the beaten path yet accessible enough to be a great place for families or simply those who want to avoid the far more popular areas closer to Goblin Valley. Wide and sandy, narrow and sandstone-y, utterly breathtaking with its beauty, this canyon is well known but not yet massively overloved. Towering canyon walls, intriguing rock formations, cool little parts where you walk on slickrock and need to find your way back down into the wash, a brief subway tunnel, and three narrows sections all conspire to make Crack Canyon a great jaunt in the San Rafael Swell.

From the signed parking area at the road, walk 0.7 mile down the wash, which meanders and curves east and southeast. A few sections lead over hills, but you can't get lost: simply aim for the large canyon walls to the southeast. The broad sandy wash enters the high walls of

Heading down Crack Canyon

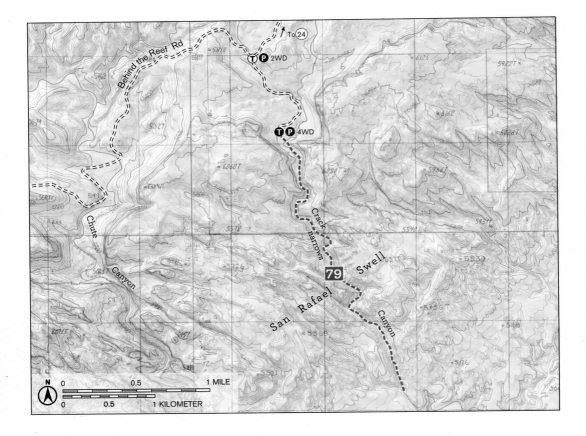

the canyon, the giant sheet of cliff recessed in places and dressed with the usual desert varnish streaks. Multiple holes in the walls, gathered in clusters that might extend for yards, draw the eye with their Swiss-cheese appearance. Very quickly you come across a mini narrows section, which can easily be bypassed to the right (west) side by walking down the terraced slickrock. Keep curving down into the high-walled canyon, which at every turn presents some new visage that is as pretty as the one before and then some.

The wash constricts, then broadens, then constricts. Trees burst out around some corners, offering shady spots to sit and relax for a minute on hot days. The three narrows sections each need to be downclimbed, but most agile people can negotiate them. Ladders constructed from large logs will offer an assist on the way back upcanyon, and some may choose to use them on the way down. You may also find knotted ropes to use as handholds on your return.

As always, check first to be sure these unmaintained poles and ropes are sturdy enough to support your weight before trusting them. Also remember that what you climb down, you must climb up on your way back. The prospect of one drop-off down a wedged boulder may prove to be the end of the hike for some, which is certainly fine, as the canyon thus far has been quite beautiful. But continue on to discover the best part. Skirting ledges under rock overhangs, sidling along sandstone slides, and ducking under boulders are all part of the exciting experience of this canyon. Once at the canyon's end, simply return back upcanyon to the parking area.

80   *Little Wild Horse and Bell Canyons*

Loop: 8.5 miles
Hiking time: 4–5 hours
Elevation gain: 700 feet
Difficulty: easy/moderate

Season: all year
Map: USGS Little Wild Horse Mesa
Contact: Bureau of Land Management, Price Field Office

Getting there: From the junction of I-70 and State Route 24, 11 miles west of Green River or 109 miles east of Richfield, go south for 24 miles on SR 24. (From Hanksville, go north on SR 24 for 19.5 miles.) Turn west onto Temple Mountain Road, which is signed for Goblin Valley. At 5.2 miles in the road splits, with the left fork leading to Goblin Valley. Turn left and drive 6 miles to a dirt road heading right (west). Turn right here and drive 5.3 miles to the signed parking area on your right (north). **Notes:** Flash flooding may occur mid- to late summer. Holidays and weekends may be excessively crowded. Vault toilet at parking area. Map reading skills helpful. Overnight camping and showers at Goblin Valley, 6 miles south.

Perhaps the most well-known pair of canyons in the beautiful San Rafael Swell, Little Wild Horse and Bell are usually hiked together to make this 8.5-mile connecting loop. They are classic Southwest slot canyons with smooth, water-carved turns; sometimes sandy bottoms; chiseled layers; and wild, wonderful mixings of colors that range from coral to pea-soup green to pearly alabaster. They are popular because they are not technically difficult, families can do them, they are easy to access, and they simply are gorgeous examples of the natural wonders that define southern Utah hiking. Carving through the heart of the Swell like sinuous, stunningly pretty arteries, these canyons attract those of nearly all ages and abilities. Sometimes those with small children or less desire to do more exploration simply head up and then back down Little Wild Horse, but the full loop connecting both canyons is recommended for a deeper appreciation of the Swell's beauty. Additionally, while Little Wild Horse can sometimes be ridiculously crowded, Bell is often virtually empty, which can give you a more serene experience. Summertime can be extremely hot, so spring and fall are the best seasons to explore these slots.

From the parking lot, head north to the signed trailhead start. Continue 0.6 mile to a small dryfall that can be climbed over or bypassed. At the canyon split, you'll find Bell to your left

(northwest) and Little Wild Horse to your right (northeast). Veer left to head into Bell Canyon. The first bit of walking is easy along a wide sandy wash, but at 1.8 miles the canyon narrows enough that you can just walk through it without needing to turn sideways. The cliff walls soar above as your path twists and turns, the canyon walls smooth in some places and ridged in others. Some minor scrambles over rocks will appear here and there before you reach the end of the canyon and find yourself back out in the flatter desert again, at 2.5 miles.

An old mining road, Behind the Reef Road, runs east to west in front of you. Follow the road right (east) for 1.6 miles, winding up and around sloping hills and jutting rock points. An easily visible information kiosk set by the road guides you into the south-running wash that leads directly into Little Wild Horse in 0.6 mile. Shortly before this turnoff into the canyon, a hiker-created shortcut down into the wash heads off to your right. It should be easy to spot, but it doesn't significantly cut off any time, so if you miss it, just continue toward the kiosk.

After you wind through the curves of the wash and get into the increasingly tighter section, there will be two places where you must negotiate downclimbs. There are cairned go-arounds if the downclimbing seems too challenging. As you head into this longer and deeper slot, 4.7 total

Hikers in Little Wild Horse Canyon

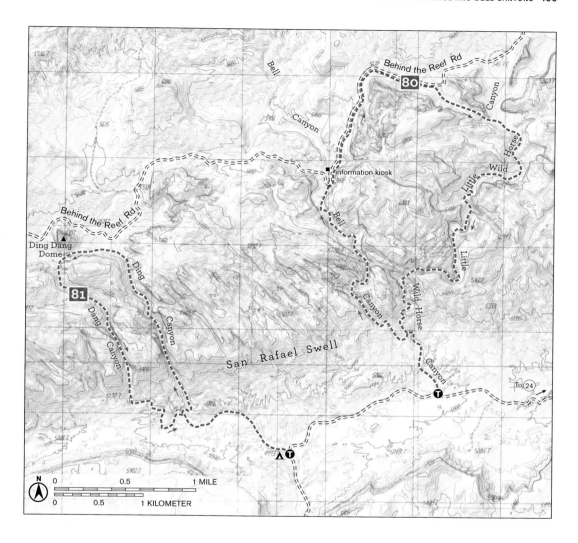

miles into your loop, you'll very soon see why so many sing its praises. While fairly wide for the first 0.5 mile, Little Wild Horse then becomes a classic slot canyon, at times narrowing down to barely foot-width on the floor while still allowing your upper body to pass through the split walls. Nooks and crannies, crevices and hollows, boulders and dips are all there for exploring and scrambling over and under, making this a sandstone playground. Ridged rock layers undulate along the narrow walls, adding to the beauty of the canyon. Light can play down into it, slicing through some sections while others remain shadowed.

There are some reasonably minor drop-offs and obstacles along the way, all of which are navigable for most. Some even hike into this canyon wearing backpack-style child carriers, although that might make some of the tighter sections more challenging to get through. At 8.1 miles, you reach the southern end of Little Wild Horse and are back at the original meeting of the two canyons. Retrace your steps 0.6 mile through the sandy wash back to the parking area.

81 *Ding and Dang Canyons*

Loop: 5.75 miles	*Season:* all year
Hiking time: 3–4 hours	*Map:* USGS Little Wild Horse Mesa
Elevation gain: 500 feet	*Contact:* Bureau of Land Management,
Difficulty: moderate	Price Field Office

Getting there: From the junction of I-70 and State Route 24, 11 miles west of Green River or 109 miles east of Richfield, go south for 24 miles on SR 24. (From Hanksville, go north on SR 24 for 19.5 miles.) Turn west onto Temple Mountain Road, which is signed for Goblin Valley. At 5.2 miles in the road splits, with the left fork leading to Goblin Valley. Turn left and drive 6 miles to a dirt road heading right (west). Turn right here and drive 6.7 miles to the large parking area on your right (north), just where the road curves south. Some cars may not make it all the way; if in doubt, you can leave your car at the Little Wild Horse parking area, adding 1.3 miles each way to your hike. **Notes:** Flash flooding may occur mid- to late summer monsoon season. Do not enter the canyons if rain threatens. Use of ropes may be required in Dang Canyon. Scrambling up and over or down wedged chockstones required. Wading through water up to chest deep or more may be required. Map reading skills may be helpful for the northern connector section. Overnight camping allowed at parking area. Vault toilet located just east at the parking area for Little Wild Horse and Bell canyons.

If you tried Little Wild Horse and Bell canyons and want even more canyon adventure in the San Rafael Swell, Ding and Dang canyons should be next on your list, as they are immediate neighbors to the west. While they are not nearly as crowded as the two more well-known canyons, it can be difficult to have total solitude in Ding and Dang during weekends and holidays. More demanding of your time and technique, these canyons present the ledges, curves, towering walls, deep pockets of twisting turns, and overall geography of classic narrow southern Utah canyons. The chockstone clambering can make this challenging for solo hikers or those less agile. The two canyons are generally done as a loop, with most people heading north up Ding, crossing west, then going back south down Dang, due mostly to technical considerations in Dang that make going down that canyon far easier than going up. Between the two you will pass a sandstone hill called Ding Dang Dome, which gives the entire hike a rhyming name that might ring in your head.

From the trailhead, go west down the sandy wash. As you curve through the wash, striped bentonite hills rise to the north, their clay sides gently bulging out and displaying their striated colors of mauve, pink, seafoam green, and pink-red. Golden-red sandstone curves down to the wash in sections. After 1 mile, you arrive at a clear break in the wash, with the choice of going either straight on or to your right. People often leave obvious cairns here. Turn right (north) to head up Ding Canyon. The first small challenge immediately appears in the form of a sloped sandstone friction slab that must be ascended. Climbing it is not difficult for those with agility and confidence in foot placement. If this gives you pause, however, you might not be ready to enter these canyons.

After ascending the slab, you will first see a sandy wash with sandstone bumps and ledges poking up here and there. The enclosing walls are low and have the look of hastily tossed-together pieces of buff-colored desert stone. Right ahead, though, the walls dramatically shoot upward in large, single-piece upthrusts, with the canyon itself seeming but a slim crack between them. Not a slot canyon in terms of being so tight you need to turn sideways, Ding

Classic San Rafael Swell scenery on the way to Ding and Dang canyons

nevertheless has a brief narrows section that is occasionally blocked by chockstones, large rocks tightly wedged between the walls that must be negotiated in order to continue. Scrambling up and over several of these is necessary through the canyon.

Soon you come across a veritable jumping-jack section of large potholes, which will be filled with water if storming has happened recently. Impressive to look at, these potholes are easily bypassed by ascending the ledges to the east. Much ledge climbing, pothole skirting, and sand-or-slickrock tread choosing present themselves the rest of the way up this canyon.

The canyon pours you out into a wide desert section at its northern end. Looking to your left (west), you'll see the roughly pyramid-shaped Ding Dang Dome; follow the trail toward it. The trail winds along, heading up a few small slopes, and curves beneath and to the left (south) of the dome. You will come to a wash leading south and

east, which usually has cairns to mark it. Follow this wash down to Dang Canyon. More potholes, ledge-skirting, and occasionally walking beneath huge leaning boulders are part of this canyon, which becomes narrow the farther down you go, although again it never reaches tight slot proportions.

The canyon walls once again leap far above your head. When you come to the first 40-foot dryfall, know that it looks more intimidating from above than it actually is. Two options for the casual day hiker present themselves: descend on the left (east) side, where there may be a piece of webbing bolted to the rock to assist downclimbing. Be very sure to test the webbing and bolt before trusting them with your safety. There is adequate footing just below the lip, so those who are confident may be able to scramble down entirely on their own. The second option is a ledge to the right (west) of the dryfall, which is negotiable by those who are agile and not fearful of exposure. If you reach this section and decide it's not doable for you, you can always retrace your footsteps to return back down Ding Canyon, although that extends the hike.

Past the dryfall, another, shorter dryfall and more chockstones, narrows, and potential water wading are present through the rest of the canyon back down to the same sandy wash you first used to enter. Once the canyon opens up to the wash and the bentonite hills, turn left and head east 1.5 miles back down the wash to the parking area.

82 *Goblin Valley*

Roundtrip: 4.9 miles
Hiking time: 2–3 hours
Elevation gain: 275 feet
Difficulty: easy

Season: all year
Map: USGS Little Wild Horse Mesa
Contact: Goblin Valley State Park

Getting there: From the junction of I-70 and State Route 24, 11 miles west of Green River, go south for 24 miles on SR 24. (From Hanksville, go north on SR 24 for 19.5 miles.) At mile marker 136, take the signed turnoff to Goblin Valley State Park on the west side of the highway. Follow the road 12.5 miles into the park. **Notes:** Fee required for both day use and overnight camping. Holidays and weekends may be excessively crowded. Campground has flush and vault toilets, yurts for rent, RV and tent camping, showers, barbecue grills, fire pits.

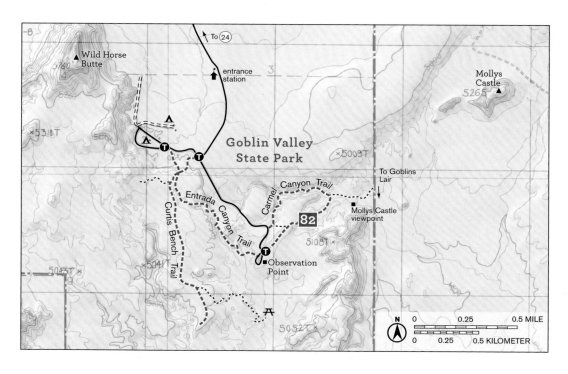

Snow-covered Henry Mountains behind Goblin Valley

Wandering through Goblin Valley is like wandering through a colorful moonscape of natural formations that are bizarre yet wondrous. The orangey-red hoodoos of this valley are a fascinating draw for their myriad shapes ranging from stunted little mushrooms to crooked rocket ships to the eponymous goblins. Whatever your imagination can make up, you will likely find within this fanciful landscape created by the congruent forces of water, wind, and time. The Jurassic-era Entrada sandstone layer eroded faster than the alternating silt and shale layers, leaving behind formations that demand creative names. Over time, spheroidal weathering smoothed and rounded the edges, leaving behind these engrossing natural formations. Although the state park encourages people to wander and play around the hoodoos, remember that these creations took millions of years to form and are now protected for the enjoyment of all. Strongly resist the temptation to knock over a hoodoo in a misguided (and illegal) attempt to keep others safe from any perceived danger of tilting or falling sandstone.

Three specific trails let you explore this area. Take Carmel Canyon, Curtis Bench, and Entrada Canyon for a total of 4.9 miles. Simply wandering though the hoodoo-filled valley itself is something you definitely want to do, however, and happily know there are no trails in there. Exploring around and behind all the mushrooming formations is intriguing enough and can truly take hours. Enjoy doing this in an extremely original little slice of Utah natural landscape.

Entrada Canyon Trail: This is really a trail for those staying in the campground who wish to walk to the hoodoos rather than drive. It is a pleasant, straightforward stroll of 1.3 miles one-way, but it really isn't an essential trail to experience if you are not camping in the park. It starts at the campground and heads southeast through a drainage to the valley just below Observation Point, where it begins to pass by the interesting hoodoos. Return along the same route.

Curtis Bench Trail: Curtis Bench has an inauspicious start at the bottom of a service road, but walking up the road really does let you have an excellent view of the surrounding landscape. Park in the pullout at the bottom of the service road right at the junction at which you can either turn left for Observation Point or right for the campground. Walk up the dirt road, which certainly looks bland cutting up a rather featureless hillside. At the top of the rise in 0.2 mile you will be able to see down into Goblin Valley itself.

Continue ambling in the generally south direction, where many sections make for scenic shots of the Henry Mountains to the south. You can descend into Goblin Valley at almost any point and from there wander your way back to the easily visible parking area at Observation Point (which rather sadly obstructs the views to the north and northeast, but at least it makes for an easy marker so you really can't get lost in the valley). Walk from Observation Point back to your car along the paved road or, if not walking down into the hoodoo lands, simply turn around and return to the parking area.

Carmel Canyon Trail: From the very northeast end of the Observation Point parking area, keep walking east along a wide finger of land. You might not think you're going the right way, but in about 0.2 mile you will see trail markers noting where you descend down a rather steep little hillside via a "stairway" fashioned from sandstone slabs. A large hoodoo outcropping is directly before you and to your left (north). The trail curves down through a little canyon, then slips behind this formation into Carmel Canyon, which isn't an exciting area, to be quite honest. If you head east toward the Mollys Castle viewpoint, it's somewhat more scenic. Signs will direct you either left (west) for Carmel Canyon or right (southeast) for Goblins Lair. Along the way to Goblins Lair you will come to the Mollys Castle viewpoint and terminus of the Carmel Canyon Trail. Return to the parking area the same way you came in.

Extending your hike: The recently discovered Goblins Lair is a fascinating little diversion, since it leads into the ground beneath the canyon for a positively spooky experience. While you can find your own way to the Goblins Lair, the trail cutoff to the cave is not marked and it is tricky to climb up to the cave entrance and then down into the cave itself in what is basically a scramble over tumbled rocks. Exercise caution if attempting this. The park offers guided hikes to Goblins Lair; inquire at the entrance booth or visitor center.

Opposite, top: Approaching Turret Arch on the Windows Loop in Arches National Park

Opposite, bottom: The view through Pine Tree Arch on the Devils Garden Primitive Loop

Southeast

Owachomo Bridge

Located in a part of the country that boasts some of the darkest night skies left visible from our well-lit world, Natural Bridges National Monument's primary claim to fame is majestic natural bridges that also shelter evidence of ancient cultures that once lived in their shadows. Just to the south is a primitive area called Grand Gulch, which holds a tremendous concentration of Ancestral Puebloan ruins within the length of its winding 50-mile canyon. Natural arches, beautiful canyon walls streaked with dark desert varnish, and the hidden oases of green riparian areas along streams that carve their way through the area lure backpackers and day hikers alike to this secluded place filled with the intriguing mysteries of the past as well as expansive mesa lands to visit.

Arches National Park and Canyonlands National Park are what most people think of when they picture the southeastern corner of Utah. The huge, graceful flow of iconic Delicate Arch framing the snow-capped La Sal Mountains is an image millions of people have seen. Home to over 2000 natural arches, Arches has justifiably made a name for itself in terms of natural beauty. The very easy entrance into the park also makes it very attractive to visitors, as do the amenities of nearby Moab and its famed mountain biking trails. Canyonlands, split into three major districts, is an almost equal draw for those who enjoy viewing the seemingly endless dips and hollows and folds of canyons and buttes and mesas, all painted with beguiling natural colors that simply beg to be photographed.

Right beside Canyonlands is Dead Horse Point State Park, home to another one of the world's most recognizable scenic images, looking down at a famous bend of the Colorado River from the park's eponymous point above. The sheer vastness of the desert canyon landscapes in these parks is breathtaking. Trails around the Moab area are plentiful and marvelous as well, sporting significant natural arches, beautiful canyons, gently lazing river eddies, and slickrock exploration opportunities that seem almost as endless as they are alluring.

83 *Natural Bridges Loop*

Loop: 8.6 miles
Hiking time: 5–6 hours
Elevation gain: 495 feet
Difficulty: easy/moderate

Season: all year
Map: USGS Moss Back Butte
Contact: Natural Bridges National Monument

Getting there: From Blanding, drive south on US Highway 191 for 4 miles. Turn right (west) onto State Route 95 and drive 35 miles to State Route 275. Turn right (north) and drive 5 miles to the visitor center on Bridge View Drive. From here, turn right onto the one-way loop road and drive 2 miles to the Sipapu Bridge trailhead parking area. **Notes:** Fee required. Vault toilets, overnight camping, paved loop road, interpretive visitor center, trail map available. Potable water at visitor center.

Sipapu Bridge as seen from the trail down to the canyon floor

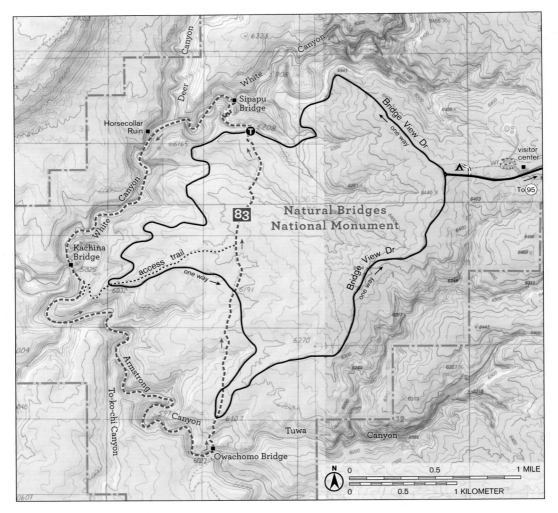

Utah's first national monument, Natural Bridges became a protected area in 1908 in order to preserve the incredible grandeur of its natural bridges. People back then wouldn't have considered that the area would also become renowned for its dark night skies many decades later; being far removed from the light pollution of more populous areas, Natural Bridges boasts some of the most stellar night-sky viewing in the Lower 48. The key attractions here, however, are the majestic bridges to discover on this loop hike. Called Sipapu, Kachina, and Owachomo to honor the native people who made this area their home centuries and millennia ago, these beautiful natural bridges, formed from Cedar Mesa sandstone, are some of the largest in the world. This trail offers viewpoints as well as allowing you to walk right beneath or beside them.

From the parking lot, the trail heads west and almost immediately drops 450 feet to the canyon floor below in 0.6 mile. The steepness of this section demands caution while descending. The monument has constructed stairs and ladders to assist your passage, and switchbacks keep the trail from being a sheer vertical drop. Partway down this trail, a spur overlook allows for good photos of the first bridge along the trail, Sipapu. Its name is the Hopi word for the opening between the worlds; previous appellations included Augusta and President. Sipapu is the largest bridge in the monument, and its enormous scale cannot truly be comprehended until you are close to it.

Once on the bottom of White Canyon, the trail turns left to go beneath the bridge, taking you in a generally southwest direction. Keep an eye out for handprint pictographs on the wall 1.4 miles along the trail, shortly before you reach Horsecollar Ruin. The many rooms of this ruin, tucked under the cliff walls, bear testament to the fact many people lived in this canyon centuries ago. A meticulously preserved site, this ruin is a fascination to explore. Remember to not touch, lean on, sit on, remove, or otherwise disturb anything here so future generations can also enjoy seeing the remnants of the culture that once flourished here.

When you are 3 miles in, the beautiful Kachina Bridge rears over the confluence of White Canyon and Armstrong Canyon. At times the bridge was known as Senator and Caroline; its present name came from petroglyphs and pictographs of dancing figures at the base of this bridge, seen by a surveyor who correctly guessed the people who'd left those marks were ancestors of the present-day Hopi peoples. In 1992, 4000 tons of sandstone dislodged from the underside of this bridge, evidence of the natural forces that shaped and continue to shape these monumental structures. Scan the nearby walls for more ruins and rock art, particularly the west side of the canyon for an impressive panel of pictographs.

From here, angle slightly left to be sure you remain heading south down Armstrong Canyon; if you find yourself walking west, you're in the wrong canyon. Continue along the trail another 3.3 miles to reach Owachomo Bridge, which stretches along the southern side of the canyon. Although it is the smallest of the three, as well as the oldest, many visitors consider this slender bridge to be the prettiest one in the monument. Its name means "rock mound" in Hopi; it was named after the protruding rock mound atop the eastern end of the bridge. Previous names for this bridge included Edwin, Little, and Congressman. From here, simply head up the trail that leads back to the top of the rim. Cross the road to follow the trail another 2.2 miles back to the trailhead where you parked.

84 Collins Canyon

Roundtrip: 10.5 miles	**Season:** all year
Hiking time: 6–7 hours	**Map:** USGS Red House Spring
Elevation gain: 370 feet	**Contact:** Bureau of Land Management,
Difficulty: moderate	Monticello Field Office

Getting there: From Blanding, drive south on US Highway 191 for 4 miles. Turn right (west) onto State Route 95 and drive for 37.5 miles to State Route 276. Turn left (south) and drive to mile marker 85. Look for signed Collins Canyon Road/County Road 260. Turn left (south) here on the dirt road and drive 6.5 miles to the trailhead. Stay right at the fork to reach the trailhead parking. **Notes:** Obtain required permit at Kane Gulch Ranger Station or self-pay tube at trailhead. Can be very hot in summer. Binoculars may be helpful for viewing distant ruins. Roads may be impassable when wet.

Spanning a period from 2500 to 700 years ago, an ancient group of people known now as Ancestral Puebloans inhabited the remote Grand Gulch Primitive Area on Cedar Mesa.

They left a rich array of evidence of their existence: incredible rock art, crumbling stone ruins perched high on cliff faces, intricate pottery and baskets, and thousands of tinier remnants still being unearthed today. This area offers hikes through beautiful canyons that showcase soulful natural beauty as well as fascinating vestiges of the long-gone people who once called it home. Collins Canyon is a little more remote than some of the other trails in Grand Gulch but certainly no less beautiful or intriguing. It's also perhaps the easiest route into the gulch itself, making this an accessible choice for most families as well as those who aren't interested in technical scrambles. Classic canyon walls, alluring ruins that still stand the test of time, and the sense of exploring where few others go make this canyon an excellent choice to explore this enthralling, isolated region.

Drop into the canyon from the Collins Spring trailhead on an easy walk in along the well-marked trail. You'll come across an old cowboy camp, testament to some of the more recent human activity in the area. Cowboys herded cattle here, and the first cowboy "archeologists" explored the ancient remains here over a century ago. Keep following the wash as the canyon walls begin to soar above, showing off reds, duns, tans, pinks, and the dark wash of desert patina tattooing permanent little waterfalls of oxides down their sides. The holes of solution cavities decorate walls and sandstone bulges here and there in random Swiss-cheese patterns. Small monoliths rise from the walls, as do rounded little knobs and reaching spires. The brush of natural forces applied to the canyon over millennia has left it etched with colors, holes, miniature arches, and seemingly endless turns as it slowly winds you along its route.

Reach the confluence with Grand Gulch in 2 miles. From here, turn right (south) to take a short 0.25-mile jaunt to the brief narrows section.

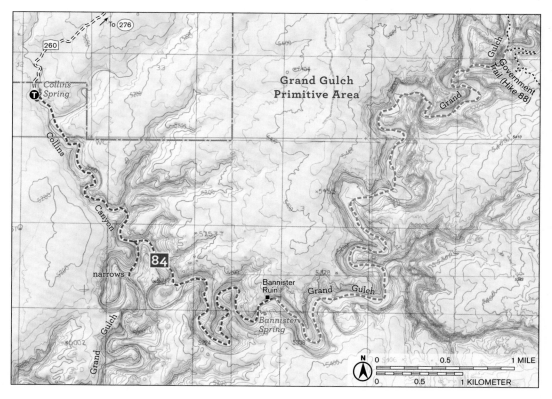

Ancient granary tucked into a small alcove

Return to the main canyon and continue generally east through Grand Gulch, winding along the stream bottom with large canyon walls gracefully leaping up overhead. In 2.7 miles you'll come across Bannister Spring, which has water only seasonally so don't count on it without first checking at the ranger station.

Just 0.3 mile beyond the spring you reach Bannister Ruin, high in the cliffs to your left (north). Exposed horizontal wood beams give this two-tiered ruin its name. The lower level sports a kiva that is double-walled and has an intact roof, which is rare to find. The ancients who lived here left behind enough ruins, rock art, pottery shards, metates and manos used for grinding, and other remnants to tease the imagination as well as prompt decades of scientific questioning for researchers. Remember to leave anything you find untouched and undisturbed so that future generations can enjoy it as well. From here, retrace your steps back to the trailhead, which will involve a bit of an uphill push at the end.

Extending your hike: Continue up Grand Gulch as it winds its way northeast another 7 miles to the junction with the Government Trail (see Hike 88). More ruins, petroglyphs, pictographs, alcoves, and sheer canyon beauty await in this section. Exit at Government trailhead (shuttle vehicle required).

85 Kane Gulch

Roundtrip: 10 miles
Hiking time: 7–8 hours
Elevation gain: 600 feet
Difficulty: moderate

Season: all year
Map: USGS Kane Gulch
Contact: Bureau of Land Management, Monticello Field Office

Getting there: From Blanding, drive south on US Highway 191 for 4 miles. Turn right (west) onto State Route 95 and drive for 28.5 miles to State Route 261. Turn left (south) and drive 4 miles to the Kane Gulch Ranger Station turnoff on your left (east). Pull in and park here. The trailhead is west across SR 261. **Notes:** Obtain required permit at Kane Gulch Ranger Station or self-pay tube at trailhead. Can be very hot in summer. Binoculars may be helpful for viewing distant ruins.

Perhaps the most popular canyon in the Grand Gulch area due to its ease of access, Kane Gulch is an easy and spectacular introduction to the area's natural and human-made gems. Soaring canyon walls, twisty canyon bottoms, ruins, pictographs, and that sense of solitude you find deep within the more remote pockets of canyon country meld together to make this a beautiful, relatively easy hike that gives you a lot of payoff for not a huge amount of effort. Junipers and pinyons flourish throughout the region, dusty-green and fragrant sagebrush is of course ubiquitous, and large cottonwoods sometimes nod over the canyon bottom, lending welcome shade on hot days. Tie this hike in with others in the area to provide a deeper experience of an area that once was a hub of human activity in a gorgeous canyon setting, many centuries ago.

Walk southwest from the trailhead, crossing sage-dotted flats to dip into the initial low depression of Kane Gulch. Walk over slickrock at the half-mile mark, then travel over sandy bottom as you head on. Don't be surprised to come across a small aspen grove 1.5 miles in, just after the canyon walls begin to rise. Although the elevation is much lower here than where aspens are usually found, glacial movement during the last ice age deposited seeds that flourished into the trees you see today. Even more interesting, this is a clone grove of genetically identical trees that have been growing here for the last 11,000 years. The canyon also presents odd-shaped boulders, shy alcoves, leaning rocks that seem to threaten a tumble down from their perches, and a proliferation of the hardy desert plants more typical here.

Kane Gulch mashes up with Grand Gulch at the 4-mile mark. Shady campsites are available here, or they may simply be nice spots to sit and rest. The first ancient-ruin focus of your hike is here as well: Junction Ruin rests in an alcove on the west side of the canyon. Easily reachable, the ruin is beguiling with its mud brick structures and walls. A multitude of architectural designs greets you, inviting speculation and imagination about the lives of the people who created them. This is one of the largest ruin sites in Grand Gulch, and as such has offered up a wealth of information about its human history. Remember to treat the ruins with care, which includes not sitting, standing, or resting on any of the fragile structures.

Head another 0.7 mile down the canyon to reach the next point of interest, Turkey Pen Ruin. Named because of holding blocks in which the bones of ancient turkeys were found, this ruin apparently was used to raise and keep birds used for food. Their feathers were also used as well, woven into capes, blankets, and the like. You will likely find an abundant scattering, or careful gathering on rocks, of potsherds, corncobs, metates, manos, and other bits and pieces of history. Leave everything where you find it so

Desert varnish decorates the canyon walls.

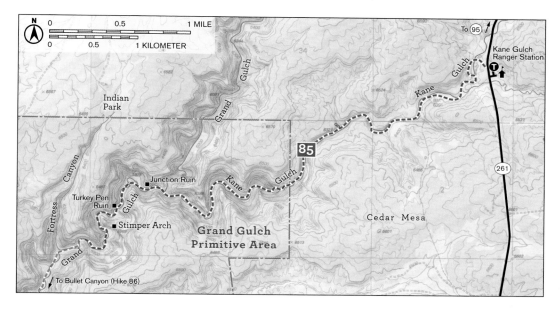

those who come here after you can equally enjoy the few remnants left. Walk another 0.3 mile for a view of Stimper Arch high in the cliffs to your left on the north rim. This thick arch marks the end of your trail; return from here back up the canyon to the trailhead.

Extending your hike: For a backpacking trip, hike another 10.7 miles down canyon to the junction with Bullet Canyon. Ruins and canyon gorgeousness continue all along the way. Walk 7.2 miles up Bullet Canyon (see Hike 86) to exit at the Bullet Canyon trailhead (shuttle car required).

86 *Bullet Canyon*

Roundtrip: 10.6 miles
Hiking time: 7–8 hours
Elevation gain: 820 feet
Difficulty: moderate
Season: all year

Map: USGS Cedar Mesa North, Pollys Pasture
Contact: Bureau of Land Management, Monticello Field Office

Getting there: From Blanding, drive south on US Highway 191 for 4 miles. Turn right (west) onto State Route 95 and drive for 28.5 miles to State Route 261. Turn left (south) and drive 4 miles to pass the Kane Gulch Ranger Station. Continue another 7.2 miles and turn right (west) at County Road 251. Drive another 1.1 miles on the dirt road to the trailhead parking. **Notes:** Obtain required permit at Kane Gulch Ranger Station or self-pay tube at trailhead. Can be very hot in summer. Rock scrambling required. Some exposure on slickrock. Rope may be useful for hauling backpacks over one section. Routefinding skills may be necessary. Binoculars may be helpful for viewing distant ruins. Roads may be impassable when wet.

Bullet Canyon is an ominous name for a stunning canyon that holds ancient treasures in the form of ruins left behind more than 800 years ago. Not only are the intriguing ruins a draw, the canyon itself is a remarkable example of southern Utah landscape and a step into geologic as well as human history. While a long day hike may work quite well for some, an overnight trip is encouraged in order to give you plenty of time to really explore the canyon and the ruins. Plenty of options to camp and take little (or big) side trips in the area exist here, but Bullet Canyon allows for a spectacular first visit to Grand Gulch and an introduction to the beauties of this remote, primitive place.

From the trailhead, walk west for 0.25 mile to reach the canyon rim. Drop into the canyon and follow the cairned route down. Here and there you'll be walking on sandstone; potholes filled with water may be scattered about during the rainy season, but don't necessarily count on any water at all being present. Just 0.25 mile into the canyon, look up to the right to glimpse an unusual square masonry tower perched up high, guarding the canyon like a sentinel.

The canyon tracks you west, the walls steadily growing in height as you descend. The classic dark desert varnish drips over the yellow and mauve walls, forming intricate patterns. Keep your eyes peeled for ruins high on the cliff walls.

At 1.7 miles in, a dry water course tumbles over what almost seems to be a slickrock slide that has natural tiers in it. Remember you will have to ascend back up this on the way out, so be sure everyone in your party is agile enough. This section may be slightly tricky with backpacks on, either up or down; bringing a short length of rope to haul packs over the large step at the bottom on the return trip may be useful.

About 2.5 miles in, a significant boulder jam demands that you follow a bypass route on the right (north) side of the canyon. Walk along a ledge high above the canyon for 0.2 mile before the bypass steeply descends back into the wash. As you wander along the canyon, sandstone bulges out, rears high above, and forms buttresses and shelves and curving walls. About 4.5 miles in, the riparian canyon floor widens considerably. Every canyon turn brings the possibility of new discoveries, not to mention a ceaseless parade of natural beauty. When you swerve around a big bend 5.2 miles from the trailhead, look for the large alcove partway up the north wall of the canyon. Find the hiker trail leading toward it to see the amazing preservation of Perfect Kiva, a highlight of this canyon.

Used as ancient ceremonial spaces, kivas were sacred to the Ancestral Puebloans who lived here so many centuries ago. A sturdy modern-day ladder allows you to descend through a square

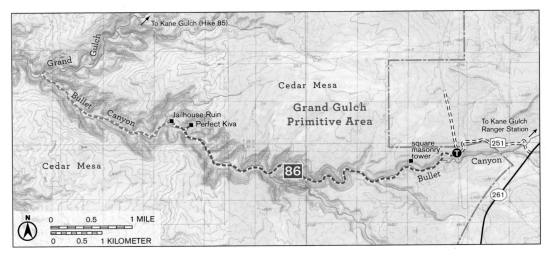

Unusual square masonry tower in Bullet Canyon

opening into the kiva. Pictographs, metates, potsherds, and dried corncobs also give testament to the fact that people once lived here. Be sure to leave everything exactly where you find it, and do not touch any wall art to avoid damaging it with the natural oils in your hands.

Back in the main canyon, continue down the trail another 0.3 mile to reach Jailhouse Ruin on the right-hand side of the canyon, so named for the wooden "bars" over a window opening. Large white pictographs decorate the walls behind the ruin, leading to further speculation about the use of this particular structure. From here, simply turn around and retrace your steps back to the trailhead, being sure to watch carefully for the boulder jam bypass route along the way.

Extending your hike: From Jailhouse Ruin, walk another 2 miles downcanyon to reach the junction with Grand Gulch. This is a good area to search for overnight campsites, particularly among the cottonwoods. Camping here allows for much more time to explore the canyons and ruins before returning to the trailhead back up Bullet Canyon. This extension adds a total of 4 miles to this trip.

87 Fish Creek Canyon and Owl Creek Canyon

Loop: 17 miles
Hiking time: 2–3 days
Elevation gain: 1450 feet
Difficulty: moderate
Season: all year

Map: USGS South Long Point, Bluff NW, Snowflat Spring Cave
Contact: Bureau of Land Management, Monticello Field Office

Getting there: From Blanding, drive south on US Highway 191 for 4 miles. Turn right (west) onto State Route 95 and drive for 28.5 miles to State Route 261. Turn left (south) and drive 4 miles to the Kane Gulch Ranger Station; stop here to obtain a permit. Drive 1 more mile and turn left (east) on County Road 253. Drive 5 miles on this dirt road to

Remains of ancient civilization in Owl Creek Canyon

the trailhead parking by an old drill hole. **Notes:** Obtain required overnight permit from the Kane Gulch Ranger Station or self-pay tube at trailhead. Routefinding skills may be necessary. Can be very hot in summer. Binoculars may be helpful for viewing distant ruins. Roads may be impassable when wet.

On the east side of the road that bisects the area, Owl Creek Canyon and Fish Creek Canyon differ from Grand Gulch in that they are deeper, steeper, and more slickrocky, and they have perennial streams flowing through their bottoms. The canyon walls soar 500 feet high, and ruins, natural arches, colorful springtime flowers, hanging gardens, and sandstone pour-offs make this an exceptionally beautiful hike through classic canyon-country landscape that features the special attraction of this rugged, remote area: ancient ruins and other signs of those people who once passed through here so long ago.

From the trailhead, follow the well-marked path 0.25 mile south to begin your loop at Owl Creek Canyon. The descent here is a little steep, so watch your footing while wearing a backpack. Be sure to scan the cliffs to the right (south) as you descend, particularly past the first significant

drop roughly 0.1 mile in, where you may spot a fairly substantial ruin. The trail gently swerves you around a few pour-offs (look for cairns and foot tracks leading you the left around these) and past other ruins before meeting with the floor of Owl Creek Canyon 1.5 miles in. The way along the canyon floor is not an exercise in level walking, as the elevation keeps dropping and the trail can still be somewhat steep in places. Large pools of water are usually found here and there, although the depth of summer (which is not a recommended time of year to do this hike) may find them fairly dry.

About 2.75 miles in, the way finally flattens out some to make for easier walking. You reach Nevills Arch 4.25 miles from the trailhead. Large and imposing in its high-walled setting, the arch presides over the canyon and several nearby ruins. Another 2.5 miles along you reach the cottonwood-laden confluence with Fish Creek

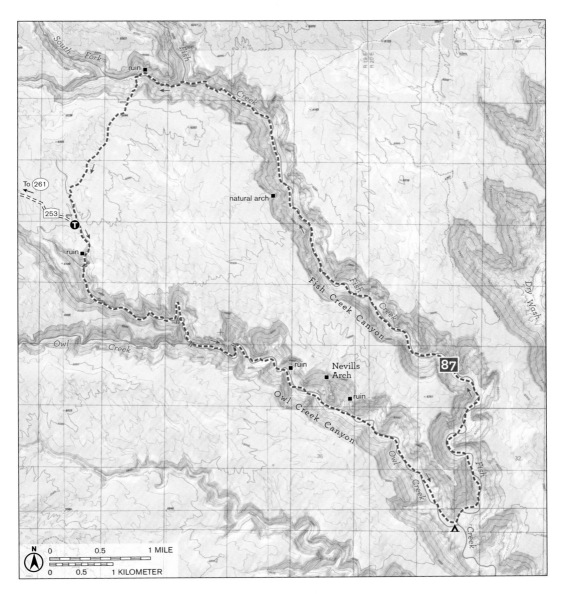

Canyon, which is a good place to find a campsite for the night.

From here you begin walking northwest up Fish Creek Canyon, steadily regaining elevation along the way. Narrower than Owl Creek Canyon, it offers an equally impressive number of ancient ruins, although you generally have to look much harder to find them high up on the ledges. This canyon features more slickrock walking as well, and its natural beauty can be even more spectacular than Owl Creek Canyon. From the confluence of the canyons, it is a total of 9.5 miles up Fish Creek Canyon all the way back to the trailhead, with 1350 feet of elevation gain, mostly along the final 2 miles. Keep a sharp eye out for the trail out of the canyon; this is where map reading and routefinding skills may come in handy. Also be prepared to rise very steeply the final 0.25 mile. Stellar views once you reach the canyon rim make up for the effort. From here it is 1.5 miles along an easy trail through the pinyons and junipers back to the trailhead.

Extending your hike: Walk southeast down Fish Creek Canyon from the confluence at Owl Creek Canyon for as long or as little as you wish. Many more ruins are scattered through this section, so it is best to take your time and look carefully. There is no real trail through here, so be prepared for bushwhacking as you explore.

88 *Government Trail*

Roundtrip: 10.6 miles	**Season:** all year
Hiking time: 7–8 hours	**Map:** USGS Pollys Pasture
Elevation gain: 740 feet	**Contact:** Bureau of Land Management,
Difficulty: moderate	Monticello Field Office

Getting there: From Blanding, drive south on US Highway 191 for 4 miles. Turn right (west) onto State Route 95 and drive for 28.5 miles to State Route 261. Turn left (south) and drive 4 miles to the Kane Gulch Ranger Station; stop here to obtain a permit. Drive another 9.7 miles to County Road 245, which is directly across from Cigarette Spring Road. Turn right (west) on the dirt road CR 245 and drive 2.9 miles to a split; take the right fork. Drive another 4.9 miles and again turn right at a road split. From here it is another 1.5 miles to the parking area by a stock pond where information kiosks and trailhead register are clearly visible. If your vehicle can't make it in all the way, simply pull over and park

Beautiful Grand Gulch on the Government Trail

before the going gets too rough. **Notes**: Obtain required permit from Kane Gulch Ranger Station or self-pay tube at trailhead. Can be very hot in summer. Binoculars may be helpful for viewing distant ruins. Roads may be impassable when wet.

Following the path of a deep canyon incised into the earth and winding in gentle, sinuous fashion through a landscape that can look, from a distance, as if it holds nothing more than sagebrush and juniper trees, Government Trail offers a beautiful example of the Grand Gulch canyon system and some of its ancient rock art. Starting at the top and dropping into the canyon, the trail is flat and easy along the canyon bottom, with both natural and human-made surprises awaiting the keen eye that carefully observes the passing scenery. Large cottonwood trees grace the area, along with rock alcoves tucked back into the walls, and a lovely pictograph panel reveals a little about this area's intriguing long-gone human occupants.

From the trailhead parking area, set off north on a long, flat, and not terribly exciting walk over the top of the mesa 2.7 miles to the canyon rim. Once at the rim, however, the beautiful and fascinating Grand Gulch opens up below, beckoning with its hint of hidden treasures. Pollys Canyon swoops in from the east, making this a veritable mashup of canyons. As you approach the rim, if you look closely across Pollys Canyon, you might see a south-facing ancient ruin, still protected from the elements after centuries beneath a rock shelter overhang on a protuberance known as Pollys Island. Drop onto the trail behind and below the sign, even though at first glance you might think the first step will hurtle you off into the abyss. The trail skirts the edge of the canyon in an easy path down the side, reaching the bottom in just under a mile. Once you reach level ground, strike off north (right) to follow the graceful curves and long straight sections.

Sandy wallows, the possibility of water pockets, shaded sections beneath tilting rock walls, and sun-exposed stretches all intermingle on this trail. Wander through here for 1.5 miles. If you examine the rock walls now and then, small panels of ancient art may reveal themselves along the way. A small arch resides high up on

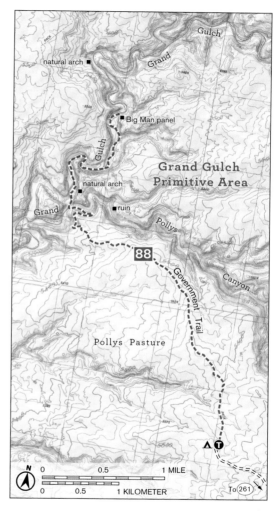

the eastern wall, though it is easy to miss. When you are 5 miles in, keep your eyes peeled for hiker trails veering off to the right and into the rocks under the east canyon wall. Clamber up over the rock slabs to reach the well-known Big Man pictograph panel.

The artwork of the ancients still fascinates today, and people might spend long minutes or even hours here, examining the handiwork of those long since passed into dust. The BLM has interpretive materials at this site you can read to gain more understanding of what you're looking at, or you can simply gaze upon it from your own perspective. From here, return the way you came back to the parking area, keeping an eye out again for ruins or other pictograph panels you may have missed on the hike in.

89 *Mule Canyon*

Roundtrip: 8 miles
Hiking time: 4–6 hours
Elevation gain: 430 feet
Difficulty: easy

Season: all year
Map: USGS Hotel Rock, South Long Point
Contact: Bureau of Land Management, Monticello Field Office

Getting there: From Blanding, drive south on US Highway 191 for 4 miles. Turn right (west) onto State Route 95 and drive for 23.5 miles to County Road 263. Turn right (north) here and drive 0.25 mile to the pullout parking area. (If from SR 95 you reach the paved entrance to Mule Canyon Ruins instead, you overshot the correct road by 0.25 mile to the west.) **Notes:** Fee required. Obtain required overnight permit from Kane Gulch Ranger Station. Routefinding skills may be necessary. Can be very hot in summer. Binoculars may be helpful for viewing distant ruins. Roads may be impassable when wet.

Mule Canyon is easy, accessible, filled with ruins, and just lovely overall. While not as spectacular in natural scenery as some other area canyons, the canyon showcases the ancient ruins and rock art of the Ancestral Puebloans who lived in this area centuries ago. Knowing,

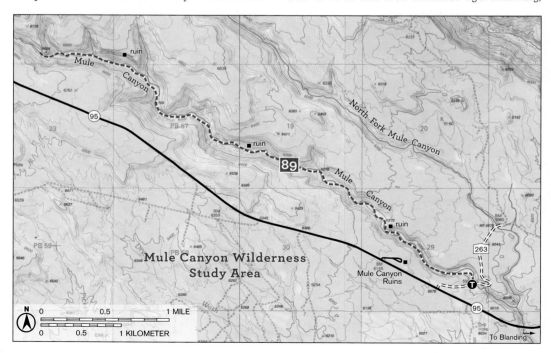

Famed House on Fire Ruin in Mule Canyon

understanding, and loving areas like this will help keep them protected for generations to come. Ancient ruins are gently tucked under sandstone alcoves. Canyon walls gently rise the farther in you get, densely decorated with pinyons, junipers, and other desert vegetation. Tall ponderosas seem to scrape the sky, also providing shady spots for rests here and there.

From the parking area, head northwest through the miniature forest of tenacious pinyons and junipers into the canyon. More a shallow depression in the earth than a canyon at first, Mule slowly becomes deeper the farther up you head. As the sandstone canyon begins to lift around you, ledges and rocky benches carve their way into it. A mere 1.5 miles in, the first and most well-known ruin will come into sight on the north side of the canyon. Known to many as House on Fire Ruin, it is so named for the flame-like appearance of the natural wall curving up and away from the human-made ruin below it. Shoot for a mid- to late-morning arrival for the best light.

Ancient structures like these housed people, food, animals, and more. Their meticulous creation with stone, sandstone bricks, mud, small pebbles for decoration, wood beams for support, and doorways made from large stone slabs (finding these is rare, as many were carted off years ago by illegal and thoughtless "collectors") is a testimony to the time as well as imagination possessed by the people who lived here so long ago. Remember to take pictures but nothing else, and refrain from touching, leaning against, or sitting upon any of these protected remnants in order to preserve them as long as possible for future generations to be able to see as well.

Continue up the canyon, beneath tall Douglas firs, around vegetation-covered bends, and under outward-jutting red walls dripping with dark streaks of desert varnish. Keep your eyes on the north side of the canyon to spot more ruins; ancients tended to build on the north sides so as to receive the southern sun for light and warmth. You should pass at least eight visible ruins in this stretch of the canyon, although you do need to keep an eye out in order to spot them all. In the springtime, the green seeps on the walls where water is present may also grace you with water-hungry wildflowers such as columbine and red monkeyflower. In the drier sections, look

221

for little yellow Chambers' twinpod and vibrant cerise-colored coral gilia.

Although you can travel farther up the canyon, turning around at the 4-mile mark is generally sufficient for seeing most of the historic treasures as well as natural beauty here, and it makes for a pleasant yet not-too-demanding amount of time for a day hike. Simply turn around and follow the canyon back down to the trailhead.

90 *Dead Horse Point Rim Trail*

Loop: 9.2 miles	**Season:** all year
Hiking time: 3–5 hours	**Map:** USGS Shafer Basin
Elevation gain: 150 feet	**Contact:** Dead Horse Point State Park
Difficulty: moderate	

Getting there: From Moab, drive north on US Highway 191 for 9 miles to State Route 313. Turn west (left) here and drive another 23 miles to the park entrance. **Notes:** Fee required. Summer can be very hot. Visitor center, restrooms, snacks available at trailhead parking lot.

Despite the grim name, Dead Horse Point State Park boasts some of the best views in the state, if not the entire country. With vistas that span from Green River to the La Sal Mountains, sweeping over the mass of wrinkled, crumpled canyons and mesas and buttes and river carvings of neighboring Canyonlands National Park, this state park packs in an amazing concentration of easy trails with mind-blowing views. The rim trail travels along exactly what it says: the rim of one of the many large upthrust plateaus that rise throughout the landscape. Although the mileage varies depending on how much of it you actually hike, the trail itself is mostly level, making this a literal stroll in the park. Soaring a grand 2000 feet above the broad Colorado River, which snakes below, the park's plateau gives you a bird's-eye view of the surrounding countryside and some of the state's most iconic images, as evidenced by the staggering number of photos that have been taken from the rim. The total mileage assumes heading out on each spur trail to see the views; you can considerably shorten this hike by not going on all or even any of the spurs, turning around at any point, or following the road straight back to the visitor center after the most famous overlook at Dead Horse Point itself.

View eastward from the Dead Horse Point Rim Trail

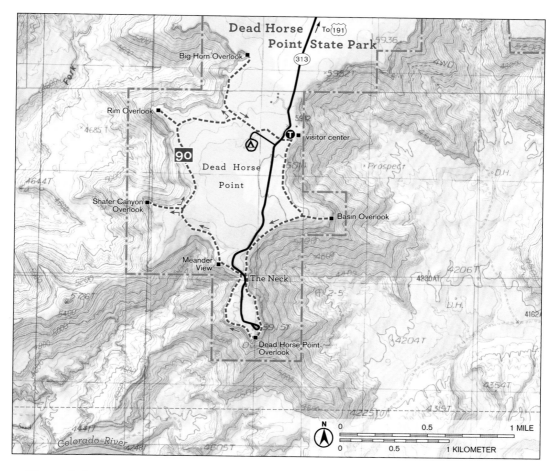

The trail departs the visitor center parking lot to the east, although it quickly curves south to follow the natural contour of the rim. The first spur trail to the left (east) takes you a few hundred feet out to Basin Overlook. After you return to the main trail, continue rambling southward. About 1 mile from the visitor center you must pass through The Neck, a super-skinny isthmus so narrow the trail shares the road. At 1.6 miles you tumble onto Dead Horse Point, which also has a parking lot and vault toilets. This is, of course, the view that most people come here to see. The sheer drop of the cliffs; the vast, jagged tumble of canyons and benches and plateaus; and the sharp bend of the Colorado all make for a view that is incredibly vast and stunning.

Take your time at this point, crowded though it may be.

From here, the trail begins to head northwesterly, still following the rim itself. The next overlook is Meander View, which, appropriately enough, overlooks the meandering river below. Shafer Canyon Overlook is the next small spur trail, followed by Rim Overlook not long after. The next spur trail is more of an actual trail, since it will take you 2.5 miles roundtrip to reach the Big Horn Overlook. The views from this one are as spectacular as the rest, although it takes a little longer to get to them. Back on the main trail, it's almost a straight shot east to finish up your loop at the visitor center parking lot.

91 *Syncline Loop*

Loop: 8.3 miles
Hiking time: 5–7 hours
Elevation gain: 1500 feet
Difficulty: moderate

Season: all year
Map: USGS Upheaval Dome
Contact: Canyonlands National Park, Island in the Sky District

Getting there: From Moab, drive north on US Highway 191 for 9 miles to State Route 313. Turn left (west) here and drive 21 miles to the Island in the Sky visitor center. From here, drive another 6.5 miles to the signed junction to Upheaval Dome; turn right and drive another 5 miles to the parking area. **Note:** Fee required. Can be extremely hot in summer. Routefinding, rock scrambling required. Exposed sections with drop-offs.

Upheaval Dome is as interesting as its name suggests, although it's not quite correct in its description. Upheaval Crater would be a more accurate designation for the main feature around which the Syncline Loop winds. A few theories abound as to the cause of this captivating landmark, which is even visible from space: the impact crater theory and the salt dome theory. For your purposes, though, what you really need to know is that this is an incredible and unique hiking area. Tumbled tawny and russet rocks, a precipitous drop into the canyon, large sandstone walls, hillocks of color-banded bentonite clay, tremendous views, and the possibility of seeing animals such as bighorn sheep all conspire to make this hike one to do for the fit, ambitious, and adventurous. The trail's start is at the Upheaval Dome parking lot, which also features a separate 2.5-mile roundtrip Overlook Trail. The overlook actually provides a better

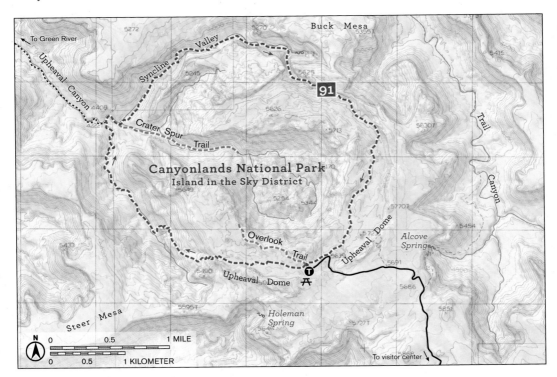

Dark summer day on the Syncline Loop

view of Upheaval Dome, but be prepared for a very challenging 10.8-mile day if you attempt it as well as the strenuous Syncline Loop trail.

From the trailhead, take the left (west) turn to begin the loop in a clockwise direction. The initial 0.8 mile is reasonably level; then you begin the abrupt 1000-foot drop into the canyon. Switchbacks lessen the impact on your knees somewhat, but you will likely still feel it. Immense, long-range views should distract from that—but do keep an eye on your footing. After the descent, you'll be in a dry wash for some time. Curve along its bottom as it carves alongside jagged rock walls, gradually taking you northwest. The junction with a trail leading through Upheaval Canyon to the Green River opens on your left (west) at 3.2 miles; stay on the Syncline Loop trail, which still curves more to the northeast. The spur trail to the crater itself appears just past that; take the 3-mile roundtrip hike in if so inclined, but it's not essential to see this area.

The main trail keeps looping back, taking you through scrub brush, tilted canyon walls, and, eventually, rock scrambling. On occasion water trickles through this area in a few riparian sections, but don't rely on it being there. The trail ascends a rocky, ledge-y, boulder-strewn cliffside on which agility is required, not to mention a sense of humor at the conditions of the "trail," which essentially is an everyone-for-themselves scramble up a rugged waterfall of giant sandstone slabs. This is, however, an exciting part of the trail for those fit enough to enjoy it. As you reach the top, a far more typical beaten path awaits, clearly stretching ahead through a small desert meadow tucked between red canyon walls. The last 1.8 miles is an easy jaunt back to the parking area.

Otherworldly formations and colors inside Upheaval Dome

92 Mesa Arch

Loop: 0.5 mile
Hiking time: 1 hour
Elevation gain: 140 feet
Difficulty: easy

Season: all year
Map: USGS Musselman Arch
Contact: Canyonlands National Park,
Island in the Sky District

Getting there: From Moab, drive north on US Highway 191 for 9 miles to State Route 313. Turn left (west) here and drive into Canyonlands National Park. Thirteen miles in, the signed parking area will be on your left-hand side. **Note:** Can be very crowded spring through fall, especially at sunrise.

Sunrise as viewed from behind Mesa Arch is a bit of a mecca trip for many visitors, professional photographers and casual snap-happy tourists alike. Even without the light of sunrise casting its reflective glow on the underside of the arch, the view through the opening is truly astounding. A mess of jumbled canyons and tilted rocks, the distant points of the La Sal Mountains—often snow-covered for even better contrast—the interlocking masses of plateaus and mesas, and the always fascinating buttes and spires of sandstone are all framed under the arch, giving ample reason why this is one of the most photographed arches in the world. A simple enough trail for the very young to complete, yet stunning enough for even the most experienced hiker to want to see, Mesa Arch is one of those a-little-something-for-everyone hikes that is an

easy yet excellent showcase of why Canyonlands is a favorite national park for so many.

After snagging a pamphlet, take the trail as it leads off to the left from the parking area. A potpourri of endemic plant varieties lie scattered alongside the trail as you walk. Pinyon and juniper clump here and there, along with the jointed fingers of Mormon tea, the sharp-tipped pads of prickly pear cactus, and clumps of soft green-gray mountain mahogany. Along the way, living cryptobiotic soil bursts up in small colonies of what seem to be dark heads of cauliflower. An essential part of dry desert landscapes that can be ferociously washed by storms, cryptobiotic soil is extremely fragile, takes an extremely long time to grow, and must be carefully avoided so you don't trample it and thus help further erode bare hillsides. The well-marked path is broad in

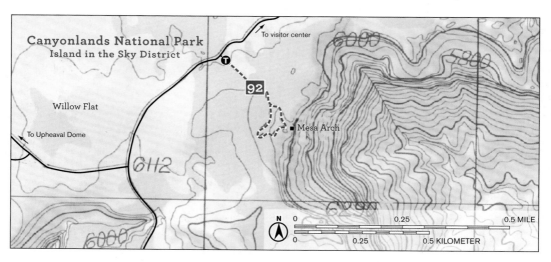

The view through Mesa Arch

some parts as it crosses sand, then somewhat less so when it gently climbs wide sandstone stairs.

In a quarter mile, you crest a small rise that allows you to see the expansive views eastward. Just several more strides bring the arch itself into view, close to the rim. Drop down and *boom*, the views through the arch are stunning and just beg for photos. While it's likely many other people had the same thought—particularly at sunrise—this trail is very much worth dealing with crowds. Look for the distinctive shape of Washer Woman Arch in the distance, to the left (north) side of your view through Mesa Arch. When you're done taking all the shots you can or simply soaking it all in, complete the small lollipop loop to return to the parking area.

93 *Chesler Park*

Loop: 10.5 miles
Hiking time: 6–8 hours
Elevation gain: 1300 feet
Difficulty: moderate

Season: all year
Map: USGS Druid Arch, The Loop
Contact: Canyonlands National Park, Needles District

Getting there: From Moab, drive south on US Highway 191 for 40 miles to the signed turnoff to State Route 211 and the Needles District of Canyonlands National Park on your right (west). Turn right here and drive 35 miles to the entrance station. Then follow signs to Elephant Hill trailhead parking. The last 3 miles are on a dirt road that may be impassable when wet. **Notes:** Fee required. Can be very hot in summer. Vault toilets at parking area. Backcountry permit required for overnight camping.

The extraordinary sandstone formations of Chesler Park

Chesler Park itself is a small desert meadow, flat and covered with sagebrush, pinyons, junipers, and other hardy plant denizens of the high Utah canyonlands. But it is also a magnificent place surrounded with gorgeous red-and-white sandstone towers whose intriguing shapes fascinate the eye and encourage exploration. This landscape can be called bizarre, even Mars-like, and it certainly is utterly spectacular. Sandstone fins, spires, and pinnacles brashly announce their presence in colorful beauty. The rocks are banded with layers in varying thicknesses, blazing out in shades similar to the colors of the sunset just before the sun falls behind the horizon. Walking on slickrock is part of the attraction of this loop hike, although the main reason is simply to see the sheer unique beauty of this place. Many possible trail combinations are available here, and you can walk for as short or as long as you prefer, even overnighting if desired, as backcountry sites are available. This loop provides an excellent immersion into this most geologically fascinating and gorgeous area.

From the parking area, head south and uphill to begin winding among, up, and around sandstone obstacles. Snaking through the landscape, you soon rise high enough to see Chesler Park's nest of needly spires in the distance. Along the trail stairways have been built through rock sections, giant sandstone slabs precariously rest on dubious ledges, and the pathway undulates over and around this rocky garden. Watch for rock cairns to be certain you stick to the trail, although it's fairly well beaten in this section. At the 1.5-mile mark you reach a signed junction offering you various choices; you want to turn right (west) for Chesler Park. Shortly thereafter you will cross a wash and begin a steep climb. When you reach 2.5 miles another junction appears; go left (south) for Chesler Park. Very quickly you'll come to yet another signed junction, at which you turn left to begin your clockwise loop of the spire-filled park.

Dropping into the park, the trail circles the meadow encircled by the spires. Once used by cowboys to graze cattle, the area has thankfully been allowed to return to its natural vegetation

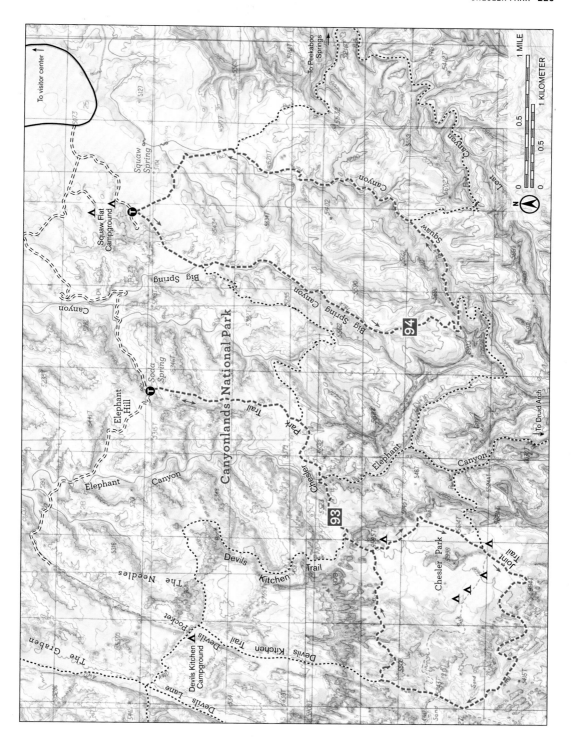

To visitor center

Squaw Spring

Squaw Flat Campground

Big Spring

Canyon

Elephant Hill

Soda Spring

Elephant Canyon

Canyonlands National Park

Park Trail

Chesler Trail

Devils Kitchen Trail

The Needles

Devils Pocket

Devils Kitchen Campground

Devils Lane

The Graben

Chesler Park

Joint Trail

Elephant Canyon

To Druid Arch

Big Spring Canyon

Squaw Canyon

Lost Canyon

To Peekaboo Springs

93

94

N

1 MILE
1 KILOMETER

0   0.5   1
0   0.5   1

state. Here the path is flat and easy, and amazing views surround you in every direction. At the 3.8-mile mark there is a signed turnoff for Druid Arch to your left; stay right to remain on the Chesler Park Trail. At 4.4 miles you are now on an intriguing section known as the Joint Trail, so named by local old-timers who saw its crack-in-the-wall section as a joint in the rock. The slot through here is very fun, with a sandy bottom along its straight shot. Little wooden ladders and small boulder obstacles lend adventure to this part of the trail, not to mention the coolness factor of walking between enormous boulders for a length of time.

At 5.3 miles the trail hooks into a 4WD road. Although loud vehicles may join you on this stretch, it's easy walking and still scenic. When you are 6.3 miles into the trail, disregard the signed Devils Kitchen Trail leading off the road directly ahead (north); instead stay to your right (east) to remain on the Chesler Park loop. When you again reach a Devils Kitchen sign at 7.8 miles, turn right for the final 2.7 miles to complete the loop back where you started at Elephant Hill.

One of many joint trail sections of the Chesler Park Trail

94 *Big Spring Canyon–Squaw Canyon Loop*

Loop: 7.5 miles
Hiking time: 3–4 hours
Elevation gain: 440 feet
Difficulty: moderate

Season: all year
Map: USGS The Loop
Contact: Canyonlands National Park, Needles District

Getting there: From Moab, drive south on US Highway 191 for 40 miles to the signed turnoff to State Route 211 and the Needles District of Canyonlands National Park on your right (west). Turn right here and drive 35 miles to the entrance station. Then follow signs to Squaw Flat Campground and trailhead parking. **Notes:** Can be very hot in summer. Vault toilets at parking area. Rock scrambling may be required. Exposed drop-offs in some sections. Walking through water may be required.

The less visited Needles District of Canyonlands is quite beautiful, and sometimes even more pleasant due to fewer crowds. The Big Spring Canyon–Squaw Canyon Loop is a perfect starter hike to discover the geologic grace and elegance of the area, and its relatively easy path

makes it a good one for families. Despite its inauspicious beginning in flat scrublands, the trail soon takes you through a slickrock section that surrounds you with pinkish-red sandstone outcroppings; upthrust pinnacles capped by white rock; flat, broad portions dimpled with

Sunset light on the Big Spring Canyon–Squaw Canyon Loop

potholes that sometimes may hold water; uneven red rock walls that are slowly eroding; and canyonland vistas that spread out as far as the eye can see. The views of the Needles—that prickly garden of Cedar Mesa sandstone spires both thick and thin—are enough to make the hike a stunner. Significantly hot in summer, this extremely satisfying hike is best enjoyed in spring and fall.

Heading south from the parking area in the Squaw Flat Campground, follow the marked trail for 150 feet to the signed fork. Take the right-hand choice toward Big Spring Canyon to begin your loop. Travel over the scrublands for 0.25 mile, then traverse a low-slung slickrock ridge with some nice views. At 1.3 miles reach another trail junction. Go left (south) for Big Spring Canyon. After you drop down, you will find yourself in the canyon for about 3 miles. Draws, terraces, and the curves and turns of walls, washes, and fins accompany you through this section. Water flows through here as well, which can be quite enjoyable on warmer days as you wander through this beautiful canyon.

At canyon's end, you must once again ascend slickrock ledges and slopes, and this is where some people may feel somewhat hesitant about the exposure. Keep an eye out for cairns and carefully pick your way up.

The terrain and views only get more beautiful in this section. Topping sandstone rises, circling around more rocky ledges, climbing over saddles, and passing the ubiquitous pop-ups of junipers and pinyons, you also occasionally get stellar views of the Needles District and the La Sal Mountains. You then drop down a saddle into Squaw Canyon; again simply be aware of your footing as you navigate down the sandstone. Once in the canyon, you head to the east/northeast. At 6.5 miles in, pass the signed junction for the Peekaboo Trail leading off to your right (southeast) while you continue walking north on the Squaw Canyon Trail back toward Squaw Flat. Head over the relatively flat slickrock ridges and ledges for a half mile before intersecting with the creek, which you will cross several times. The trail ends back in the campground from which you started.

95 *Windows Loop and Double Arch*

Roundtrip: 2 miles
Hiking time: 1–2 hours
Elevation gain: 290 feet
Difficulty: moderate

Season: all year
Map: USGS Arches National Park
Contact: Arches National Park,
The Windows Section

Getting there: From Moab, drive 5.2 miles north on US Highway 191 to the well-marked turnoff road to Arches National Park on the right (east) side of the highway. (From Green River, drive 20 miles east on I-70, then 30 miles south on US 191 to the turnoff.) From the fee station, drive 9 miles along Arches Scenic Drive to The Windows Section turnoff and turn right. Drive another 2.5 miles to the parking area. **Notes:** Can be very hot in summer. Can be very crowded. Vault toilets at parking area.

The Windows Loop is a perfect short introduction to Arches National Park, ideal for those with limited time who still want to soak in the beauty of the area. North Window, South Window, Turret Arch, and Double Arch all command attention and are quite lovely to see and explore around. Well known and accessed often, these arches offer an excellent first perspective on the beauties to be found in this national park. The sandstone is shot through with cream, pale gold, burnished umber, light peach, and the dark streaks and falls of desert varnish, all of which bedazzle the eye, particularly during the incredible light of sunrise and sunset hours. Don't let the crowds sway you from walking this brief loop—if they do, plan to visit in the

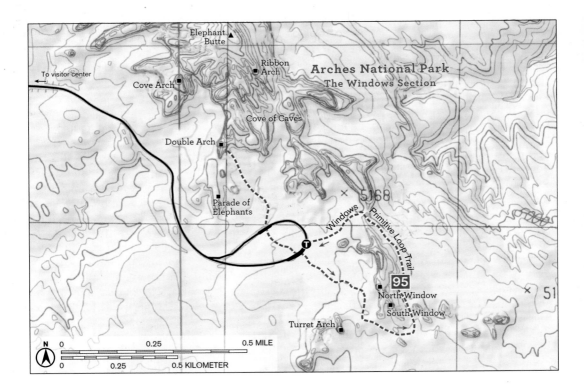

One of many arches visible from the Windows Loop

colder months or very early in the morning. Just because they're highly visited doesn't mean these classic Utah arches are not highly worthwhile. As a solitude bonus, be sure to take the Primitive Loop Trail, which far fewer people travel and which thus tends to be the most serene part of this area.

From the parking area, set out southeast along the trail to first approach Turret Arch in 0.25 mile. The trail here is wide and relatively flat, although it soon begins to rise a bit. Turret Arch is named for the turret-like rock that rises beside the arch; a small arch carves through the rock just to the side of the main arch. At just under 0.5 mile, a junction allows you to decide whether you will complete the small loop between the three arches or head out on the Primitive Loop. Turn right to continue on another 0.1 mile to South Window and the

Primitive Loop. North Window is just beyond. Make sure to get here to see Turret Arch framed in North Window. When you tackle the Primitive Loop, keep an eye out for cairns on this less traveled section. This is the perfect part of the trail to add if you really want to get some distance from the crowds as well as see more incredible Arches scenery. The trail circles around north and then back east to the parking lot:

Once back at the parking area, walk north on the road to the trailhead for Double Arch. Take a good look at the whimsically named Parade of Elephants formation along the 0.3-mile trail to the arch; it really does look like what the name implies. Once at Double Arch, enjoy the spectacle of two arches virtually on top of each other, the only such ones in this area. Return to the parking area the same way you came in.

96 *Devils Garden Primitive Loop*

Roundtrip: 7.2 miles
Hiking time: 3–5 hours
Elevation gain: 280 feet
Difficulty: moderate

Season: spring–fall
Map: USGS Arches National Park
Contact: Arches National Park

Getting there: From Moab, drive 5.2 miles north on US Highway 191 to the well-marked turnoff road to Arches National Park on the right (east) side of the highway. (From Green River, drive 20 miles east on I-70, then 30 miles south on US 191 to the turnoff.) From the entrance station there, drive 18 miles along Arches Scenic Drive to the Devils Garden parking area. **Notes:** Can be very hot in summer. Vault toilets located at parking area.

Devils Garden in Arches is a tantalizing slickrock playground that beautifully showcases the main reason Arches is a national park, because here you will find the enormous profusion of natural arches that brings millions of footsteps every year. Natural arches were shaped by millions of years of weathering in a confluence of relatively weak sandstone, abrasive wind, and relentless water. Slipping between giant fins of rock; watching the sunlight dance over the terra cotta, vermilion, and creamy salmon shades; gazing in awe at the wildly differing shapes of the arches—all this and more is why Devils Garden is such a popular delight for so many. You almost certainly will be vying with many others for optimal photographs, but it's well worth being part of the crowds to see this place. If you'd rather experience it with a modicum of solitude, try for a winter visit, or at least as early a start time as possible in the day. Many people really love the sunset hour, however, so if you want that light, be prepared to share the glory with plenty of other people if you're here during the busy season—basically March through October.

Famed Landscape Arch near the start of the trail

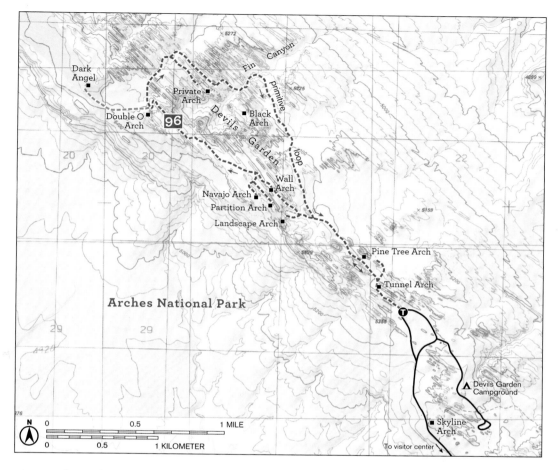

From the parking lot, grab a park trail guide and set out northwest along the well-marked trail to the 0.3-mile point, where you reach the spur trail leading off right to Pine Tree Arch and Tunnel Arch. It is worth the little jaunt out to see these young, photogenic arches. On the main trail, in 1 mile you reach popular Landscape Arch. Long, thin, and appearing as if it will come crashing to the ground at any second, Landscape Arch has a 306-foot span, making it the longest one in Arches National Park. Abide with the crowds to see this pretty, skinny arch, knowing that the vast majority of people will return to their vehicles after this stop and the numbers of other hikers will dwindle as you head on. The trail keeps going northwest, sometimes passing over slickrock and then back to loose, sandy depths. At 1.3 miles there is a junction with a spur trail that takes you to secretive little Navajo Arch; another spur trail off this one leads to Partition Arch. Take the time to make the extra 0.7 mile to see both these arches.

Back on the main Devils Garden Trail, keep heading northwest toward Double O Arch. This beautiful arch is really two, a smaller one tucked beneath a larger one. Many spectacular vistas are possible around these arches, the larger one of which frames quite the background behind it. After visiting Double O Arch you can choose to take a 1-mile spur trail to Dark Angel, a rock monolith that really does rather resemble a brooding celestial being. If you are here for the arches, though, skip the angel and stay to the right for the primitive loop trail, which gives you more visual bang for your hiking buck. Be certain to take the 0.4-mile marked spur trail to Private Arch, which is lovely.

Not the best trail for rank hiking newbies or those uncertain of their footing (if that describes you, simply return to the trailhead on the main Devils Garden Trail), the primitive loop is a heck of a lot of fun, with scrambling on slickrock and walking beneath and through the large sandstone fins

in what is known as, quite accurately, Fin Canyon. This is perhaps the best part of the entire loop hike, and luckily it's also the least crowded. Enjoy the trip through this astounding area while remaining cautious of slickrock sections that seem icy or just too much for your party. You can always turn back at any time, although, of course, that will increase your total mileage. The primitive loop eventually meets up with the main Devils Garden Trail again, at which point it is 0.9 mile back to the parking area.

97 Delicate Arch

Roundtrip: 3 miles
Hiking time: 2–3 hours
Elevation gain: 600 feet
Difficulty: easy/moderate

Season: spring, fall
Map: USGS Arches National Park
Contact: Arches National Park

Getting there: From Moab, drive 5.2 miles north on US Highway 191 to the well-marked turnoff road to Arches National Park on the right (east) side of the highway. (From Green River, drive 20 miles east on I-70, then 30 miles south on US 191 to the turnoff.) From the fee station, drive 12 miles along Arches Scenic Drive to the signed Delicate Arch turnoff. Drive another 1.2 miles to the parking area. **Notes:** Can be very crowded on weekends and holidays. Can be hot in summer. Vault toilets located at parking area.

Certainly an iconic symbol of Utah, Delicate Arch is often the first exposure many people have to the state's outstanding natural wonders, since it has probably appeared in photographs and other images more than just about any other from the Beehive State. Curving up to kiss the sky, this freestanding arch attracts tons of visitors every year who want to snap pictures of its beauty. Framing the La Sal Mountains, Delicate Arch really is the perfect choice for a classic Utah image. Hiking up to the arch itself (rather than just the shorter trail to a viewpoint) is virtually a requirement for both residents and visitors. Despite potential crowds, this trail is truly breathtaking and also diverse as it covers slickrock walking, skims you past hanging gardens of bursts of greenery, and, at its end, offers

Iconic Delicate Arch

a wide-ranging viewpoint that really is stunning. Winter can be a lovely time to visit the arch, because the crowds are far diminished and any snow on the arch and surrounding slickrock vistas can simply be breathtaking, with a stark contrast between red and white.

From the trailhead starting immediately before the historic Wolfe Ranch cabin, cross the bridge over Salt Wash. Right after the bridge there is a junction to a petroglyph panel; turn left here to take the short spur trail to see the panel. Loop back to the Delicate Arch trail and continue in a generally northeast direction, admiring the views across Cache Valley. The dirt trail winds around in little curves, steadily climbing. After ascending a brief but leg-burning hill, you will begin the slickrock portion of the hike. At 0.8 mile the trail heads up the rock itself, marked by cairns and occasional grooved steps cut right into the rock. The final 0.4 mile is along a broad ledge right on the side of the cliff. It is perfectly safe but may call for keeping small, active children in your immediate sight due to the drop-offs.

Stone stairs along the trail

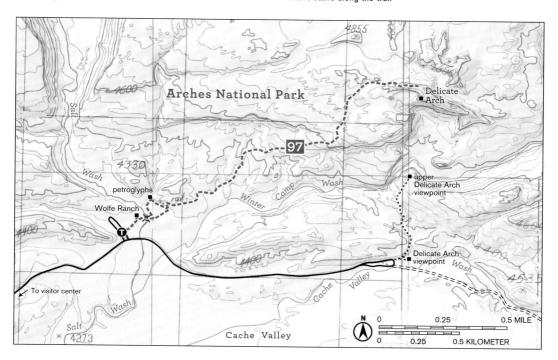

When you head over the final rise, Delicate Arch is in your sights. This immediate view often stops people in their tracks as they grab their cameras, but after you've squeezed off a shot or ten, keep heading on. The views beyond the arch are nearly as impressive, adding to the overall jaw-dropping beauty of the spot. You can head down into the sandstone bowl from which the arch rises, which many people do in order to get a picture of themselves standing directly under the arch. This is a somewhat precarious but great way to fully grasp the massive scope of this icon, which rises 65 feet at the top (48 feet at the opening) and spans 32 feet. Take in your fill of the view before retracing your steps to the parking area.

98 Corona Arch

Roundtrip: 3 miles
Hiking time: 2–3 hours
Elevation gain: 557 feet
Difficulty: easy

Season: all year
Map: USGS Gold Bar Canyon, Moab
Contact: Bureau of Land Management, Moab Field Office

Getting there: From Moab, drive north on US Highway 191 for 4 miles to Potash Road. Turn left (west) here and continue another 10 miles to the signed trailhead for Corona Arch. Parking is on the right (north) side of the road. **Note:** Summer can be very hot; trail is mostly exposed.

Tall enough to fly a small plane through—not that that's remotely advisable—Corona Arch is a really breathtaking arch just outside Moab. Not in any of the national parks, this arch is still popular due to its gorgeous shape as well as the relative ease of access. With its 335-foot span and 140-foot height, not to mention its sinuous curve as it delicately reaches out from the sandstone

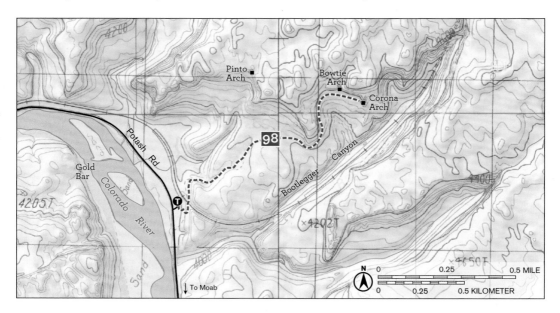

Corona Arch

rock of which it once was fully a part, Corona Arch is one of the most beautiful examples of a natural arch to be found in all of Utah. The fact that your trail to and from the arch is mostly slickrock only adds to the appeal of this hike. Interestingly enough, this arch is also the closest one to reach from Moab, and it certainly holds its own with even the most spectacular arches in nearby Arches National Park. Corona Arch is on BLM land, in what is rather fascinatingly known as Bootlegger Canyon.

You almost immediately ascend on the trail from the parking area, heading directly up a rather steep slope, although this is switchbacked. After crossing railroad tracks (which are still used; as noted by the sign there, exercise caution as you cross) you will be on a disused old road in rough shape that slices right through the slickrock. Once you've passed through the gap,

follow the cairns through a wash as you angle northeast. From here the trail meanders through low desert scrub, sand, and slickrock. High on the northern cliff walls rises Pinto Arch, which is also very scenic. At 0.8 mile you will be at the base of a slickrock climb, where cables are attached to the rock to help people up should they need the extra support on the potentially slick surface. The drop-offs would make for more of a slide rather than a free fall, so this shouldn't be a nerve-racking area for most.

Just beyond these first cables you will be able to see your first glimpse of Corona Arch in all its freestanding glory. Just under 1 mile in you reach the next set of cables, which assist you up another, steeper slickrock slope. Footholds have also been carved into the rock, all of which makes this climb relatively simple. If anyone in your group has a pronounced fear of heights, however, this may signal the end of the hike for them. Just beyond these cables a ladder against the sandstone rise again assists in getting over this obstacle; as usual, be certain the ladder is safe before using it. From this point on you are on a wide, mostly flat bench, which makes for a simple stroll the rest of the way. At 1.2 miles you will pass beneath Bowtie Arch, a very pretty pothole arch 100 feet overhead in the cliffs. Keep going to Corona Arch, 1.5 miles in. Situated in a sandstone bowl with miniature valleys and dips, the arch is positioned just right against the cliff wall for beautiful viewing. You can walk directly beneath this massive arch, which gives you an excellent idea of its scale and scope. Return to the parking area via the same route.

99 *Negro Bill Canyon/Morning Glory Natural Bridge*

Roundtrip: 4.5 miles
Hiking time: 3–4 hours
Elevation gain: 400 feet
Difficulty: moderate

Season: all year
Map: USGS Moab
Contact: Bureau of Land Management, Moab Field Office

Getting there: From Moab, drive north on US Highway 191 for 2 miles to State Route 128. Head east for 3.1 miles to the parking area on the right (south) side of the road.
Notes: Can be very hot in summer. Walking through water may be required. Beware of poison ivy.

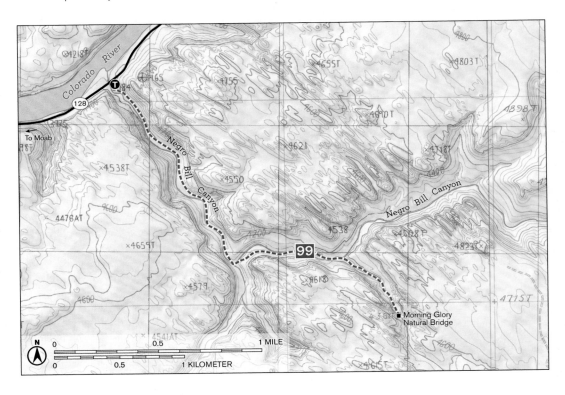

Looking down Negro Bill Canyon

William Grandstaff (or Granstaff, depending on which historical resources you consult), the man for whom this canyon was named, had an interesting history—at least what we know of it. The first black settler in the Moab area, he ran cattle here during the late 1870s, primarily using the canyon that now bears at least part of his name. In later years, after he moved to Colorado, he was also a prospector, an elected constable, and a highly respected town member. The canyon's name has been controversial over the years, for both the far cruder original term and what it is currently called. But no matter your views on the nomenclature, the canyon itself is simply stunning and well deserves a visit. The beautiful Morning Glory Natural Bridge (technically, it's actually an arch) is another attraction in the canyon. At 243 feet long, it's the sixth-longest natural rock span in the United States. With a perennial water source streaming through it, this wet canyon can be soothing on a hot day,

although you should hike it in the early spring or in the fall for the best weather.

The trail leads beside the stream initially, then demands that you cross it multiple times. The classic towering Navajo sandstone walls are drizzled in desert varnish, surrounding the life on the canyon floor that newly burgeons as soon as winter slips away. Cottonwoods and willows provide respites of shade. A century after William Grandstaff ran his cattle here, a different sort of controversy literally ripped into the canyon when land conservationists and vehicular recreationists had decidedly differing viewpoints on the best use of the canyon. After barriers, bulldozers, threats and anger broke the peaceful sanctity of this canyon, a lawsuit eventually ensured that only footsteps would enter it, to the gratitude of hikers everywhere.

Enjoy the sounds of the water and the sights in the canyon as you walk through it. After 1.8 miles a large side canyon enters from the right; turn southward into this canyon to reach

Morning Glory, just 0.4 mile in. Nestled into the back wall of the canyon, this natural rock span can be hard to distinguish from the rock alcove until you are close to it. The natural spring beneath it is another cooling spot on a hot day, although poison ivy can grow there, so beware. Once you've taken in the beauty of Morning Glory, return to the main canyon and turn left to retrace your steps back to the parking area.

100 *Fisher Towers*

Roundtrip: 4.5 miles
Hiking time: 2–4 hours
Elevation gain: 740 feet
Difficulty: moderate

Season: all year
Map: USGS Fisher Towers
Contact: Bureau of Land Management, Moab Field Office

Getting there: From Moab, drive north on US Highway 191 for 2 miles to State Route 128. Turn right (east) and drive 21 miles to the marked Fisher Towers turnoff. Turn right (east) and drive another 2.1 miles to the trailhead parking area. **Notes:** Summer can be very hot; trail is mostly exposed. Vault toilet at parking area.

Fisher Towers is a beautiful hike far enough removed from general civilization to discourage the masses but easy enough to access that it doesn't dissuade the casual adventurer. Well known to rock climbers, the area is somewhat less popular with day hikers, but it is a fantastical foray into the geologic wonders that stun those who visit. Huge, relatively thin slabs of Wingate sandstone soar skyward, and the towers catch the eye from miles around, whetting

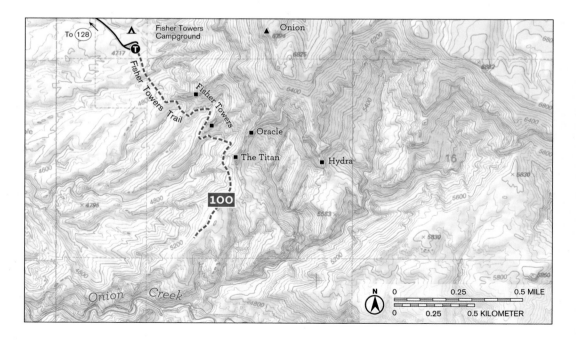

Fisher Towers from the trail

the imagination as you conjure up cityscapes made from the rocks, bizarre cities that might be found on a planet far, far away. Framed against the grandeur of the La Sal Mountains to the east, Fisher Towers is a marvelous area to explore. Luckily, it is part of the National Trails System, so it offers a perfectly charming, maintained trail to wander along.

The beginning of the trail initially drops down some steps as it leads you south to a slickrock ridge. The first 0.25 mile takes you in and out of arroyos (dry washes), meandering up and down as it goes in and out of these water cuts through the soil. Then the trail gradually rises as it takes you to the base of the towers, curving around and near them. The sculpted nature of the sandstone monoliths, formed by millennia of erosion by wind, rain, and rushing water, is always in sight, lending dramatic visual appeal to the entire trail.

Corkscrewing around, reaching high into the sky, and covered by slabby chunks that seem precarious, the towers are each individual and interesting. A much-coveted destination for rock climbers, the towers often sport seemingly tiny figures suspended from ropes as they attempt to conquer the heights.

You will pass by the fluted towers in a zigzag fashion much of the way, reaching the base of the largest, The Titan, after 1.5 miles. The red sands of the trail and the dark red of the towers might further this area's resemblance to a different planet. From the base of the 900-foot tall Titan, the trail takes you southwest and up onto another ridge, from which you will be able to command stellar views of the wider area. This is the trail's marked terminus, at 2.25 miles. From here simply return to the parking area the same way you came in.

Secretive Navajo Arch on the Devils Garden Primitive Loop

Recommended Resources

NATIONAL FORESTS

Ashley National Forest
www.fs.usda.gov/ashley

Duchesne/Roosevelt Ranger District
85 West Main
Duchesne, UT 84021
(435) 738-2482

Flaming Gorge/Vernal Ranger District
355 North Vernal Avenue
Vernal, UT 84078
(435) 789-1181

Dixie National Forest
www.fs.usda.gov/dixie

Box–Death Hollow Wilderness
Escalante Ranger District
755 West Center
Escalante, UT 84726
(435) 826-5400

Cedar City Ranger District
1789 North Wedgewood Lane
Cedar City, UT 84721
(435) 865-3200

Pine Valley Ranger District
196 East Tabernacle St. #38
St. George, UT 84770
(435)-652-3100

Red Canyon Visitor Center
(435) 676-2676

Fishlake National Forest
www.fs.usda.gov/fishlake

Beaver Ranger District
575 South Main Street
Beaver, UT 84713
(435) 438-2436

Fremont River Ranger District
138 South Main Street
Loa, UT 84747
(435) 836-2800

Uinta-Wasatch-Cache National Forest
www.fs.usda.gov/uwcnf

Evanston–Mountain View Ranger District
1565 Highway 150 South, Suite A
Evanston, WY 82930
(307) 789-3194

Heber-Kamas Ranger District
Heber Office
2460 South Highway 40
Heber City, UT 84032
(435) 654-0470

Kamas Office
50 East Center Street
Kamas, UT 84036
(435) 783-4338

Logan Ranger District
1500 East Highway 89
Logan, UT 84321
(435) 755-3620

Pleasant Grove Ranger District
390 North 100 East
Pleasant Grove, UT 84062
(801) 785-3563

Salt Lake Ranger District
6944 South 3000 East
Cottonwood Heights, UT 84121
(801) 733-2676

Spanish Fork Ranger District
44 West 400 North
Spanish Fork, UT 84660
(801) 798-3571

NATIONAL PARKS, MONUMENTS, AND RECREATION AREAS

Arches National Park
P.O. Box 907
Moab, UT 84532
(435) 719-2299
www.nps.gov/arch/index.htm

Bryce Canyon National Park
P.O. Box 640201
Bryce Canyon, UT 84764
(435) 834-5322
www.nps.gov/brca/index.htm

Canyonlands National Park
2282 SW Resource Blvd.
Moab, UT 84532
(435) 719-2313
www.nps.gov/cany/index.htm

Capitol Reef National Park
16 Scenic Drive
Torrey, UT 84775
(435) 425-3791
www.nps.gov/care/index.htm

Cedar Breaks National Monument
2390 West Highway 56, Suite 11
Cedar City, UT 84720
(435) 586-0787
www.nps.gov/cebr/index.htm

Life must be tenacious in the rugged country of the Cedar Mesa area.

Dinosaur National Monument
4545 East Highway 40
Dinosaur, CO 81610
(435) 781-7700
www.nps.gov/dino/index.htm

Glen Canyon National Recreation Area
P.O. Box 1507
Page, AZ 86040
(928) 608-6200
www.nps.gov/glca/index.htm

Grand Staircase–Escalante National Monument
669 South Highway 89A
Kanab, UT 84741
(435) 644-1200
www.blm.gov/ut/st/en/fo/grand
    _staircase-escalante.html

Natural Bridges National Monument
HC-60 Box 1
Lake Powell, UT 84533-0001
(435) 692-1234
www.nps.gov/nabr/index.htm

Vermilion Cliffs National Monument
345 East Riverside Drive
St. George, UT 84790-6714
(435) 688-3200
www.blm.gov/az/st/en/prog/blm_special
    _areas/natmon/vermilion.html

Zion National Park
Springdale, UT 84767-1099
(435) 772-3256
www.nps.gov/zion/index.htm

BUREAU OF LAND MANAGEMENT
Cedar City Office
176 DL Sargent Drive
Cedar City, UT 84721
(435) 865-3000
www.blm.gov/ut/st/en/fo/cedar_city.html

Escalante Interagency Visitor Center
755 West Main Street
Escalante, UT 84726
(435) 826-5499
www.blm.gov/ut/st/en/fo/grand
    _staircase-escalante/Recreation
    /visitor_centers/Escalante
    _Interagency_Visitor_Center.html

Fillmore Field Office
95 East 500 North
Fillmore, UT 84631
(435) 743-3100
www.blm.gov/ut/st/en/fo/fillmore.html

Moab Field Office
82 East Dogwood
Moab, UT 84532
(435) 259-2100
www.blm.gov/ut/st/en/fo/moab.html

Monticello Field Office
365 North Main Street
Monticello, UT 84535
(435) 587-1510 (Kane Gulch Ranger Station)
www.blm.gov/ut/st/en/fo/monticello.html

Price Field Office
125 South 600 West
Price, UT 84501
(435) 636-3600
www.blm.gov/ut/st/en/fo/price.html

STATE PARKS
Antelope Island State Park
4528 West 1700 South
Syracuse, UT 84075
(801) 725-9263
http://stateparks.utah.gov/parks
    /antelope-island

Dead Horse Point State Park
P.O. Box 609
Moab, UT 84532
(435) 259-2614
http://stateparks.utah.gov/parks/dead-horse

Goblin Valley State Park
P.O. Box 637
Green River, UT 84525
(435) 275-4584
http://stateparks.utah.gov
    /park/goblin-valley

Kodachrome Basin State Park
P.O. Box 180069
Cannonville, UT 84718
(435) 679-8562
www.stateparks.utah.gov/park
    /kodachrome-basin

Snow Canyon State Park
1002 North Snow Canyon Road
Ivins, UT 84738
(435) 628-2255
http://stateparks.utah.gov/parks
    /snow-canyon

CITY PARKS
Sandy City Parks & Recreation
440 East 8680 South
Sandy, UT 84070
(801) 568-2900
http://sandy.utah.gov/government
    /parks-and-recreation/parks-division
    /parks-pavilions/bell-canyon-reservoir
    .html

Natural "stairway" on the Bullet Canyon Trail

Index

Huge, ghostly figures of Barrier Canyon–style art in Horseshoe Canyon's Great Gallery

About the Author

Julie Trevelyan is a writer, outdoor guide, horsewoman, and general champion of wild spaces. Since 1999 she has lived in southern Utah, land of slinky canyons, wind-whipped mesas, unparalleled views, and lots of red sand. Ever since she created her first book as part of a second-grade classroom project, she's been hooked on writing. She now mostly writes about outdoor Utah. At age nine she successfully tackled her first backpacking trip and also began riding horses. Julie counts working as an outfitter, backpacking guide, horseback riding instructor, backcountry horse guide, wilderness therapy program instructor, camp program director, camp counselor, and more among the wonderfully fun "jobs" she's held. Currently, Julie is a wilderness guide in southern Utah with her company Sundance Adventure Guides (www.sundanceadventureguides.com) and also sometimes pens random, scattered thoughts about writing and outdoor adventuring on www.julietrevelyan.com. She lives near the red rocks and wild canyons of Capitol Reef National Park with her horses, cats, and Pippin the wonder dog.

recreation · lifestyle · conservation

MOUNTAINEERS BOOKS is a leading publisher of mountaineering literature and guides—including our flagship title, *Mountaineering: The Freedom of the Hills*—as well as adventure narratives, natural history, and general outdoor recreation. Through our two imprints, Skipstone and Braided River, we also publish titles on sustainability and conservation. We are committed to supporting the environmental and educational goals of our organization by providing expert information on human-powered adventure, sustainable practices at home and on the trail, and preservation of wilderness.

The Mountaineers, founded in 1906, is a 501(c)(3) nonprofit outdoor activity and conservation organization whose mission is "to explore, study, preserve, and enjoy the natural beauty of the outdoors." One of the largest such organizations in the United States, it sponsors classes and year-round outdoor activities throughout the Pacific Northwest, including climbing, hiking, backcountry skiing, snowshoeing, bicycling, camping, paddling, and more. The Mountaineers also supports its mission through its publishing division, Mountaineers Books, and promotes environmental education and citizen engagement. For more information, visit The Mountaineers Program Center, 7700 Sand Point Way NE, Seattle, WA 98115-3996; phone 206-521-6001; www.mountaineers.org; or email info@mountaineers.org.

Our publications are made possible through the generosity of donors and through sales of more than 600 titles on outdoor recreation, sustainable lifestyle, and conservation. To donate, purchase books, or learn more, visit us online:

MOUNTAINEERS BOOKS

1001 SW Klickitat Way, Suite 201 · Seattle, WA 98134

800-553-4453 · mbooks@mountaineersbooks.org · www.mountaineersbooks.org

 Mountaineers Books is proud to be a corporate sponsor of the Leave No Trace Center for Outdoor Ethics, whose mission is to promote and inspire responsible outdoor recreation through education, research, and partnerships. · The Leave No Trace program is focused specifically on human-powered (nonmotorized) recreation. · Leave No Trace strives to educate visitors about the nature of their recreational impacts and offers techniques to prevent and minimize such impacts. · Leave No Trace is best understood as an educational and ethical program, not as a set of rules and regulations. · For more information, visit www.lnt.org or call 800-332-4100.

OTHER TITLES YOU MIGHT ENJOY FROM MOUNTAINEERS BOOKS

Best Hikes with Dogs: Utah
Dayna Stern
The best dog-friendly trails in Utah
for the most doggone fun!

**Backcountry Ski & Snowboard
Routes: Utah**
Jared Hargrave
In Utah, the question isn't, "Where in
the backcountry can I ski?" but,
"Where's the book that shows the
best places?" Hey, here it is!

**100 Classic Hikes in Colorado,
3rd Edition**
Scott Warren
The most popular guidebook
to Colorado

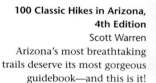

**100 Classic Hikes in Arizona,
4th Edition**
Scott Warren
Arizona's most breathtaking
trails deserve its most gorgeous
guidebook—and this is it!

**Mixed Emotions: Mountaineering
Writings of Greg Child**
Greg Child
The first collection of work from one of
the world's finest mountaineering writers

Postcards from the Ledge
Greg Child
Selections of the best writing
from the elite mountaineer
Greg Child

www.mountaineersbooks.org